Ambivalence and the Structure of Political Opinion

Ambivalence and the Structure of Political Opinion

Edited by

Stephen C. Craig

and

Michael D. Martinez

AMBIVALENCE AND THE STRUCTURE OF POLITICAL OPINION
© Stephen C. Craig and Michael D. Martinez, 2005.

First published in 2005 by
PALGRAVE MACMILLAN™
175 Fifth Avenue, New York, N.Y. 10010 and
Houndmills, Basingstoke, Hampshire, England RG21 6XS
Companies and representatives throughout the world.

PALGRAVE MACMILLAN is the global academic imprint of
the Palgrave Macmillan division of St. Martin's Press, LLC and of
Palgrave Macmillan Ltd. Macmillan® is a registered trademark
in the United States, United Kingdom and other countries.
Palgrave is a registered trademark in the European
Union and other countries.

ISBN 1–4039–6571–4

Library of Congress Cataloging-in-Publication Data

Ambivalence and the structure of political opinion / edited by
Stephen C. Craig and Michael D. Martinez.
    p. cm.
Includes bibliographical references and index.
ISBN 1–4039–6571–4
    1. Public opinion—United States. 2. United States—Politics and
government—Public opinion. 3. Ambivalence. I. Craig, Stephen C.
II. Martinez, Michael D.

HN90.P8A5 2004
303.3'8'0973—dc22   2004049005

A catalogue record for this book is available from the British Library.

Design by Newgen Imaging Systems (P) Ltd, Chennai, India.

First edition: January 2005

10 9 8 7 6 5 4 3 2 1

Printed in the United States of America.

For
Diane and Wanda

Contents ᴖ

List of Tables ﾟ

List of Figures ⤳

Notes on Contributors ◟

Bethany Albertson is a doctoral candidate in the Department of Political Science at the University of Chicago. Her research interests include public opinion, political psychology, and race and religion in American politics. She has worked at the National Opinion Research Center studying citizens' emotional response to 9/11, and is currently writing her disseration on the effect of religion and religious rhetoric on political attitudes in the United States.

R. Michael Alvarez is Professor of Political Science at California Institute of Technology. He has focused most of his research on the study of electoral politics in the United States, and is author of *Information and Elections* (1997) and co-author of *Hard Choices, Easy Answers: Values, Information, and American Public Opinion* (2002, with John Brehm) and *Point, Click, and Vote: The Future of Internet Voting* (2004, with Thad E. Hall).

Brandon Bartels is a Ph.D. student in the Department of Political Science at The Ohio State University. His research interests include judicial politics, in particular Supreme Court decision making; public opinion and processes of institutional evaluation; and quantitative methods.

John Brehm is Professor of Political Science at the University of Chicago. He is author of *The Phantom Respondents: Opinion Surveys and Political Representation* (1993), and co-author of *Working, Shirking, and Sabotage: Bureaucratic Reponse to a Democratic Public* (1997, with Scott Gates) and *Hard Choices, Easy Answers: Values, Information, and American Public Opinion* (2002, with R. Michael Alvarez). His research focuses mainly on the study of political psychology as manifested in public opinion and political organizations.

Jack Citrin is Professor of Political Science at the University of California, Berkeley. He is co-author (with David O. Sears) of *American Identity and the Politics of Multiculturalism* (2004), *Tax Revolt: Something for Nothing in California* (enlarged edition, 1985), and numerous journal articles and book chapters on political trust, national identity, immigration and language politics, and various other topics.

Stephen C. Craig is Professor of Political Science at the University of Florida, as well as director of the university's Graduate Program in Political Campaigning. He is author of *The Malevolent Leaders: Popular Discontent in America* (1993), as well as numerous journal articles and book chapters dealing with attitude measurement, partisan change, campaign effects, and other aspects of contemporary public opinion and political behavior in the United States.

Jason Gainous is a Ph.D. student in the Department of Political Science at the University of Florida. His dissertation deals with Americans' ambivalence about social welfare issues, and he has co-authored several conference papers and journal articles dealing with public opinion, voter behavior, and the psychology of political attitudes.

Allyson L. Holbrook is Assistant Professor of Public Administration and Psychology at the University of Illinois at Chicago. She received her Ph.D. from The Ohio State University in 2002. Her research deals primarily with the social and cognitive psychological processes that affect answers to survey questions, processes by which information is combined to form attitudes, and moderators of the impact of attitudes on thoughts and behaviors.

William G. Jacoby is Professor of Political Science at Michigan State University. He received his Ph.D. from the University of North Carolina at Chapel Hill. His areas of interest include public opinion, voting behavior, state politics, and quantitative methodology. Professor Jacoby is currently editor of *The Journal of Politics*.

James G. Kane is president of the *Florida Voter* polling organization, and an adjunct professor with the Graduate Program in Political Campaigning at the University of Florida. He has co-authored journal articles, book chapters, and conference papers dealing with various aspects of public opinion and voting behavior in the United States.

Jon A. Krosnick is Professor of Psychology and Political Science at Ohio State University. He is the author of four books and over 100 articles focusing on the psychology of political behavior; attitude formation, change, and effects; and the optimal design of survey questionnaires. He has taught courses around the world at universities, as well as for various corporations and government agencies, and has served as a consultant to such organizations as Home Box Office, the Office of Social Research at CBS, the News Division of ABC, the National Institutes of Health, NASA, NOAA, the U.S. Bureau of the Census, and the Urban Institute. His scholarship has been recognized with the Phillip Brickman Memorial Prize for Research in Social

Psychology, the Midwest Political Science Association's Pi Sigma Alpha Award, the Erik Erikson Early Career Award in Political Psychology, and a fellowship at the Center for Advanced Study in the Behavioral Sciences.

Samantha Luks is Assistant Professor of Political Science at the University of Minnesota. She has published articles on trust in government, voting behavior, and welfare dynamics. Her other research interests include African-American partisanship and political participation, age-period-cohort models of political attitudes, and residual votes in U.S. elections.

Michael D. Martinez is Associate Professor of Political Science at the University of Florida. His research on partisanship, voting behavior, ideology, and attitudinal ambivalence has appeared in numerous academic journals, including *American Journal of Political Science, Canadian Journal of Political Science, Political Behavior, Political Research Quarterly*, and others. He has been a Fulbright Scholar at the University of Calgary, and a Visiting Associate Professor at the University of British Columbia.

Kathleen M. McGraw received her Ph.D. in psychology from Northwestern University in 1985, and is currently Professor of Political Science, Psychology, and Journalism and Communication at The Ohio State University. She received the 1994 Erik Erikson Award from the International Society of Political Psychology for distinguished early-career contributions to political psychology. Her broad research interests lie in the areas of political psychology and public opinion.

Ian McGregor received his Ph.D. in social psychology from the University of Waterloo in 1998, and spent the following year conducting post-doctoral research at Northwestern University. He is now an Associate Professor of Psychology at York University in Toronto, Canada. His most recent research, published in the *Journal of Personality and Social Psychology*, has experimentally demonstrated that uncertainty and ambivalence about the self can cause compensatory conviction and zealous extremism about social issues.

Ian R. Newby-Clark received his Ph.D. from the University of Waterloo in 1999. Following stints as a Social Sciences and Humanities Research Council of Canada postdoctoral fellow at Cornell University, and member of the faculty at the University of Windsor, he currently is an Assistant Professor of Psychology at the University of Guelph. His research focuses on the psychology of attitudes (especially ambivalence), and the psychology of thinking about the future (especially plans and predictions for self-change).

Mark P. Zanna is Professor and former chair of the Department of Psychology at the University of Waterloo. He has served as president of the Society of Experimental Social Psychology (1985) and the Society of Personality and Social Psychology (1997), co-editor of the *Ontario Symposium on Personality and Social Psychology* (since 1981), and editor of *Advances in Experimental Social Psychology* (since 1991). He received the Donald O. Hebb Award from the Canadian Psychological Association (1993), and the Donald T. Campbell Award from the Society of Personality and Social Psychology (1997), both for distinguished scientific contributions. In 1999, he became a Fellow of the Royal Society of Canada. Current research is in the area of communication and persuasion, focusing on topics related to the overcoming of resistance to change (e.g., subliminal priming and persuasion, self-affirmation and persuasion, and narrative persuasion).

1. Pros and Cons ⟿

Ambivalence and Public Opinion

Michael D. Martinez, Stephen C. Craig,
and James G. Kane

> *Ambivalence is a wonderful tune to dance to. It has a rhythm all its own.*
>
> Erica Jong

In retrospect, it seems rather simplistic to think of attitudes as always being unidimensional. After all, who hasn't experienced "mixed feelings" about people, places, and things that we have encountered or visited in our lives. Take cars, for example. Talk to anyone who drives an older-model Jaguar and he or she will probably go on about the intrinsic beauty of its design, its stability taking corners, and especially the guttural resonance of that legendary double-overhead cam engine. It is equally likely, however, that the same individual will also recount the car's finicky behavior, and its celebrated unreliability and high maintenance. In the end, most owners of an older Jag will say they both loved and hated the car. Asked to rate the car overall on a traditional bipolar continuum, they would find such a scale inadequate to describe their feelings for the beautiful but mischievous cat.

As obvious as it may be that conflicted feelings do exist, for most of the twentieth-century researchers in both social psychology and political science (e.g., see Eagly and Chaiken 1993; Zaller and Feldman 1992) generally conceptualized attitudes as being unidimensional. Thurstone's early seminal work on attitude measurement, for example, characterized attitudes as bipolar, ranging from positive (or favorable) to negative (or unfavorable), with a neutral point in between (Thurstone 1928; Thurstone and

Chave 1929). In his review of attitude research, Gordon Allport (1935) even suggested that the bipolarity of attitudes (favorable versus unfavorable) was their most distinct feature. This seemed to make perfect sense at the time because on most issues people undoubtedly did think in bipolar terms. They either liked the car or they didn't. In political commentary, candidates and elected officials were described ideologically as being either "liberal" or "conservative" (or perhaps "middle-of-the-road")—and, depending upon their own predispositions, voters were thought to react accordingly, that is, positively or negatively, but probably not both at the same time. Research over the years, though, has made it clear that the unidimensional model does not capture the entire story.

THE CONCEPT OF AMBIVALENCE

At first glance, describing something as both good *and* bad, or a candidate as both liberal *and* conservative, would seem improbable—or at least inconsistent. But in real life we can, and often do, evaluate objects as if they contained separate components. Politicians, for example, are seen as being liberal on some issues but conservative on others, with the *summation* of these perceptions presumably telling us whether they fall, overall, into one category or the other. Feldman (1995) described this process as the "distributions of considerations" and argued that an opinion expressed in response to a survey question provides only an estimate of the *central tendency* of an individual's attitudes or beliefs on that subject. Thus, when a person's distribution of considerations includes contradictory or inconsistent evaluations, beliefs, or emotions, we can describe him or her as being *ambivalent* (Craig *et al.* 2002; McGraw *et al.* 2003; Cacioppo *et al.* 1997; Alvarez and Brehm 1995; Eagly and Chaiken 1993; Zaller and Feldman 1992).

As we point out in chapter 4 of the present volume, the concept of ambivalence is not new. Social psychologists, based upon studies using experimental data, were the first to question the bipolar model. Looking at inconsistencies in beliefs, Scott (1969: 262) concluded that "an ambivalent image is one that includes both desirable and undesirable characteristics." Later, Abelson and his colleagues (1982) found that positive and negative affective reactions clustered separately on a factor analysis—in other words, these reactions formed two factors that were only weakly (negatively) correlated with one another. Accordingly, they concluded that having good feelings toward, say, Ronald Reagan, did not necessarily imply an absence of bad feelings toward him. Although scholars working in conflict theory

(Mowrer 1960; Brown and Farber 1951) were among the first to define ambivalence, it was Scott's (1966, 1969) research that led to the notion of ambivalence as a property of an attitude (Thompson *et al.* 1995).

WHAT AMBIVALENCE IS NOT

While the fact that people's orientations toward classic cars, candidates, and political issues can have both positive and negative dimensions implies that ambivalence is an important attribute of attitudes, we must distinguish ambivalence from other such attributes. As some have correctly pointed out, ambivalence is not the same thing as indifference or uncertainty about an attitude object (Alvarez and Brehm 1995, 2002; McGraw *et al.* 2003), though all three of these attributes might lead someone to score at the mid-point on a traditional bipolar scale (Eagly and Chaiken 1993). Someone who is *ambivalent* can have strong opinions about a subject and perhaps even know more about it than most experts, but nevertheless feel conflicted. In contrast, an individual who is *uncertain* does not have enough information to form a reliable opinion but may arrive at one when provided with additional information. *Indifference* refers to a state of having neither positive nor negative attitudes toward an attitude object. Although responses from ambivalent, uncertain, and indifferent respondents may be similar on traditional survey-based scales, the underlying reasons for their response are not.

Likewise, other attitude attributes may be related to ambivalence (often negatively) but conceptually distinct from it. One would expect that this is the case for many aspects of attitude strength: *attitude importance*, reflecting the degree to which people care deeply about an issue and its significance to their daily lives (Krosnick and Abelson 1992; Krosnick 1988a, 1988b; Boninger *et al.* 1995b); *elaboration*, referring to whether someone has given thoughtful consideration to the underlying attitude (Petty and Cacioppo 1986b; Petty *et al.* 1995); *extremity*, connoting distance from the midpoint on traditional attitude scales (Abelson 1995; Krosnick and Abelson 1992; Krosnick *et al.* 1993); and *intensity*, indicating the extent to which an attitude is accompanied by emotional reactions (Krosnick and Abelson 1992; Krosnick *et al.* 1993). At the opposite end of the strength spectrum, Philip Converse (1964) suggested that many people may have *non-attitudes*, or an absence of underlying convictions that are frequently masked by survey respondents' attempts to cooperate with interviewers by providing guesses to opinion questions.[1]

Most of these attitude attributes are related to one another, though factor analyses of experimental data have confirmed that ambivalence is empirically distinct from the others (Lavine *et al.* 1998a). It is reasonable, then, to assume that each attribute has independent effects on attitude stability, and that each operates differently in amplifying or moderating the relationships between attitudes and behavior. In practice, the challenge has been to develop measures that capture the essence of ambivalence (i.e., the concurrent positive and negative attitudes) while at the same time maintaining the distinction between ambivalence and other related constructs. Let us quickly review some of the approaches that have been employed in the literature.

MEASURING AMBIVALENCE

Defining ambivalence is one thing, but measuring it is quite another. As ambivalence received greater attention in recent years from political scientists and survey researchers generally, scholars have developed and tested a variety of different approaches. Some of these approaches are indirect and inferential. Zaller and Feldman (1992), for example, asked survey respondents to state whatever thoughts came to mind as they answered two traditional closed-ended policy questions; based upon the mix of answers given, the authors concluded that "most people possess opposing considerations on most issues, that is, considerations that might lead them to decide the issue either way" (p. 585; also see Zaller 1992). This was described as the *ambivalence axiom* which, according to Zaller and Feldman, helps to account for the over-time response instability often found in opinion surveys (Converse 1964). However, the ability to identify arguments on both sides of an issue may actually reflect *elaboration* (consideration of multiple sides of an argument) more than it signifies the presence of an underlying cognitive conflict that we would associate with ambivalence (see Alvarez and Brehm 1995, 1997, 1998; Craig *et al.* 2002).

Using a very different approach, Alvarez and Brehm (1995) inferred the presence of ambivalence in citizens' attitudes about abortion from the patterns of error variance in heteroskedastic probit models of binary choice. They argued that ambivalence, uncertainty, and equivocation can be detected by observing the effects of concurrent predispositions and new information on error variances in models of issue preference. The general public's ambivalence on an issue is indicated when error variance is increased by coincident predispositions (or value conflict) and by an increase in information relevant to the issue. On the other hand, uncertainty on an issue is assumed to be present when information reduces error variances in the model, but the existence of conflicting predispositions has no discernible effect. Finally, equivocation is apparent when coincident predispositions and information both reduce error variances in the model (Alvarez and Brehm 2002: 58; see also chapter 2 in this volume). While this measurement strategy has been helpful for understanding differences in the structure of public opinion on abortion (Alvarez and Brehm 1995), racial issues (Alvarez and Brehm 1997), and bureaucracy and the Internal Revenue Service (Alvarez and Brehm 1998), inferences about *individual-level* concepts (such as ambivalence and uncertainty) based upon *aggregate-level* data (patterns of error variance in binary choices) are problematic for at least two reasons: First, while the inferential approach can be used to estimate the general levels of ambivalence that exist on an issue, it does not allow us to differentiate levels of ambivalence between individuals in the mass public. Second, the relationship between value conflict and ambivalence is one that must be assumed in this model; it is not susceptible to empirical testing.

There have been numerous attempts to measure ambivalence directly at the individual level, using both objective and subjective indicators. Objective ambivalence measurement began when Kaplan (1972) tried to interpret what it meant for an individual to choose the "neutral" point on a semantic differential scale (Osgood *et al.* 1957). He reasoned that a neutral response could mean "neither positive or negative" (indifferent) or, alternatively, "both positive and negative" (ambivalent). His method of distinguishing between indifference and ambivalence was both simple and elegant: To collect both positive and negative responses, Kaplan split the semantic differential scale at the neutral point and asked subjects to indicate separately how positive and how negative they felt about the same attitude object. Thus, to measure positive attitudes about object Y, subjects were asked, "Considering only the positive qualities of Y and ignoring its negative ones, evaluate how positive its positive qualities are on a 4-point scale: (1) not at all positive; (2) slightly positive; (3) quite positive; or (4) extremely positive." The question was then repeated, only this time substituting "negative" for "positive."

Kaplan found that subjects could indeed evaluate an attitude object in both positive and negative terms, and that the correlations between these scales were remarkably independent of one another (a mean correlation of only −0.05).[2] One could argue, of course, that the apparent independence of the various scales masked a significant amount of random and systematic response error (Green 1988; Green and Citrin 1994). However, Thompson, Zanna, and Griffin's (1995) LISREL analysis showed that latent variables representing both positive and negative components were *not* more highly correlated after controlling for both random and systematic error.

Although Kaplan's method of collecting positive and negative responses captured the component (i.e., conflicting) parts of ambivalence (Priester and Petty 1996; Thompson *et al.* 1995; Eagly and Chaiken 1993), his formula for combining the different parts proved to be problematic. Kaplan saw the amount of ambivalence as a function of the *total affect* directed by a person toward an attitude object (positive plus negative reactions) less the *polarity* of those reactions (absolute value of positive minus negative responses). The difficulty with this measure, as others have pointed out (Priester and Petty 1996; Thompson *et al.* 1995), is that it fails to account adequately for the presence of *polarized beliefs*. For example, someone who rates an attitude object as "4" on the positive component, and "2" on the negative component, is probably experiencing less ambivalence than someone who answers "2" on both. Yet according to Kaplan's measure, each of these individuals receives an identical score on the overall measure. Common sense suggests that any operational definition of ambivalence should account for the degree of polarization, or else risk overestimating the amount of ambivalence that actually exists.

Thompson *et al.* (1995) corrected for this deficiency by reformulating Kaplan's measure so as to include both similarity and intensity of components, that is, reasoning that increased similarity between positive and negative components reflects greater ambivalence. At the same time, they proposed that when similarity is held constant, increased intensity should result in greater ambivalence.[3] While their formula (discussed in chapters 4 and 7 of this volume) for combining separate positive and negative elements varies from the original, objective measures of ambivalence still follow Kaplan's lead in relying on separate assessments of positive and negative reactions to the same attitude object.

Another approach to measuring ambivalence directly is simply to ask a subject the degree to which he or she feels conflicted or discomforted about an attitude object (Priester and Petty 1996; Thompson *et al.* 1995; Tourangeau *et al.* 1989b). In the literature this is referred to as *subjective*, *direct*, or *felt* ambivalence (Fazio and Olson 2003).[4] Tourangeau and his colleagues (1989a), for example, asked survey respondents how important several issues were to them, and whether or not they felt conflicted with regard to those issues ("would you say that you are mostly on one side or another . . . or would you say your feelings and beliefs are mixed?"). Similarly, Holbrook and Krosnick (see chapter 5 in this volume) measured subjective, or meta-psychological, ambivalence by asking people how "mixed" and "decisive" their thoughts and feelings were about a particular issue.

It should be noted that the correlation between subjective and objective measures of ambivalence is not usually very strong. In trying to validate their model, Thompson *et al.* (1995) compared subjects' objective scores with their personal assessments regarding feelings of conflict (i.e., "I find myself feeling 'torn' between two sides of the issue of euthanasia"). Although Thompson and her colleagues found the objective measure (sometimes referred to as the Similarity Intensity Model, or SIM) to be better at predicting subjective ambivalence than other indicators, its correlation with subjective ambivalence still did not exceed 0.40. Based upon similar results, Priester and Petty (2001: 29; also see Priester and Petty 1996) concluded that objective measures "account for only a moderate amount of the variance associated with the reported psychological experience of ambivalence."

Thompson *et al.* (1995) correctly noted that more work needs to be done in validating both subjective and objective indicators. Low correlations might suggest that the latter do not fully capture one's true level of ambivalence on a given issue, that people are often unaware of their ambivalent feelings and cannot report them accurately when asked (Greenwald and Banaji 1995), or both. Alternatively, objective and subjective measures may be capturing different aspects of ambivalence, a possibility explored by Holbrook and Krosnick in chapter 5 of this volume.

THE SOURCES OF AMBIVALENCE

Why are some people ambivalent and others not? Many scholars have suggested that value conflict plays a central role in creating ambivalence (e.g., Alvarez and Brehm 1995, 2002; Feldman and Zaller 1992; Zaller 1992; Katz and Hass 1988). In recent years, researchers have increasingly become aware of the central role played by core values in structuring citizens' behavior and their views on specific political issues. Empirically, Feldman (1988) found that core beliefs about equality of opportunity, economic individualism, and the free enterprise system contributed significantly to voters' policy and candidate preferences. Feldman and Zaller (1992) reported that the social welfare policy views of survey respondents are based partly upon their beliefs about the proper role of government, individualism, humanitarianism, and other abstract values and principles. Sniderman and Piazza (1993) discovered that the core values of individualism and authoritarianism are important in shaping Americans' racial attitudes. Peffley and Hurwitz (1993; also Hurwitz and Peffley 1987) identified "general postures" relating to militarism and authoritarianism that are associated with attitudes on foreign and defense policy issues.

Although it is generally believed that ambivalence occurs when there is a *conflict* involving a person's core values (Alvarez and Brehm 1995; Eagly and Chaiken 1993; Katz and Hass 1988), the evidence showing this to be the case is extremely limited. In their study of political tolerance, for example, Peffley and his associates (2001) assumed that value conflict and ambivalence are interchangeable terms, yet they failed to demonstrate an actual link between the two using either objective or subjective measures of ambivalence. Craig, Kane, and Martinez (2002) approached the question more directly and found greater ambivalence among individuals with conflicting views on the values of moral traditionalism and marriage roles (whether a wife should look after the home and family rather than pursuing a career of her own)—but only on the elective, as opposed to the traumatic, dimension of abortion (above; also see Alvarez and Brehm 1995; Schnell 1993). Given such ambiguous results, we concluded that "future research needs to take a closer look at the extent to which ambivalence is truly grounded in value conflict" (Craig *et al.* 2002: 295).

Values are usually assumed to be deeply seated cognitions, so the presupposition that ambivalence stems from value conflict suggests that the former is a chronic condition for some individuals on some issues. However, some recent evidence suggests that ambivalence fluctuates over time and varies across contexts. Jewell (2003), for example, found that ambivalence tends to increase as an approaching deadline sharpens the salience of negative aspects of a generally positively regarded behavior, such as donating blood. If deadlines are associated with higher levels of ambivalence, we might hypothesize that ambivalence in public opinion will also crest as one gets closer to election day, that is, the deadline for voters' decisions.

Most work on ambivalence is rooted in a cognitive framework, but Huckfeldt, Mendez, and Osborn (2004) have suggested that an individual's social networks can influence the level of ambivalence that he or she feels about political candidates. Respondents in the 2000 American National Election Study named up to four political discussion partners; those naming partners who were unanimous in their presidential preference (for either Gore or Bush) tended to express less ambivalence about the candidates than did those whose discussion network included both Gore and Bush supporters. From this perspective, ambivalence about candidates is a function of conflict (or disagreement) among the people within one's social network rather than of some underlying attitudinal conflict within an individual.

In sum, our knowledge about the origins of ambivalence is incomplete. Perhaps most importantly, there is mixed evidence from prior research regarding the value conflict hypothesis that has dominated discussion of this question. Moving beyond values, however, we can safely say that a great deal of the variance in ambivalence, both across individuals cross-sectionally and over time, has yet to be identified.

THE CONSEQUENCES OF AMBIVALENCE

The most critical element of the research agenda, in our view, has to do with the impact of ambivalence on both attitudes and behavior. When people are ambivalent, how is that likely (if at all) to shape the way they think about politics or to influence their actions within the political realm? Here the literature is beginning to uncover evidence that ambivalence does matter at least some of the time and under certain circumstances. There are indications, for example, that ambivalence is associated with the direction of attitudes, that it affects the relationship between specific attitudes and general beliefs, that it contributes to the instability of attitudes over time, and that it mediates the relationship between attitudes and behavior.

The idea that ambivalence about a candidate might be positively or negatively related to overall candidate evaluation is somewhat perplexing at first glance. After all, ambivalence is conceptualized as the presence of both positive and negative sentiments resulting (one would think) in an overall neutrality toward the attitude object. In this light, a finding that ambivalence is associated with *moderate* evaluations of candidates is entirely understandable (Meffert *et al.* 2000). Yet some recent studies have suggested that ambivalence about an attitude object may actually lead to *negative* evaluations overall. In one such study, McGraw, Hasecke, and Conger (2003) found that ambivalence toward a hypothetical candidate for the U.S. Senate was associated with more negative assessments of that candidate. A possible explanation for this finding is that ambivalence necessarily connotes the presence of some salient negative aspects of the attitude object— and that in comparison with other generally positively regarded attitude objects, the negative cognitions tend to stand out and lower a person's overall evaluation (see Lau 1982, 1985; Klein 1991, 1996; Cacioppo *et al.* 1997; Holbrook *et al.* 2001).

If the lack of ambivalence is an aspect of attitude strength, and we argue that it is, ambivalence might be expected to destabilize attitudes over time. Because ambivalent attitudes have both positive and negative components, variations in the salience of those components over time would be expected to make the attitudes more prone to change. The evidence, however, is decidedly mixed. Some survey analysts (Zaller and Feldman 1992; Hill and Kriesi 2001; Craig *et al.* in chapter 4) and experimenters (Bargh *et al.* 1992) have concluded that ambivalence contributes to attitude instability, susceptibility to persuasive communications (Armitage and Conner 2000), and context effects within surveys (Tourangeau *et al.* 1989b). In contrast, other research has failed to uncover a link between ambivalence and instability. Bassili (1996b) noted that ambivalence regarding quotas, pornography, and hate expressions did not significantly reduce the stability of those attitudes over a ten-day to two-week period. Similarly, Armitage and Conner (2000) concluded that health-care workers who were ambivalent about eating a low-fat diet were no less stable in their attitudes over a period of five to eight months than those who were not ambivalent. Thus, despite an elegant theory and a fair amount of circumstantial evidence suggesting that there is a connection between ambivalence and stability, the inconsistent empirical findings to date leave room for doubt. It is conceivable that the destabilizing effects of ambivalence—to the extent they exist at all— are either domain-specific or dependent upon the presence of other attitude characteristics.

Finally, there is evidence that ambivalence mediates the relationship between attitudes and behavior, or at least between specific attitudes and general orientations. A series of studies by Christopher Armitage and his colleagues demonstrated that relatively non-ambivalent people are more likely to show higher levels of attitude–behavior correspondence with regard to eating a low-fat diet (Armitage and Conner 2000; Conner *et al.* 2002), consuming alcohol, and donating blood (Armitage 2003). In our survey of Florida voters, we found that ambivalence on gay rights policy attitudes weakened the relationship between those attitudes and overall evaluations of the incumbent governor (Craig *et al.* 2005). Findings such as these reaffirm the political relevance of ambivalence.

AN OVERVIEW OF THE BOOK

In this introductory chapter, we have raised more questions than we have answered, and we have suggested that many strands of the research agenda remain ripe for further investigation. The authors of the chapters that follow address (without necessarily providing a definitive answer for) some of the important questions that have arisen concerning the conceptualization and measurement of ambivalence, its effects on attitude stability and the impact of attitudes on evaluations of candidates and policies, and its relationship to attitudes about political institutions and regimes.

In chapter 2, Bethany Albertson, John Brehm, and Michael Alvarez provide a review of various perspectives in political science and psychology as to what constitutes ambivalence, as well as a discussion of competing measures. They argue that not all forms of attitude conflict are necessarily ambivalence, which connotes a high degree of internalized conflict. The authors elaborate on what they believe to be the appropriate criteria against which to assess measures of ambivalence, and then provide empirical validations of the inferential measure of ambivalence that they presented in *Hard Choices, Easy Answers* (Alvarez and Brehm 2002).

In chapter 3, Ian Newby-Clark, Ian McGregor, and Mark Zanna also contend that potential ambivalence, or the mere existence of conflicted evaluations, is not necessarily felt ambivalence. Following from the classic theory of cognitive dissonance, they assert that felt ambivalence occurs only when positive and negative evaluations of the same attitude object are *simultaneously accessible* in memory. Felt ambivalence, but not potential ambivalence, is said to be a psychologically uncomfortable state that triggers distraction, suppression, compensatory conviction, or other processes that might relieve the discomfort.

In chapter 4, we address the relationship between ambivalence and overtime attitude stability using a panel survey of abortion attitudes in Florida. We show that there are two separate dimensions of ambivalence about abortion, based on whether the conditions under which a woman seeks an abortion are "traumatic" or "elective." More to the point, ambivalence on each dimension is shown to be associated with response instability on that dimension across the two waves of our panel, controlling for a variety of other aspects of attitude strength.

In chapter 5, Allyson Holbrook and Jon Krosnick consider whether meta-psychological (or subjective) and operative (or objective) measures of ambivalence are capturing the same phenomenon. Low correlations between those measures in previous studies suggest that they may be tapping separate constructs and, similar to the argument presented by Newby-Clark and his colleagues in chapter 3, Holbrook and Krosnick posit that operative ambivalence may be a necessary but not a sufficient condition to produce meta-psychological ambivalence. Based on data gathered from 654 Ohio State undergraduates, they contend that operative and meta-psychological ambivalence are distinct concepts with different consequences for information gathering, false consensus effects, shaping candidate evaluations, and political activism.

In chapter 6, Kathleen McGraw and Brandon Bartels use data from the 1997 American National Election Study Pilot Study to explore the extent of Americans' ambivalence about the institutions of the national government (Congress, the president, and the Supreme Court), as well as the relationships between ambivalence and basic political orientations of trust, efficacy, and support for democratic processes. McGraw and Bartels suggest that ambivalence has different consequences for the mass public's evaluations of Congress than it does for evaluations of the Supreme Court and President Clinton, a finding that is best understood in terms of the "default," or baseline, opinions that citizens hold toward these institutions, that is, the baseline is (or was in 1997) largely negative in the case of Congress, but largely positive in the case of the president and Supreme Court.

In chapter 7, Jack Citrin and Samantha Luks develop a measure of emotional ambivalence about America based on respondents' positive and negative emotional reactions to the nation as expressed in the 1996 General Social Survey. Based on that measure, it appears that ambivalence toward the country is more widespread than some might expect—and that it is equally prevalent among men and women, blacks and whites, and not much different across age and income groups. Citrin and Luks also assess the relationships between emotional ambivalence about the country, on the one hand, and national identity and patriotism, on the other.

Finally, in chapter 8, William Jacoby sounds a cautionary note that scholars who are looking for ambivalence might be too prone to find it. That is, many analyses of public opinion show a great deal of attitude conflict, but some of the conflict is less real for citizens than researchers assume to be the case. While at first glance it may appear, for example, that a large segment of the public holds contradictory attitudes *both* opposing large government *and* favoring public spending increases in many policy areas, an analysis of the 1992 American National Election Study shows that attitudes toward welfare and non-welfare spending are shaped by different factors; this finding, in turn, leads Jacoby to conclude that the apparent contradiction disappears when respondents' subjective interpretation of government spending is understood to mean welfare spending in particular.

The collection of essays presented here provides an important retrospective on the state of our knowledge about ambivalence and public opinion, while at the same time charting new directions for future research. Taken together, these chapters confirm that ambivalence is an attitude attribute with the potential to help us better understand some of the apparent conflicts and complexities uncovered by the existing literature on public opinion. The research presented in these pages, however, also suggests that there may be conditioning effects on ambivalence, as well. Though our authors take different approaches to the question of how to assess ambivalence, all agree that it represents an internalized conflict of attitudes. The salience of that conflict to the individual, and the role it plays in rendering potential ambivalence into felt ambivalence, may be a key to identifying when, how, and why ambivalence structures information seeking, attitude stability, general evaluations, resistance to persuasion, and other aspects of public opinion. Perhaps only when the proud owner of our prototypical Jaguar attaches importance *both* to the car's responsive power *and* to its maintenance demands will we see the effects of ambivalence.

NOTES

1. Alvarez and Brehm (2002: 125) also discuss the impact of equivocation, or speaking with two distinct but mutually reinforcing voices, in promoting more firmly fixed individual opinions about public policy issues.

2. Whereas Kaplan argued that no filler was needed between questions that tap positive and negative reactions, Thompson and her colleagues (1995) reported a correlation of roughly 0.40 between the scales. The latter study also indicated that more filler between positive and negative assessments resulted in less covariation between them.

3. For an alternative revision of the Kaplan measure, see Priester and Petty (1996).

4. Greenwald and Banaji (1995) refer to subjective accounts as explicit, and objective measures as implicit.

2. Ambivalence as Internal Conflict ᶜᶳ

Bethany Albertson, John Brehm, and R. Michael Alvarez

Political scientists and psychologists recognize the presence of ambivalence in our attitudes, but conceptions of ambivalence are widely varied. Is ambivalence common or rare? Is it a *subjective* feeling that can only be measured by asking the individual, or is it an *objective* property of an attitude that can be measured without the respondent's knowledge? Answers to this question may depend on the way ambivalence is defined. In the discussion that follows, we compare some of the various definitions of ambivalence that have been offered by scholars in the past. We argue that the concept has been employed too loosely in earlier research, and suggest a number of ways in which it can be defined in a more precise and productive manner. Specifically, we argue that "ambivalence" should be restricted to instances of strong internalized conflict which lead to increased response variability that cannot be reconciled as a function of additional information.

In political science, the term ambivalence is often used to imply value conflict. Using in-depth interviews, Hochschild (1981: 238) found that "given the opportunity, people do not make simple statements; they shade, modulate, deny, retract, or just grind to a halt in frustration." Yet Hochschild was clear that not all value conflicts result in ambivalence. An individual might, for example, sort the importance of different norms among different domains. In Hochschild's work, individuals experienced ambivalence when they weren't able to resolve the conflict; however, she did not separate out similarly conflictual states. Ambivalence was manifested in helplessness, anger, inconsistency, or confusion. Feldman and Zaller (1992) also viewed ambivalence as a manifestation of value conflict. In their study, respondents' answers to open-ended survey questions indicated that liberals tend to be more ambivalent regarding social welfare issues than are conservatives. The authors concluded that this was due to the difficulty experienced by liberals in reconciling their pro-welfare views with their simultaneous support for individualism and limited government—two sets of values that are widely shared in American society.

Although ambivalence represents a type of conflict in each of these works, neither addresses the question of intensity, or personal importance. For example, one individual could be "conflicted" about whether there should be a flag burning amendment but want more information before making up his or her mind. Another might feel "conflicted" and yet not care a great deal because the issue is thought to have little impact on his or her life. A third person might care deeply while also feeling "conflicted," perhaps because s/he strongly believes that freedom of expression should be protected *and* that flag burning hurts national pride (the latter being highly valued). When asked about flag burning, then, all three individuals might evince value conflict, and appear ambivalent, under that definition.

To muddy the conceptual waters even further, there has been a tendency in political science to use the term ambivalence less to describe individual citizens and their attitudes than as a characteristic of public opinion as a whole. It is common to read impressionistic reports of poll results in the media, or to hear talking heads debate the "ambivalence" of the public, when the data being discussed actually show disagreement in the aggregate about some policy. Page and Shapiro (1992), for example, noted that aggregate shifts in support for welfare versus support for the poor might reflect ambivalence. Similarly, Myrdal (1944) drew upon aggregate-level analysis to suggest that Americans are internally conflicted over racial issues. However, when half the public supports a policy which the other half opposes, such a division indicates a conflicted nation rather than a nation of conflicted individuals.

Psychologists usually define ambivalence more narrowly. For Cacioppo and Berntson (1994), ambivalence is a state of simultaneous high positive and high negative evaluation of an attitude object. Importantly, they assert that positive and negative evaluations are not necessarily coupled as the traditional bipolar scale implies.[1] People can hold a very positive evaluation and little in the way of negative feelings towards the same attitude object, or they could hold low negative and low positive feelings, or perhaps even high negative and high positive feelings simultaneously. This last state is their version of ambivalence. Bassili (1998) also measured ambivalence by asking respondents about positive and negative feelings separately, and observing the amount of conflict between the two. He found that the higher the conflict (or potential ambivalence), the slower people are to express their opinions.

Some political science conceptions of ambivalence are closer to the perspectives found in psychology. Craig, Kane, and Martinez (2002; also see chapter 4 in this volume), for example, measured ambivalence by asking respondents to rate positive and negative evaluations separately; ambivalence was then calculated by adding positive and negative evaluations (intensity) and then dividing by the difference between the two (similarity). McGraw, Hasecke, and Conger (2003) included subjective and objective measures of ambivalence and uncertainty in a study of on-line and memory-based candidate evaluation. Their objective measure of ambivalence was the intensity–similarity measure used by Craig and his colleagues, while their subjective measure was a simple agree/disagree with the statement, "I have both positive and negative feelings about [candidate]." Interestingly, they found that the subjective experience of ambivalence was related to a memory-based judgment strategy, meaning that people were more likely to rely on information that was readily accessible (as opposed to their on-line tally). They also discovered that the subjective measure of ambivalence was directly related to candidate evaluation for participants low in political sophistication, but not for participants high in political sophistication. In contrast, the objective measures of ambivalence were moderately related to candidate evaluation for more sophisticated participants and unrelated for less sophisticated participants. Though the causal mechanism here is not obvious (does memory-based judgment cause feelings of ambivalence, or do feelings of ambivalence cause memory-based judgment?), the McGraw study points out an interesting relationship between subjective and objective measures of ambivalence and evaluation, as well as compelling evidence that the measures are capturing distinct phenomena.

Alvarez and Brehm (2002) defined ambivalence as strong internalized conflict. It was said to occur when "[c]oincident predispositions induce wider response variability [and when] information widens response variability. Ambivalence results when respondents' expectations or values are irreconcilable . . . ." (p. 58). In our operationalization, we think of ambivalence as a condition experienced by the individual at the moment of an interviewer's question, which reveals itself because of characteristics of prior information about the person's choices (in the form of their value orientations and state of informedness) and is detected via an inferential statistical approach (also see Alvarez and Brehm 1995).

Clearly, then, there are important distinctions in the ways that scholars use the term "ambivalence." Some view it as a general state of confusion, while others restrict it to instances of high evaluative conflict. Depending upon which definition is used, ambivalence is thought to be either common or rare in public opinion. Another key distinction is between the subjective experience of feeling ambivalent, and ambivalence as a property of an attitude (as measured by combining separate indicators of positive and negative evaluations). Prior research indicates that the correlations between subjective measures of ambivalence and simultaneous positive/negative evaluations are modest in magnitude (Newby-Clark *et al.* 2002; Priester and Petty 2001)—a finding which suggests that ambivalence may have different antecedents and different consequences depending upon which definition and which measurement is used. Newby-Clark, Ian, McGregor, and Zanna (2002) concluded, for example, that both simultaneous accessibility and preference for consistency moderated the relationship between potential ambivalence (separate positive and negative evaluations) and felt ambivalence (measured subjectively). Similarly, Priester and Petty (2001) found that felt ambivalence can be partially explained by interpersonal attitude discrepancy with a liked other.

WHY THESE CONCEPTIONS COMPETE

These various conceptions of ambivalence drawn from political science and social psychology might strike some readers as a matter of splitting hairs. To the contrary, we argue that they imply quite different things about the state of respondents' or subjects' political attitudes. Furthermore, we continue to believe that it is useful to confine the concept of ambivalence strictly to conditions of internalized conflict.

What does the simple, simultaneous presence of both positive and negative attitudes (or "likes" and "dislikes") encompass that might be at variance from an internalized conflict notion of ambivalence? At a very basic level, simultaneous likes and dislikes about an attitude object might be better characterized as a feeling of being "bittersweet" (Cacioppo and Berntson 1994) than as a sense of conflict. College seniors on graduation day serve as an archetypal example. These young adults typically experience a mix of emotions, including a sense of excitement and anticipation at the prospect of moving to a new phase of their lives combined with a wistfulness borne of the knowledge that they are leaving close friends behind. Save for the extent of actual "conflict" present in one's emotional state, such sentiments meet the classic dictionary definitions of ambivalence, for example, "the simultaneous existence of conflicting emotions, such as love and hate, towards a person or object" (*Webster's New Universal Unabridged Dictionary*, p. 56).

There are perhaps few opportunities in the political realm that might cause people to adopt bittersweet attitude states. Among the exceptions, at least for partisans who were fans of their respective administrations, the conclusions of the Reagan and Clinton presidencies appear to have been occasions when many citizens experienced both sadness at the end of an era but also a feeling of uplift at what these leaders had accomplished. In fact, three of the last four U. S. presidents have benefited from late upward movement in their approval ratings: Ronald Reagan (despite his involvement in Iran–Contra), George H. W. Bush (despite the nation's sour economy), and Bill Clinton (despite the Monica Lewinsky scandal). Only Jimmy Carter's low ratings, which stemmed largely from the ongoing hostage crisis in Iran, persisted through the last month of his Administration (readily observable in Gallup presidential approval data; see Gronke and Brehm 2002).

Elsewhere (see Alvarez and Brehm 2002; Alvarez *et al.* 2003), we have argued that a person's political attitudes are far more likely to be in a state of *uncertainty* than of true ambivalence. That is, there are hosts of policy questions where individuals might recognize the existence of at least two sides to the debate while still coming quite firmly to one position. Welfare reform, environmental protection, immigration laws, school prayer, and many other topics appear to involve issues where a single dimension of conflict dominates—and where, at best, there are high levels of uncertainty rather than of ambivalence among the general public (Alvarez *et al.* 2003). Most provocatively, we contend that Americans' attitudes towards race and racial policy are really ones of uncertainty, not ambivalence (Alvarez and Brehm 1997, 2002). Although scholars and citizens have long recognized that the ideals of equality and freedom sometimes conflict with policies that explicitly benefit certain minority groups and not others (Schuman *et al.* 1985), these "principle-implementation" gaps do not appear to stem from an internalized, intra-psychic state in people's minds so much as from an externalized, inter-psychic conflict among political groups.

Even attitudes about abortion, the quintessential example of internalized conflict, are often better characterized as reflecting states of uncertainty than of ambivalence. In our first article on the subject (Alvarez and Brehm 1995), and in our recent book (Alvarez and Brehm 2002), we explicitly identified circumstances under which respondents would be able to rationalize away one side or another of the potential conflict. Regarding the legality of an abortion sought for purposes of protecting the health of the mother, for example, we noted that supermajorities of respondents to the General Social Survey supported such a position, and did so without any evidence of internalized conflict. At the other end of the spectrum, for an abortion conducted long after the beginning of the third trimester (a time-span outside of protections from *Roe v. Wade*) people generally were able to rationalize the procedure as being undeserving of moral protection. It is only when abortion was framed as a matter of personal choice, without any external justifications, that respondents displayed the kind of intrapsychic conflict that we argue constitutes ambivalence (Alvarez and Brehm 2002: 88).

For that matter, the simultaneous presence of positive and negative emotional evaluations of an individual or policy problem also need not identify ambivalence. From the 1960s forward, social psychologists have wrestled with the notions of imbalance (Heider 1946) and cognitive dissonance (Festinger 1957) by noting that subjects appear to be willing to carry around such contradictory feelings without a trace of internalized conflict. Although imbalance and cognitive dissonance were thought to be noxious states that people would be motivated to avoid, we actually are equipped with a variety of mental mechanisms to facilitate the separation of seemingly inconsistent cognitions. For example, it was commonly said that many Americans were appalled at President Clinton's conduct in his personal life while at the same time being pleased with his handling of the national economy. Were all of these Americans ambivalent? The two aspects of performance were in conflict, but many citizens probably were able to separate out multiple dimensions of presidential evaluation. Some may have reconciled their conflicting feelings about Clinton by prioritizing those dimensions, for example, by deciding that policies trump character issues or, conversely, that character is what matters most in politics. Others perhaps concluded that a disliked aspect of the president was idiosyncratic while a liked aspect was more enduring. And some individuals may have made a situational attribution for positively evaluated characteristics (a good economy) but a dispositional attribution for negatively evaluated characteristics (little self-control). We contend that characterizing all of these individuals as ambivalent is too loose an application of the concept. Simply holding simultaneous positive and negative evaluations of an attitude object does not necessarily indicate that one is conflicted.

If coexisting positive and negative evaluations do not always reflect ambivalence, then the claim that the dictionary definition presented earlier captures the central core of the concept becomes weaker still. Although one might subjectively label some attitudes held by a respondent or subject as both positive and negative, the individual may put little emotional investment behind those attitudes. For example, we know that people differ substantially in their need for cognition. As subjects are permitted to expand upon their answers to open-ended questions, they become more likely to give both positive and negative assessments of the attitude object almost as a matter of course (Larsen *et al.* 2001). Prior research also tells us that respondents can be induced to elaborate their answers by incentives (e.g., prompts) provided by the interviewer or experimenter, creating a larger number of responses to such open-ended questions as the traditional candidate and party "likes" and "dislikes" in the American National Election Study surveys (Brehm 1993).

Given relatively easy-to-induce elaborations, it is not surprising that respondents/subjects sometimes invest very little in their offered responses. This means that measures of ambivalence such as response latency are suspect: While these may be terrific measures for assessing the accessibility of attitudes, the idea that they reflect conflict is problematic. Bassili (1995) argued that some attitudes are more potentially conflictual than others, and hence take longer for respondents to access. Yet some attitudes may simply be more obscure or less immediately comprehensible than others, perhaps due to nothing more than the familiarity that the respondent has with politics (see Delli Carpini and Keeter 1996).

To recap our objections to the manner in which this loosely defined concept is typically employed: We prefer to treat ambivalence as an individual-level attribute ascribing internalized conflict, rather than using the term to refer to states of mind that may (1) include psychological states devoid of internalized conflict (e.g., being bittersweet); (2) represent conditions where people are willing to trade off nominally competing predispositions (e.g., being uncertain); (3) invoke states of mind that are easily reconciled; or (4) be stimulated in ways that confound loquacity with internal conflict. Our goal here is to focus the concept of ambivalence upon those necessarily few moments when we are faced with truly difficult choices between incommensurable alternatives.

ANALYSIS

As we hope is clear from the previous discussion, there are multiple conceptions of ambivalence within the disciplines of both political science and psychology. These conceptions may not all refer to the same thing. How, then, do we adjudicate among them? One approach would be to identify a series of potential confounds of the measures, and to assess the strengths and weaknesses of the various approaches by examining their relative vulnerability to those confounds. To make clear that our difficulties with the concept of ambivalence apply not only to work done by other scholars but also to our own earlier research, we offer three examples drawn from the 1998–99 Multi-Investigator Study.[2] These examples are part of a larger project on the limited effects of framing in survey responses, though the questions serve to illustrate our broader point.[3]

The central idea in the experiments we conducted was to randomly assign the respondents to two of three broad policy categories.[4] Specifically, we asked the following questions:

1. *Affirmative action and minority set-aside programs*
   - When it comes to setting aside a certain number of government construction contracts for businesses that are owned and operated by minorities, are you for or against this?
   - How do you feel about allowing state universities to have flexible admissions standards in order to promote racial diversity? Are you for or against this?

2. *Women with children and welfare*
   - How do you feel about requiring women with children to work at a job in order to stay on welfare? Are you for or against this?
   - Are you for or against limiting the number of months a woman with children can stay on welfare?

3. *Immigrants and welfare*
   - How do you feel about allowing legal immigrants from other countries, who are here legally, to receive welfare in the U. S.? Are you for or against this?
   - How do you feel about providing public education to the children of illegal immigrants who are in this country illegally? Are you for or against this?

Ambivalence was measured in three distinct ways. First, we relied heavily upon our inferential measure of ambivalence (see Alvarez and Brehm 1995, 2002). Using a variety of maximum likelihood techniques, this measure estimates the implicit variance in the probability of choosing one specific alternative among several possibilities. The idea is to conceive of response variability as the range of plausible responses to a survey question. Respondents with narrower response variability tend to answer questions in largely consistent ways (perhaps reflecting better crystallized belief systems), while those with wider variability tend to answer questions in an inconsistent fashion (appearing to have less crystallized belief systems). This is, of course, an inference about a single respondent's plausible range of responses based upon attributes such as the coincidence of predispositions (here, specific values) and state of political information. To be clear, it is not the variance itself that defines ambivalence, but rather the sign on key covariates: What is the effect of the condition where a respondent exhibits equal levels of support for two or more predispositions? Does this sign indicate a wider variance (i.e., positive, suggesting ambivalence) or a narrower variance (i.e., negative, suggesting the absence of ambivalence)? We also employed a second measure of "ambivalence" using response latency timers. As soon as the interviewer finished asking a question, he or she hit a key which initiated a timer; then, once the respondent began to answer, the interviewer hit another key stopping the timer. A longer interval between the two actions (reported in milliseconds) supposedly indicated ambivalence. Finally, a third measure of "ambivalence" was obtained by asking respondents to assess subjectively the difficulty of each attitudinal question: "How hard was it for you to make up your mind on that last question—not hard at all, not very hard, somewhat hard, or very hard?"

Readers may at this point have well–formed opinions about the comparative strengths of these measures, but we wish to point out some areas of concern. Consider first the subjective ambivalence measure, which appears to have the advantage of being a direct evaluation of an attitude report. Presumptively, respondents will find the question either relatively easy to answer or relatively difficult. Yet this mode is fused with other difficulties. For example, the subjective measure confounds the comprehensibility of the question (did the respondent understand the terms?) with his/her difficulty in providing an answer. Although one can imagine a series of follow-up questions (how confusing was this last question? what do you mean by "not very hard" when you answered my last question?), one might also imagine that this approach would further confuse people. Another potential problem with the subjective measure is that respondents' evaluations need not invoke very deep emotional investment. Research suggests, for example, that this question may be the attitudinal equivalent of asking for directions, with men being less likely than women to admit they are "ambivalent" (Alvarez and Brehm 2000). How much reflection is involved in reporting on the difficulty of the question, and how accurately does that reflection document self-investment?

The response latency approach may appear to have advantages as well. Unlike subjective difficulty, respondents who are identified here as being "ambivalent" differ in physically measurable ways from those who are not "ambivalent," that is, it takes them longer to conjure appropriate answers to the questions posed. By necessity, however, this approach confounds the accessibility of predispositions with the length of time it takes for people to reconcile multiple predispositions. Indeed, one of the leading scholars of ambivalence uses response latency indicators to assess the accessibility of predispositions, not the degree of conflict between them (see Bassili 1995; Bassili and Fletcher 1991).

These points are readily observable in several related analyses of our data. For the inferential method, we use heteroskedastic probit (see Alvarez and Brehm 1995).[5] Because the subjective ambivalence question asks respondents to place themselves into one of four ordered categories, we rely on ordered probit in our tests of that particular item.[6] And since timers for the response latency approach report results in milliseconds, with values varying from small through large integer numbers, we employ a standard event history method (the Weibull distribution) to model its effects.[7] In each case, what is purportedly "ambivalence" needs to be modeled in such a way that we can observe some basic interactions. Our contention is that ambivalence is indicated when the effect of both additional information and the coincidence of nominally conflicting predispositions tend to *increase* response variability. We measure information by combining respondents' acquired level of education with a summary tally of their successes in answering a series of questions about politics.[8] Coincidence between two values, (v_1, v_2), is measured by

$$1 - |v_1 - v_2|$$

In this regard, we employ an index of egalitarianism and an index of support for law and order[9]—two value dimensions that are nominally in conflict with one another (e.g., Reider 1985).[10] (As the reader will shortly see, however, the evidence suggests that they are not and that a better characterization of people's attitudes is one of "uncertainty" rather than "ambivalence.") We also wish to illustrate the potential for gender effects on subjective reports of ambivalence, so that is included in our model as well. Results are presented in three tables, one for each of the measures of ambivalence described earlier.

Table 2.1 documents our inferential measure of ambivalence as modeled with heteroskedastic probit. Heteroskedastic probit *is* conditional on the model for choice here, which we treat as a function of three separate predispositions: egalitarianism, women's rights, and "law and order." We also include controls for gender, whether the respondent is currently working, and party identification, as well as the coincidence measure reported in the preceding paragraph. Note that the choice model behaves in a largely sensible manner. Feminists support pro-minority policies like reserving government contracts or adopting flexible admission standards, are less supportive of requiring work for welfare or setting time limits on the receipt of welfare, but tend to be indifferent on immigration. The most interesting story in the choice model concerns the coincidence of egalitarianism and conventional (law-and-order) authoritarianism where those who

Table 2.1 Heteroskedastic probit as measure of ambivalence

Variable	Government contracts	Admission standards	Require work	Limit welfare	Immigrant welfare	Immigrant education
Choice Model						
Constant	0.28	0.02	−0.29	−0.02	−0.22	−0.16
	(0.19)	(0.00)	(0.03)	(0.01)	(0.01)	(0.00)
Male	−0.68	−0.31	0.64	0.61	0.37	0.05
	(0.07)	(0.01)	(0.03)	(0.01)	(0.13)	(0.00)
Education	0.16	0.06	0.08	−0.02	0.05	0.00
	(0.02)	(0.00)	(0.00)	(0.00)	(0.00)	(0.00)
Working	−0.29	−0.05	0.00	0.10	−0.07	−0.03
	(0.02)	(0.00)	(0.00)	(0.00)	(0.00)	(0.00)
Party ID	0.27	0.04	0.01	−0.05	0.10	0.03
	(0.02)	(0.00)	(0.00)	(0.00)	(0.01)	(0.00)
Women's Rights	0.19	0.06	−0.10	−0.10	0.04	0.01
	(0.01)	(0.00)	(0.00)	(0.00)	(0.00)	(0.00)
Egalitarianism	−0.03	−0.04	0.05	0.03	−0.04	−0.01
	(0.01)	(0.00)	(0.00)	(0.00)	(0.00)	(0.00)
Law and Order	−0.11	−0.02	0.01	−0.03	0.02	0.00
	(0.05)	(0.00)	(0.01)	(0.01)	(0.01)	(0.00)
Concidence	−1.13	−0.36	1.05	0.83	0.28	0.17
	(0.08)	(0.01)	(0.03)	(0.03)	(0.01)	(0.01)
Variance Model						
Education	−0.71	−2.22	−1.27	−1.41	−0.67	−0.69
	(0.34)	(0.42)	(0.19)	(0.30)	(0.34)	(0.45)
Information	−0.69	0.28	−0.36	0.10	−0.92	−0.71
	(0.10)	(0.15)	(0.04)	(0.06)	(0.12)	(0.32)
Male	0.85	0.68	−0.48	0.20	−0.69	−1.36
	(0.18)	(0.12)	(0.11)	(0.06)	(0.18)	(0.58)
Coincidence	0.04	0.29	0.04	−0.12	0.23	−0.16
	(0.06)	(0.08)	(0.02)	(0.05)	(0.08)	(0.07)
χ^2	21.06	13.98	52.90	38.89	9.94	7.13
Heteroskedasticy Test	14.33	8.97	8.80	7.55	10.46	12.17
Number of cases	1067	1067	1067	1067	1067	1067

Note: Data are from 1998–99 Multi-Investigator Study (see n. 2). Table entries are estimated coefficients and associated standard errors (in parentheses).

experience the greatest degree of coincidence of these two predispositions, controlling for their main effects, demonstrate relatively low levels of support for affirmative action in set-asides and university admissions, and relatively high levels of support for welfare reform and immigration reform. It is also worth noting from the controls that men are more likely to oppose pro-minority policies, but support welfare and immigration reforms.

One can readily understand what many would regard as the "typical" pattern of support or opposition in these related policy domains: Men, for example, tend to fit the stereotype of opposing more generous social policies and favoring more restrictive ones, while feminists are frequently in the reverse. The patterns for egalitarians and law-and-order authoritarians are more complex, yet typify someone who is both socially egalitarian and believes in the importance of social order, opposing policies that benefit outsiders like blacks, the poor, and immigrants.

The lower panel of table 2.1 presents the variance model (our inferential measure). What this rather clearly demonstrates is that the notion that these six questions induce an ambivalent internal conflict between egalitarianism and conventional authoritarianism is a mixed case at best. We define two criteria for determining the presence of ambivalence, that is, information and the coincidence of values should lead to increasing response variance. Two measures of political informedness are employed: education and the respondent's score on our information scale (see n. 8). In four of the six cases, the higher one's level of education, the lower the variance: for the pro-minority and anti-welfare policies, the magnitude of the variance coefficients on education are substantial, especially relative to every other coefficient in the model. (Perhaps a more relevant condition is the marginal effects, or partial derivatives of the variance component evaluated at the mean, plus a standard deviation change in the variable. Here the computed marginal effects of information are indeed greater than those of the other variables in these conditions, but only in a very large way for the "admissions standards" and "limited months on welfare" questions.[11]) In the last two conditions, pertaining to anti-immigrant policies, the signs on the coefficients again counter-indicate ambivalence, although the magnitude does not exceed conventional statistical significance thresholds. The effect of political information is not nearly as impressive, and is a bit less consistent. There is, however, only one condition where greater information leads to increasing response variance, and it is for the flexible admission standards question. Thus far, then, we have *no* reason to believe that the respondents experienced ambivalence.

How about the second criterion (which happens to be much closer to many of the competing conceptions of ambivalence found in the literature), that coincidence of values leads to increasing variance? Results in table 2.1 show the signs to be correct in four of the six conditions, but only statistically significant in two: flexible admissions standards and allowing welfare access to immigrants. In the remaining two conditions, coincidence not only leads to decreasing variance but does so to a statistically significant degree. One would have to conclude from the results of the inferential method of assessing ambivalence over these policy domains that respondents are not ambivalent, but instead are much more likely to be "uncertain" (a condition where additional information is the dominant effect in the inferential model, substantially reducing response variance).

While readily conceding that there are other ways to operationalize what could fairly be dubbed "ambivalence," we nevertheless wish to speculate about two possible side difficulties associated with measures based on subjective assessments (gender effects) and response latency (accessibility). As documented in tables 2.2 and 2.3, there is very strong evidence that there are serious problems in both instances. Table 2.2 reports the ordered probit models for subjective ambivalence, that is, how hard it was for the respondent to answer the prior questions. The most important finding here is the highly consistent effect of gender: Men are much less likely to profess ambivalence than are women, with five of the six coefficients being negative (though one of these as well as one positive coefficient, each involving welfare reform, fall short of achieving conventional levels of statistical significance). It also is interesting to note that gender has a systematic impact on response latency, with men being quicker to respond. The results here suggest that men may be more accurately reporting the state of their mind, and doing so more quickly, than women.

Table 2.2   Subjective assessment of ambivalence

Variable	Government contracts	Admission standards	Require work	Limit welfare	Immigrant welfare	Immigrant education
Education	0.16	0.02	0.63	0.11	−0.13	0.16
	(0.03)	(0.03)	(0.03)	(0.03)	(0.03)	(0.04)
Information	−0.08	0.17	0.26	0.59	0.56	0.27
	(0.03)	(0.03)	(0.03)	(0.03)	(0.03)	(0.04)
Male	−0.14	−0.27	0.01	−0.01	−0.23	−0.18
	(0.01)	(0.01)	(0.01)	(0.01)	(0.01)	(0.01)
Coincidence	0.10	0.09	0.04	0.01	0.06	−0.01
	(0.00)	(0.00)	(0.00)	(0.00)	(0.00)	(0.01)
a_1	0.40	0.50	0.98	0.84	0.68	0.80
	(0.01)	(0.01)	(0.01)	(0.01)	(0.01)	(0.02)
a_2	0.75	0.86	1.31	1.14	1.01	1.13
	(0.01)	(0.01)	(0.01)	(0.01)	(0.02)	(0.02)
a_3	1.77	1.62	2.10	2.05	1.91	1.89
	(0.02)	(0.02)	(0.02)	(0.02)	(0.02)	(0.02)
χ^2	13.09	11.49	37.36	25.02	14.29	12.34
Number of cases	1067	1067	1067	1067	1067	1067

Note: Data are from 1998–99 Multi-Investigator Study (see n. 2). Table entries are estimated coefficients and associated standard errors (in parentheses).

Table 2.3   Response latency as measure of ambivalence

Variable	Government contracts	Admission standards	Require work	Limit welfare	Immigrant welfare	Immigrant education
Education	−0.30	−0.25	0.05	−0.19	−0.16	−0.16
	(0.03)	(0.04)	(0.03)	(0.03)	(0.03)	(0.04)
Information	−0.19	−0.12	−0.07	−0.09	0.23	−0.36
	(0.03)	(0.03)	(0.03)	(0.02)	(0.03)	(0.03)
Male	−0.09	−0.02	−0.07	0.10	−0.20	0.01
	(0.01)	(0.01)	(0.01)	(0.00)	(0.00)	(0.01)
Coincidence	0.00	0.03	0.02	−0.07	0.00	0.00
	(0.00)	(0.00)	(0.00)	(0.00)	(0.00)	(0.01)
Constant	6.64	6.33	6.21	6.46	5.97	6.32
	(0.01)	(0.01)	(0.01)	(0.01)	(0.01)	(0.01)
$\ln(p)$	−0.14	−0.22	−0.19	−0.06	−0.06	−0.24
	(0.00)	(0.00)	(0.00)	(0.00)	(0.00)	(0.00)
χ^2	15.08	4.22	3.15	6.12	8.20	7.40
Number of cases	1067	1067	1067	1067	1067	1067

Note: Data are from 1998–99 Multi-Investigator Study (see n. 2). Table entries are estimated coefficients and associated standard errors (in parentheses).

Further, we observe an odd but rather consistent effect for the informed-ness coefficients: Respondents with higher levels of education, and better scores on the political information items, generally profess greater difficulty answering the questions. And those respondents who are *both* egalitarian *and* conventional authoritarians admit to greater subjective ambivalence, though the magnitude of this relationship is rather modest (especially relative to the effect of political information).

Estimates for the response latency model appear in table 2.3, where the pattern of coefficients strongly indicates that response latency is a rather poor method for measuring ambivalence. First, for virtually all coefficients on the information variables (education and political information), we find that as information increases, response latency falls; that is, respondents who are better educated and/or more familiar with elite political discourse simply answer these policy questions much more rapidly. There are two exceptions: (1) Better educated respondents have slightly greater response times for the question on requiring work for welfare recipients; and (2) Individuals scoring higher on political information tend to take longer in expressing their opinions on welfare for immigrants. These relationships do not, however, seem to be part of the larger picture. The effect of the coincidence of predispositions is negligible. As noted earlier, we observe that men are quicker to answer their questions than are women (a finding consistent with men being either less subjectively ambivalent, as per table 2.2, or less hesitant to answer).

In sum, the record is quite mixed regarding this small assortment of ambivalence measures, and far from clear as to whether they actually are multiple indicators of the same psychological construct.

DISCUSSION: WHY AMBIVALENCE IS INTERNAL DIFFICULTY

As argued at the outset, the mere fact that an individual holds two separate feelings about an object at the same time does not mean that he or she is ambivalent. We all have experience with holding multiple and distinct feelings about objects. Most of us in our childhoods owned plush toys, but simply because they induced feelings of warmth and feelings of fuzziness does not mean that we felt ambivalent about our stuffed animals. At a minimum, ambivalence would seem to involve a state of mind in which the existence of those two feelings are in opposition to one another—a state of mind that would presumably make it difficult for a person to evaluate the object. Former President Clinton, for example, may have induced in many Americans feelings of loathing for his policies as well as dismay at his personal failings, and yet we could not possibly attribute ambivalence to anyone with this particular configuration of sentiments. Although they represent two distinct feelings about the president, ambivalence surely is not the appropriate term for describing an individual who possesses such uniform (negative) but complex attitudes.

Further, even if the two feelings about the object are in opposition, one would still have to require that there be some kind of tension between those feelings. Feminist Democrats who were able to rationalize their support for the decidedly unfeminist actions of Bill Clinton were not meaningfully ambivalent about him. Likewise, apologists for scandals that occurred during the Nixon (Watergate) and Reagan (Iran–Contra) administrations could simply say, "Everyone does it, this president just happened to be caught." In both cases, positive feeling toward the incumbent triumphed over negative understandings about their actions in other areas.

Thus, it is not meaningful to talk about an ambivalent subject or respondent without also taking into account that person's state of informedness. If ambivalence is intended to refer to something more than a muddleheaded frame of mind, the concept needs to explain why some individuals have harder choices the more they think about the nature of that choice, and the more information that they have about its consequences.

Likewise, in our perspective ambivalence should reflect a specific choice or specific evaluation of the attitude object. It is not especially meaningful, in our understanding, to describe as ambivalent a respondent who experiences both positive and negative feelings not simultaneously but in seriatum, alternating between likes and dislikes about parties or candidates or policies.

We therefore contend that the inferential approach to measuring ambivalence is better than its competitors: It has allowed us to document the effect of two policy areas simultaneously, and to demonstrate that additional information served both to make response variability increase and to demonstrably change the nature of choices made by respondents. Moreover, the choices involved had to do with specific policies and conditions. Unlike the subjective measure of ambivalence, gender effects washed away. Unlike the response timers, we did not pick up simply how readily a respondent can make a choice. We can conceive of circumstances where one could modify the subjective ambivalence or response latency measures by purging the effects of gender or of accessibility. For the present, though, the inferential approach offers too many advantages.

NOTES

1. Norris, Larsen, and Cacioppo (2003) have a novel and interesting way to test the separability of positive and negative evaluations by utilizing something called the "affect matrix." This measurement, which requires a capacity for spatial response, entails the subject locating his or her opinion in a grid where one dimension represents a positive reaction and the perpendicular dimension a negative reaction to the same stimulus. Ambivalence, then, is a state of simultaneous highly positive and highly negative reaction to a particular stimulus. Since our experiments were conducted in a telephone survey, direct reproduction of their method would not have been possible; indeed, we were unaware of this approach at the time of our study.

2. This unique dataset is from a national random-digit telephone survey conducted from June 21, 1998 through March 7, 1999 by the Survey Research Center (SRC) at the University of California, Berkeley. The survey population was defined as all English-speaking adults, eighteen years or older and residing in households with telephones, in the 48 contiguous states. There were 1,067 completed interviews, with a response rate of 55.8 percent.

3. Because of our study design, everyone did not answer each and every question: Repondents were randomly assigned to sets of questions and, within sets of questions, randomly assigned to different treatments. As a result, we have a significant fraction of missing data; although the missingness mechanism is "ignorable" (Little and Rubin 2002), it nevertheless benefits from compensatory

imputation. (Technically, since the missingness is because of random assignment, it falls into the category of being "Missing At Random," or MAR). We resolved this problem by application of the program *Amelia* (King *et al.* 2001), which replaces missing elements by multiple imputation.

4. Within each category (race, welfare, or immigration), the respondent was assigned to one of four conditions: (a) a single, pro-policy "stem" for the question; (b) a single, anti-policy stem; (c) both stems; or (d) neither. The hypothesis tested here is that the two-sided stems are more likely to induce ambivalence than the one-sided or zero-stem conditions.

5. Heteroskedastic probit is an increasingly common tool which varies the familiar probit model for dichotomous choice, by noticing that the errors of the dichotomous choice model cannot be assumed to be constant (and set to 1 by a scale factor). Instead, the model permits the assumption that choices have a heterogeneous error structure. As with all maximum-likelihood models (and, indeed, a very large class of statistical models generally), the estimates for this model are obtained by iterative search over the parameter space

$$\log L(\beta, \gamma \,|\, y) \;=\; \sum_{i}^{N} \left(y_i \log \Phi \left(\frac{X_i \beta}{\exp (Z_i \gamma)} \right) \right.$$
$$\left. - \, (1 - y_i) \log \left[1 \, - \, \Phi \left(\frac{X_i \beta}{\exp (Z_i \gamma)} \right) \right] \right)$$

where y_i is the dichotomous dependent variable, X_i are a family of causal variables for the choice component, β is a vector of coefficients for the choice model variables, Z_i are a family of causal variables for the variance component, and γ is a vector of coefficients for the variance model variables.

6. Ordered probits are a common and appropriate statistical tool for estimating models with ordered categorical dependent variables. Again, this is a maximum likelihood model where the parameter estimates are obtained by iterative search over

$$\log L(\mu, \beta \,|\, y) \;=\; \sum_{i}^{N} \sum_{j}^{M} y_{ji} \log \left[\Phi \left(\mu_j \,|\, X_i \beta, 1 \right) \, - \, \Phi \left(\mu_{j-1} \,|\, X_i \beta, 1 \right) \right] y_i$$

where y_{ji} is the categorical dependent variable of respondent i in category j, X_i represents the variables in the choice function, β are the choice function parameters, μ_j are the estimated "thresholds" between choice categories j, and $\phi(a|b,1)$ is the cumulative normal density of a as a function of b with variance fixed at 1.

7. Weibull is a respectable approximation for the general event history problem, with the advantage that we can analyze the rate of change in the hazard function instead of assuming, as does the exponential, a constant hazard (or instantaneous probability of a "failure," in this case, the answer to the question). Weibull

models are a class of models for event count data. The Weibull density assumes a monotonically* decaying (or increasing) event history rate, and is a highly suitable method for the analysis of response latencies, which are themselves expressed as counts. We search over

$$\log L(\beta|y) = \sum_i (\beta X_i - 1) \log y - y^{\beta X_i}$$

where y_i is the count (dependent) variable, X_i are the variables of the event count model, and β are the coefficients of the event count.

8. The information items asked respondents to indicate (a) which party had the most members in the U. S. House of Representatives; (b) how much of a majority is required for the Senate and House to override a presidential veto; (c) whether the Democratic or Republican Party is more conservative; (d) which branch of government determines whether or not a law is constitutional; (e) how many four-year terms a president can serve; (f) how many members sit on the U. S. Supreme Court; and (g) what office was then held by Al Gore. Correct answers to each question were scored as 1, incorrect answers as 0.

9. Egalitarianism was measured by combining answers to two questions: "Which would you say is more important—narrowing the gap between rich and poor, or economic growth," followed by an indicator of the degree to which this view was held (much more, somewhat more, or only a little more important). Attitudes regarding law and order were measured in a similar fashion: "Which is more important—guaranteeing law and order in society, or securing individual freedom," followed by the degree question. Each scale was coded so that scores ran from -1 (inegalitarian, libertarian) to $+1$ (egalitarian, authoritarian).

10. There are other conceivable pairings of predispositions that we might have examined, including egalitarianism vs. either libertarianism or economic individualism. The egalitarianism vs. law and order pairing was chosen because the conflict between these two values is allegedly part of the decline of New Deal liberalism, with law-and-order values leading former egalitarians increasingly to reject redistributive social policies that benefit blacks, immigrants, and welfare recipients. See Rieder (1985) for a thoughtful if controversial accounting of this ambivalence in some American communities.

11. We will provide full tables of the marginal effects in an appendix available on our website (see http://hardchoices.caltech.edu).

3. Ambivalence and Accessibility ⌒

The Consequences of Accessible Ambivalence

Ian R. Newby-Clark, Ian McGregor,
and Mark P. Zanna

Values reflect, and can drive, human strivings (Verplanken and Holland 2002). We value peace and strive for a less violent world. We value benevolence and strive to be loving. We value independence and strive for autonomy. Sometimes, however, our values conflict (e.g., Schwartz 1996; Tetlock *et al.* 1996). The nature of psychologists' taxonomies of values reflects this psychological reality. According to Schwartz, values fall along two dimensions. The first dimension, *openness to change* versus *conservation*, reflects the chronic conflict between one's need to be stimulated and self-directed, and the equally important need for stability. A first year undergraduate student may, for example, feel exhilarated at the prospect of an independent lifestyle when he arrives at the residence hall on the first day of class. Yet there may well be some ambivalence when that same student realizes that the reliable routines and security of home life are a thing of the past (at least until vacation). The second dimension, *self-enhancement* versus *self-transcendence*, reflects a similarly fundamental conflict between the need for power and achievement and the need to be benevolent. A manager wants to do well at her job and to exercise power when interacting with her subordinates. At the same time, workplaces are social milieus where positive interpersonal relationships also tend to be valued; as a result, the manager will likely feel conflicted from time to time.

Given the dialectic complexity of most social and political issues, the study of political attitudes provides a rich forum for investigating the implications of value conflict. For example, in his study of value-based ambivalence, Bassili (1996a) showed that ambivalence regarding affirmative action reflected relatively high valuing of the merit principle (that people should be rewarded according to the quality of their work) and an equally pronounced desire for equality (e.g., redressing the historic plight of women in the workplace). In a similar vein, ambivalence about abortion could be construed as a conflict between respect for life (regardless of whether or not a fetus is considered fully human) and the valuing of personal freedom. To the extent that it is grounded in values, ambivalence about political issues is by no means a trivial or transient phenomenon. Indeed, values are central and relatively permanent aspects of the self (Rokeach 1973, 1979) that guide decisions and actions (Carver and Scheier 1990). Accordingly, for many of us, chronic ambivalence about political issues is virtually inevitable.

Despite this inevitability, we must sometimes state a definite opinion or behave in accord with either our positive or negative evaluation of some pertinent issue. The university student must either resolve to go it alone or call for rescue. The manager must either discipline a friend or relinquish authority. Similarly, plebiscites on capital punishment and abortion typically do not include an "undecided" category. It is not readily apparent, though, under what circumstances an ambivalent person will express a positive or negative opinion about a certain political issue, or cast a vote in favor or against a particular referendum. In this chapter, we focus on the well-established psychological concept of *accessibility*. In so doing, we hope to account for thought and behaviors related to evaluatively complex issues.

By accessibility, psychologists mean the ease with which a thought (or thoughts) comes to mind. It is our contention that the ease with which one's ambivalence, either in whole or in part, comes to mind has implications for the expression of opinion, behavior, and the experience of uncomfortable ambivalent feelings. We begin with a consideration of the role of accessibility in ambivalence about minorities. Our analysis of an early study leads us to argue that rendering racially ambivalent people's positive attitudes toward blacks accessible causes more positive responses toward the minority than when negative attitudes are at the forefront of consciousness. Later work on ambivalence about minorities supports this contention, as does some recent work on ambivalence about feminists. In the case of *simultaneously accessible* ambivalence, the psychological effects are somewhat different. We argue that when one's extremely positive and negative evaluations are in awareness simultaneously, psychological discomfort results. In support of our contention we review cognitive dissonance theory and findings, as well as our own and others' work regarding the relation between ambivalence and negative emotional states. We then discuss various means by which these unpleasant ambivalence-related feelings can be reduced or eliminated, and the psychological implications associated with some of those means.

AMBIVALENCE ABOUT MINORITIES: AMPLIFICATION EFFECTS

Racial Attitudes and Values

Irwin Katz, his colleagues, and other social scientists noted that white people's attitudes toward blacks are not evaluatively "simple" (see Katz *et al.* 1986). They reasoned that whites' complex attitudes toward blacks were best understood as ambivalent, and that this ambivalence was based on conflicting values. Specifically, whites' negative attitudes toward blacks were the result of the former's endorsement of the Protestant work ethic, whereas their positive attitudes toward blacks were the result of their support for humanitarian-egalitarian values. These values came into conflict because blacks were viewed as deviant (due to apparent lack of effort on their own behalf) *and* disadvantaged.

Katz and Hass (1988) tested their hypothesis in a survey of white undergraduates at eight U.S. college campuses. Respondents were asked about their endorsement of humanitarian-egalitarian values, their endorsement of the Protestant work ethic, and their pro- and anti-black attitudes. Relations among the values and attitudes were then assessed. Reflecting the presence of complex racial attitudes, the correlation between pro- and anti-black attitudes was low. Also, as Katz and Hass hypothesized, the correlations between humanitarian-egalitarian values and pro-black attitudes, and between Protestant work ethic values and anti-black attitudes, were stronger than the other two value–attitude correlations.

Ambivalence Amplification

Katz and colleagues demonstrated that people's ambivalent attitudes toward blacks could result in *amplification* of one's positive or negative evaluations, as manifested in actions directed at members of that minority. In a seminal study by Katz, Cohen, and Glass (1975), research assistants telephoned white male residents of New York City, ostensibly for a brief consumer attitude survey. Respondents' impression of the racial identity of the research assistant was systematically manipulated. For some of his phone calls, the assistant created the impression that he was black by saying, "I am in the *Negro* Students' Self-Help Program at the City College of New York. . . ." (p. 966; emphasis added). For other phone calls, the research assistant said the same phrase but without the word "Negro." Also, the assertiveness of the request for help with the consumer survey was systematically manipulated. Within each of the two racial identification conditions (Negro vs. white), one-third of respondents were asked, "Would you mind answering a few questions about men's shoes?" Another third were told, "I'm sure you won't mind answering a few questions about men's shoes." Research assistants were even more assertive with the last third of respondents, saying, "I'm sure that you can give me five minutes of your time. I want you to answer some questions about men's shoes."

The key measure here is whether or not people agreed to help out by taking part in the survey. In general, the frequency of helping went down as the caller became increasingly assertive. More relevant to our concerns, respondents overall helped the Negro caller more than the white caller—though racial differences were not the same at all three levels of assertiveness. When the caller was least assertive, Negro callers were helped significantly more often than were white callers; for medium and high assertiveness, this difference disappeared. In other words, the response to Negro callers became precipitously less positive (compared to that for whites) as requests became more assertive. Katz and his colleagues argued that respondents' ambivalence toward blacks was amplified in a negative direction as the assertiveness of the request became more pronounced.

THE ROLE OF ACCESSIBILITY

The foregoing study, we believe, illustrates the role of *accessibility* in ambivalence amplification. It would appear that the interviewer's self-label of "Negro" reminded respondents of their sympathy for blacks. When the interviewer was more assertive, however, respondents were reminded of their hostility and responded accordingly. Katz and Hass (1988) more directly demonstrated the importance of the accessibility of individuals' value-based ambivalence. The researchers made a particular set of values accessible by asking participants to fill out a series of questions tapping either humanitarian-egalitarian or Protestant work ethic values. As expected, rendering whites' humanitarian-egalitarian values accessible resulted in more pronounced pro-black attitudes, while rendering Protestant work ethic values more accessible resulted in more pronounced anti-black attitudes.

Other scholars have documented the role of accessibility in ambivalence amplification. Bell and Esses (2002), for example, manipulated the accessibility of positive or negative aspects of ambivalent attitudes toward Canadian native persons. This manipulation was achieved by having participants read essays that either favored or did not favor native land claims.[1] Bell and Esses found that participants who read a message opposed to land claims reported a more negative attitude toward native people than did participants who read a positive message. Of importance, there was no effect among participants who were not ambivalent initially, presumably because some of them had no highly positive attitudes and others had no highly negative attitudes that could be rendered accessible.

Amplification, Accessibility, and Behavior

The implications of the effects of rendering either positive or negative components of an ambivalent attitude accessible are striking. In the study by Katz *et al.* (1975), respondents' willingness to help a black person was apparently influenced by more or less accessible sympathetic and hostile attitudes. In the Bell and Esses study (2002), priming ambivalent participants' negative or positive thoughts about native persons led to more or less positive attitudes toward native land claims.

MacDonald and Zanna (1998) went further by obtaining evidence that hiring decisions about a stigmatized group—feminists in this case—could be affected by rendering accessible either the positive or negative aspect of ambivalence toward that group. The authors suspected that ambivalence toward feminists would take a certain form. Specifically, they proposed that people who are ambivalent about feminists respect but, at the same time, dislike them. As hypothesized, a survey of males' ambivalence toward feminists revealed that they admire, but have little affection for, feminists.[2]

MacDonald and Zanna (1998) also investigated the effects of making either respect or liking for feminists accessible. The researchers recruited men and women who were prescreened some weeks earlier as being either ambivalent or not ambivalent about feminists. When participants arrived for the experiment, they were told that the study involved hiring decisions and presented with the résumés of three ostensibly real female job applicants. One of the résumés made it clear that the applicant was a feminist; the other two applicants were not so identified. Before presentation of the résumés, ambivalent and nonambivalent participants were exposed to one of two experimental conditions. For half, thoughts related to respectability were made salient; for the other half, thoughts related to likeability were made salient.[3] Participants were then asked about their intentions to hire the three applicants. Those in the first (respectability) group were more likely to hire the feminist than those in the second (likeability) group.

Broader Implications

As is pointed out elsewhere in the current volume (e.g., see chapters 4, 5, and 6; also McGraw *et al.*, 2003; Haddock 2003), people who are ambivalent about a particular political issue respond and behave in ways different than those who hold the same attitude but are not ambivalent. Ambivalence amplification theory, and our analysis of the role of the accessibility construct, brings deeper insight by highlighting the conditions under which an ambivalent person will respond in accord with his/her positive (or negative) evaluation of an issue. If, by dint of recent political events, the positive (or negative) aspects of an evaluatively complex political issue become accessible, ambivalent individuals' opinion, and sometimes their behavior, may be amplified in the direction of the accessible thoughts.

As a possible case in point, consider Carla Faye Tucker, the first woman to be put to death by the state of Texas since the Civil War (Pedersen 1998). Ms. Tucker's crime could not have been more brutal. In a drug-induced stupor she pick-axed a sleeping man to death and, by her own account, experienced sexual pleasure in doing so. In the 14 years that passed following the murder, Ms. Tucker underwent a radical personality change. She became a born-again Christian, made anti-drug videos for teenagers, and married a prison minister. As her date with the executioner approached, her case garnered international attention and public outcry against her sentence reached a crescendo. Shortly after her execution, an opinion poll showed that support for the death penalty among Texans had reached a historic low (Walt 1998). The Tucker case is remarkable because of the extent to which Tucker was portrayed in a sympathetic light, much to the chagrin of death penalty advocates (Walt 1998). Those humanizing portrayals arguably made people's valuing of life more accessible than the valuing of vengeance.

SIMULTANEOUS ACCESSIBILITY

Up to now, our analysis has focused exclusively on those instances in which an ambivalent person's positive *or* negative evaluation is accessible. There are times, though, when one's positive *and* negative evaluations are in awareness simultaneously. In other words, the ambivalence is *simultaneously accessible* (Bassili 1996a). Ambivalence may be simultaneously accessible when, for example, a person who is ambivalent about capital punishment watches a news magazine program in which both sides of the issue are presented. What effect would such a broadcast have on the conflicted individual? We propose that people experience uncomfortable *feelings of ambivalence* when ambivalence is high in simultaneous accessibility. In order to understand why we hypothesize such an effect, research on cognitive dissonance (Festinger 1957) bears consideration.

Cognitive Dissonance

Cognitive dissonance theory was originally conceived by Leon Festinger (1957) to account for what transpires when a person is faced with his or her conflicted thoughts. Over the decades there have been various clever ways of causing people to have conflicted cognitions. One particular methodology was designed to emulate those situations in which we make a hard choice between two more or less equally attractive consumer products. Who among us has not been in such a situation? Perhaps we had to decide between two cars with different but equally appealing features (e.g., good fuel efficiency versus a large size). Unless we are made of money, a choice must be made. Once that happens, we become aware that we have freely chosen not to purchase a product we were attracted to initially.

If you are like us, this psychological situation can be grating: We feel uncomfortable, perhaps even irritable. But our feelings of discomfort soon subside as we begin thinking less than generous thoughts about the passed-over car. If we buy the fuel-efficient car, we derogate the "gas guzzler." If we made the opposite choice, we think of the fuel-efficient car as "pokey" and inconvenient for long trips. Social psychologists have observed this situation in many studies and shown that there is a *spread of alternatives* after a free choice is made between equally attractive options. That is, two more or less equally valued items become differently valued when one of them is chosen over the other. The chosen item is more highly valued, and the unchosen item is valued less. It is proposed that derogation of the passed-over item is in service of eliminating, or at least reducing, the psychological discomfort experienced initially (Eagly and Chaiken 1993).

Simultaneously Accessible Cognitive Dissonance

Zanna, Lepper, and Abelson (1973) conducted a study that highlights the important role of simultaneous accessibility in situations that arouse cognitive dissonance. They studied children in a nursery school and used the now-classic "forbidden toy" paradigm (e.g., Aronson and Carlsmith 1963). This design is based on the supposition that children who are threatened with a severe punishment for playing with a favored toy will not have conflicting cognitions because the reason for their not playing with the toy is clear: big trouble! However, children who are threatened with only a mild punishment will have dissonant cognitions because the censure is strong enough to keep them away from playing with the toy, yet too weak to justify their not playing with it. Ultimately, the children are left feeling ambivalent about whether or not to play with the toy.

In their study, Zanna and his colleagues (1973) assigned half the children to a severe-threat condition and the other half to a mild-threat condition. Within each of these, the children's awareness of their inconsistency (or lack thereof) was manipulated systematically by assigning them to one of two groups: Children in the awareness condition were reminded, during a temptation period, that they were not playing with a favorite toy even though the punishment for doing so was relatively mild (or severe), while others were not given such a reminder. As the authors hypothesized, children in the mild-threat condition derogated the forbidden toy more than did those in the severe-threat condition. Among children in the mild-threat condition, those who were reminded of their inconsistency derogated the once-favored toy more than did children who were not so reminded. Zanna, Lepper, and Abelson reasoned that the more pronounced reduction of cognitive inconsistency in the awareness condition occurred because children in that condition experienced more negative emotions when their inconsistency was made salient. They were like the car buyer who was reminded by her husband that she, of her own accord, chose to forgo purchasing the "gas guzzler" despite its comfort and suitability for long drives.

Ambivalence and cognitive dissonance, though traditionally studied separately, are similar in that cognitive dissonance concerns conflicted thoughts and ambivalence concerns conflicted evaluations (McGregor *et al.* 1999). On the basis of this similarity, and thanks to Bassili's introduction of the notion of simultaneous accessibility, we hypothesized that ambivalent people whose ambivalence is simultaneously accessible would experience uncomfortable feelings of ambivalence. Also, if our hypothesis was confirmed, we might be able to shed light on a long-standing puzzle in ambivalence research. . . .

Two Kinds of Ambivalence

Ambivalent attitudes are often measured by separately asking people about their positive and negative evaluations of an attitude object. Such evaluations are obtained by instructing respondents to ignore their positive evaluations of an attitude object when giving their negative evaluations, and vice versa (Kaplan 1972; see chapter 4 in this volume). For example, someone might be asked, "Considering only the favorable aspects of capital punishment and ignoring the unfavorable aspects, how favorable is your evaluation of capital punishment?" (Newby-Clark *et al.* 2002). The individual first indicates the extremity of his favorable evaluation, and then gives his unfavorable evaluation in a similar manner. Responses are put into a mathematical formula that produces an attitudinal ambivalence score (e.g., Priester and Petty 1996; Scott 1968; Thompson *et al.* 1995). As positive and negative evaluations become increasingly and equally extreme, attitudinal ambivalence increases. Ambivalence is lowest among respondents who have an extremely positive evaluation of an attitude object and no negative evaluation, or vice versa (Kaplan 1972; Priester and Petty 1996; Scott 1968; Thompson *et al.* 1995).

Sometimes ambivalence researchers are interested more in the *experience* of ambivalence (i.e., felt ambivalence[4]). Feelings of ambivalence are measured with self-report scales that assess how torn or conflicted people feel about a certain attitude object (Jamieson 1993; Priester and Petty 1996; Thompson *et al.* 1995). A respondent might, for example, be asked to rate the extent of her agreement with a statement such as, "I have strong mixed emotions both for and against capital punishment, all at the same time." As might be expected, attitudinal ambivalence is positively correlated with feelings of ambivalence. Of importance, though, the correlation is not particularly high. Thompson and her colleagues (1995) found that attitudinal ambivalence correlated at only $r = 0.40$ with feelings of ambivalence (for a similar finding see Priester and Petty 1996). Yet if a person holds conflicted evaluations of an attitude object, should it not follow that s/he also *feels* conflicted?

When Ambivalence is Simultaneously Accessible

We hypothesized that people's feelings of ambivalence are determined in part by the simultaneous accessibility of their ambivalence. We re-labeled ambivalence as measured by the positive and negative attitude questions as *potential ambivalence*,[5] reflecting our expectation that it represents only the possibility that a person will feel ambivalent. Just as in the Zanna *et al.* (1973) forbidden-toy study, this potential to feel torn and conflicted should manifest itself more strongly when the ambivalence is high in simultaneous accessibility.

In our first study (Newby-Clark *et al.* 2002), we conducted a telephone survey of students' attitudes toward capital punishment and abortion. The students were asked questions that measured their potential ambivalence about both issues; they also were asked how torn and conflicted they felt about both issues, that is, their felt ambivalence. The simultaneous accessibility of respondents' potential ambivalence was measured as well. To do this, a computer was used to time participants' responses to our potential

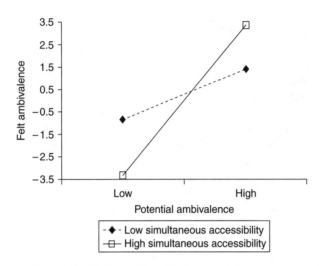

Figure 3.1   Potential ambivalence, felt ambivalence, and simultaneous accessibility

Note: Data are from telephone interviews of college students (see Newby-Clark *et al.* 2002). Depicted is the relationship, for abortion, between felt ambivalence and potential ambivalence as a function of simultaneous accessibility.

ambivalence questions;[6] faster times indicated higher accessibility (Fazio 1995). When the interviewer uttered the last syllable of a potential ambivalence question, she pressed a key to start a timer. When the respondent began to answer the inquiry, the interviewer pressed a key to stop the timer. The speeds of responses were combined mathematically into a measure of simultaneous accessibility.[7] Similar to various ambivalence measures, simultaneous accessibility scores increase as the conflicting unipolar evaluations come to mind more quickly, and equally quickly.

As expected, when potential ambivalence was relatively high in simultaneous accessibility, people's potential ambivalence about either capital punishment or abortion was generally borne out in corresponding feelings of ambivalence (a potential ambivalence/felt ambivalence correlation of $r = 0.73$ for high simultaneous accessibility versus $r = 0.32$ for low simultaneous accessibility; see figure 3.1 for an illustration). We confirmed our results in a second study using a lab-based methodology. The causal role of simultaneous accessibility, though, was still at issue because we measured but did not manipulate it in the first two studies. Thus, in a third study we randomly assigned participants to one of two conditions: In the high simultaneous-accessibility condition, participants were asked to repeatedly express their potential ambivalence, thereby increasing the simultaneous accessibility of that ambivalence (something we confirmed). Participants in the low simultaneous-accessibility condition did not repeatedly express their potential ambivalence. As was found in the first two studies, the relation between potential and felt ambivalence was more pronounced when potential ambivalence was high in simultaneous accessibility.

There is still further evidence for the role of simultaneous accessibility in ambivalence processes. Bassili (1998) studied ambivalence about affirmative action in a telephone survey of Toronto residents. Reflecting their experience of "intra-psychic conflict," ambivalent respondents were slower to express their opinion about affirmative action than were nonambivalent respondents. More to the point, the relation between that response latency and potential ambivalence was more pronounced for those whose contradictory values (i.e., merit versus equality) were relatively high in simultaneous accessibility.[8]

Racial Ambivalence Revisited

Hass, Katz, Rizzo, Bailey, and Moore (1992) examined racial ambivalence and the role of simultaneous accessibility, though they did not name it as such. In one of their studies, participants were randomly assigned to one of two conditions: In the high-salience condition (i.e., high simultaneous accessibility), whites living in New York were reminded about the Howard Beach incident, in which an armed gang of teenagers, on December 20, 1986, chased and brutalized three black men. Specifically, participants listened to an audiotape that they were told contained interviews with residents of Howard Beach; in reality, experimenters had created the recordings themselves. Some purported interviewees talked about their sympathy for the black men who were beaten, whereas others discussed the validity of the white youths' concerns. Participants in the low-salience condition (i.e., low simultaneous accessibility) did not listen to an audiotape at all. Those in both conditions subsequently completed a cleverly disguised measure of their mood.[9] Consistent with our findings, individuals who were reminded of the Howard Beach incident were in a more negative mood than were those in the low-salience condition. Most importantly, this effect was more pronounced for whites who reported feeling high levels of ambivalence about blacks.[10]

DEALING WITH THE EFFECTS OF SIMULTANEOUS ACCESSIBILITY: AVOIDING UNCOMFORTABLE FEELINGS

As we have shown, cognitive dissonance and potential ambivalence are similar in that both can give rise to uncomfortable feelings when the dissonance or ambivalence is simultaneously accessible. But what might be done when these negative feelings are actually experienced? Cognitive dissonance research points to various modes of resolution that may have relevance for the elimination of ambivalent feelings. We next consider various modes of resolution, from both the ambivalence and dissonance literatures, in turn.

Helping Behavior

Katz, Glass, Lucido, and Farber (1979) studied participants' behavioral responses to a disabled woman. A confederate (someone who worked for the experimenters unbeknownst to the participants) posed as a graduate student administering the experiment. Half the time she was in a wheelchair, and half of the time she was not. Under the guise of the development of a personality test, a group of participants answered various sentence-completion items. After ostensibly scoring participants' responses, the confederate announced that one of them had not provided candid responses and that his/her data was therefore not usable—a development that was of great inconvenience to her, and to her progress through graduate school. Participants then received private feedback on their responses to the personality test. On a randomly determined basis, some were informed that they had responded inappropriately and others were told that their responses were adequate.

Katz and his colleagues expected that participants who had unintentionally harmed the disabled research assistant would experience uncomfortable feelings because their actions supposedly created problems for someone toward whom they felt sympathetic. The researchers then provided a method by which the disagreeable feelings could be eliminated: Participants in all conditions were given the opportunity to volunteer their time to assist the confederate with her dissertation research. As expected, those who believed that they had harmed the ostensibly disabled research assistant reported a greater intention to help her than did participants in the other conditions. As the authors pointed out, these results could not be explained by concluding that there is greater sympathy for people in wheelchairs because participants who were told that their performance had been adequate did not volunteer to help out with the same frequency. Also, a guilt explanation was inadequate because participants who had unintentionally harmed a non-disabled confederate did not volunteer more than those who had not harmed the same confederate.

Denigrating Blacks

In the study just described, participants were given a *helping* opportunity as a means of resolving their uncomfortable feelings. A pro-social response is not one's only recourse, however. Indeed, Katz, Glass, and Cohen (1973) showed that the experience of uncomfortable feelings about harming a black person can lead to increased denigration. In another study, whites were assigned to the role of "sender" in an ESP experiment. Their job was to send messages to a "receiver." On a randomly determined basis, the receiver was either a black or white confederate. Senders were instructed to administer an electric shock to the receivers when the latter did not correctly report what had been sent. The set up in the laboratory was such that participants were persuaded that shocks were being delivered when, in fact, none were. For half the participants in each race-of-receiver condition, the shocks that they ostensibly delivered were understood to be mild; for the other half, the shocks were said to be strong.

The authors reasoned that white participants who delivered strong shocks to black receivers would experience uncomfortable feelings because they were aware that they were harming a person for whom they felt sympathy. A mode of resolution was then provided: All participants were asked to rate the personality of the confederate. As the researchers expected, those whites who had delivered strong shocks to black receivers gave more negative ratings than participants in the other three conditions. In a second experiment, Katz *et al.* (1973) showed that this effect was due primarily to participants who were racially ambivalent. In this case, then, participants resolved the inconsistency between their behavior and their sympathy for blacks by becoming less sympathetic.

Resolving Hypocrisy

Accessible dissonant cognitions may bring people to view themselves as hypocritical, which is surely an uncomfortable emotional state. In their investigation of personal hypocrisy, Stone, Aronson, Crain, Winslow, and Fried (1994) demonstrated that if research participants were made aware of their pro-safer-sex attitudes, and of the fact that they did not always consistently engage in safer-sex practices (again, witness the role of simultaneous accessibility), those individuals tended to respond by indicating a greater intention to engage in such practices in the future.[11]

In a similar vein, Son Hing, Li, and Zanna (2002) studied the implications of hypocrisy among ostensibly nonprejudiced people. The authors made participants simultaneously aware of their nonprejudiced attitudes and past prejudiced behaviors. In the hypocrisy-induction condition, participants completed an essay on the importance of fair treatment of minorities, including Asians, and were then asked to recall incidents when they reacted more negatively to an Asian than they believed they should have.

Next, on an apparently unrelated task, participants were asked to fill out a ballot concerning funding cuts to various student organizations, including an Asian student association. Those in the hypocrisy-induction condition made substantially fewer cuts to the Asian student association and, almost half the time, cut other clubs disproportionately so that the Asian club could receive an increase in funding. In other words, rendering hypocrisy simultaneously accessible led to a "bending over backwards" as individuals attempted to undo the hypocrisy.

Trivializing

Sometimes people can trivialize the source of their cognitive conflict, and thereby avoid negative feelings. Trivialization likely occurs when changing an inconsistent cognition to a consistent one is difficult to accomplish. In a set of studies, Simon, Greenberg, and Brehm (1995) had participants write an essay supporting mandatory comprehensive exams. Some participants wrote the essay under low-choice conditions; that is, they were told they must write an essay in support of the exams. Other participants wrote the essay under high-choice conditions; that is, they were told they could write an essay either in support of or against the exams, though the experimenters would prefer they choose the former.

While all participants in the high-choice condition wrote in support, the fact that they were presented with an option gave them an impression of choice. There was arguably no cognitive dissonance in the case of the low-choice condition, since participants were writing a pro-exam essay because they were instructed to do so. In the high-choice condition, however, there was cognitive dissonance because participants perceived that they chose to write an essay with which most of them disagreed.[12] In each of the two conditions, a random half of participants were reminded of their negative attitude toward mandatory exams. When they were not reminded of their attitude, researchers correctly anticipated that, as has been found in numerous cognitive dissonance studies, participants' attitudes toward the comprehensive exams would become more positive, thus resolving their dissonance (Eagly and Chaiken 1993). But when that mode of dissonance reduction was prevented by making their negative attitude salient, participants chose another route of resolution, that is, they trivialized the importance of the issue.[13]

THE PROBLEM OF AMBIVALENCE

Resolution of cognitive inconsistency, or trivialization of it, may not always be desirable. Indeed, in the case of ambivalence based on personal values, resolution may not even be possible. Consider a person who is ambivalent about abortion because s/he values both life and personal freedom. It is unlikely that such an individual will simply resolve his/her ambivalence by valuing personal freedom (or life) less, or by deciding that the issue is an unimportant one. Attitudes, ambivalent and nonambivalent alike, are often the product of deep-seated values, and are therefore highly stable over time (Eagly and Chaiken 1993). How, then, do people fulfill their motive of reducing uncomfortable feelings?

Distraction

Uncomfortable feelings caused by simultaneously accessible ambivalence could be reduced via self-distraction. In a clever study conducted by Brock (1962), non-Catholic Yale students wrote an essay entitled, "Why I Would Like to Become a Catholic," under conditions of low or high choice. Participants in both conditions were then assigned to reorder the sentences of their essays with regard to either the number of syllables each contained or the persuasiveness of the content. Those who focused on the syllables were presumably distracted from the content of their essays. Brock found a typical dissonance effect for the nondistracted participants; that is, people in the high-choice condition were more positive toward becoming a Catholic than those in the low choice condition. In the distracted condition, however, there was no such effect (see also Zanna and Aziza 1976).

How might distraction manifest itself in day-to-day life? One possibility is that individuals who are fundamentally ambivalent (because of conflicting values) might try to avoid situations in which their latent conflict is rendered accessible. For example, a Catholic feminist who is ambivalent about abortion might prefer to interact with either Catholic non-feminists or non-Catholic feminists—but not with members of both groups simultaneously (and perhaps not with other Catholic feminists).

Suppression

A psychological process that may operate in addition to, or in concert with, distraction is known as suppression (sometimes known as repression; for a discussion of this issue, see Singer 1990). Cooper and Stone (2000) reasoned that self-identified evangelical Christians would be unable to resolve and/or trivialize having voluntarily read statements aloud into a tape recorder that favored Buddhism as a superior religion; the centrality of their religious identity would prevent it (and the data bore this out). Yet, because their dissonance would need to be resolved, perhaps they could simply forget the words they had spoken. Indeed, that is what the researchers found: In a memory test, evangelical Christians in the high-choice condition recalled substantially less of the pro-Buddhist passage than did other participants. Nonevangelical Christians who read the pro-Buddhist statements under high-choice conditions, in contrast, became more positive toward Buddhism and showed no memory deficit.

Harkening back to the research described earlier regarding ambivalence toward feminists, we suggest that suppression of simultaneously accessible ambivalence may be more likely to occur when ambivalence is "cross-dimensional" than when it is within a single dimension (MacDonald and Zanna 1998). In other words, it may be easier to suppress ambivalence when a person is admired but not liked, as opposed to when a person is both admired and not admired. Similarly, in the political realm it may be easier to suppress ambivalence about capital punishment if it is favored for value-related reasons but not favored for pragmatic reasons, as opposed to being favored and disfavored due to a discrepancy in personal values. In our view, suppression (and distraction, for that matter) works because these processes, in effect, reduce simultaneous accessibility.

THE COST OF SUPPRESSION: SOME PROVOCATIVE DATA

Research in another area of social psychology leads us to speculate that there may be costs associated with suppression of ambivalence, necessary though it may be. Recent work by Roy Baumeister and colleagues on self-regulation has led them to conclude that people's "strength of will" is a limited resource that has the properties of a muscle (for a review see Muraven and Baumeister 2000). That is, when strength of will is exerted, one's ego strength becomes depleted and less strength remains for subsequent self-regulatory tasks.

In a series of clever studies, Baumeister, Bratslavsky, Muraven, and Tice (1998) put their theory to the test. In one particularly memorable experiment, participants first took part in a "taste-test study" before they moved on to a second, ostensibly unrelated, study on problem solving. In the taste-test phase, participants were assigned to one of two experimental groups: (1) the chocolate chip cookies condition; or (2) the radishes condition. All participants were hungry because they had been instructed to skip the meal that they would normally eat before the experiment. Also, the irresistible smell of freshly baked chocolate chip cookies wafted through the laboratory. On the table in front of them were a bowl of radishes and a plate of chocolate chip cookies; they were instructed to taste and rate one or the other, according to their condition. Participants in the chocolate-chip-cookies condition were instructed not to eat any radishes (probably an easy thing to resist), while participants in the radishes condition were told not to eat any cookies. The experimenters expected that participants in the radishes condition would need to exert a certain amount of willpower to resist eating the chocolate chips cookies, especially given the fact that they had not eaten recently and the smell of cookies was ubiquitous. After participants in the two food conditions had tasted and rated their assigned food, they moved on to the supposedly unrelated problem-solving task, where the main measure of the study was taken.

In the problem-solving portion of the study, participants were asked to complete a puzzle that, unbeknownst to them, was unsolvable. Every time someone ran into a dead-end in his/her attempt to solve the puzzle, the research assistant gave them an opportunity to make another attempt; the person was free to stop making attempts at any point. Baumeister and his colleagues (1998) reasoned that the number of attempts that participants made would be inversely related to the amount of will power that remained within them. Thus, they expected that participants in the radishes condition would make fewer attempts than participants in the chocolate-chip-cookies condition. In fact, that is precisely what they found. To rule out the possibility that participants in the chocolate-chip-cookies condition did not make more attempts than normal (possibly because of a sugar high!), experimenters included a control condition in which participants only took part in the problem-solving portion of the study. As expected, participants in the control condition made the same number of attempts as participants in the cookies condition.

It also appears that suppressing thoughts requires self-control and is similarly depleting. In two studies conducted by Muraven, Tice, and Baumeister (1998), some participants were instructed not to think about a white bear and others were assigned to a control condition. As Wegner (1994) has shown, trying not to think about something can be difficult. Subsequent measures of self-control—including, in this instance, persistence at an unsolvable task or suppressing laughter while watching amusing videos—revealed that earlier thought suppression led to depleted self-control.

For those who do achieve suppression of unwanted cognitive conflict, it may not last. Indeed, as Wegner (1994) demonstrated in a series of experiments, suppressed thoughts can often "rebound" and be in awareness as or more frequently than was originally the case. This rebound is especially pronounced when people's attentional resources are taxed in other ways. For example, if a person is suppressing cognitive conflict about abortion or capital punishment and then turns his/her attention to other matters that demand concentration, there may be a resultant resurgence of the unwanted thoughts.

There is some hope, though, for individuals who must constantly suppress their contradictory evaluations of a particular attitude object. In accord with their conceptualization of self-control as a muscle, Muraven, Baumeister, and Tice (1999) demonstrated that it is possible to strengthen people's self-control abilities through repeated exertion. Participants who had repeatedly exerted self-control over a two-week period were shown to have more of the limited resource available following a thought suppression task than participants in a control condition, who had not been required to exert self-control; however, the possibility of a rebound effect will always remain.

Compensatory Conviction

If suppression is often and ultimately ineffective, distraction holds some promise as a means of reducing or eliminating aversive feelings. Indeed, a particular kind of distraction may provide constant and reliable relief: People can draw their attention away from disturbing inconsistencies in their attitudes and values by instead focusing on unrelated but deep personal convictions. This "compensatory conviction" has been shown by McGregor and colleagues to be an effective way to distract oneself from the aversive experience of being aware of uncertainty in one's life. In one study (McGregor and Marigold 2003), for example, all participants wrote about a troubling dilemma they were currently facing in their lives. Participants in the conviction condition then wrote a paragraph describing their convictions about a social issue. Participants in the control condition instead wrote a paragraph describing someone else's convictions. So that the researchers could ascertain the accessibility of each individual's thoughts, participants then rated the salience of their personal dilemmas. McGregor and Marigold hypothesized and found that dispositionally "defensive" people who had been given the opportunity to engage in compensatory conviction reported less subjective salience of the original dilemma than did those in the control condition. In related experiments, McGregor and Marigold (2003) demonstrated that defensive participants spontaneously exaggerated their personal convictions as a way to distract themselves from personal uncertainty.

This fact may in some sense account for why people tend to hold their values as sacred and engage in rather hostile actions if they believe those values are under fire. Research on "moral cleansing" and "moral outrage" has found that after being induced to consider value-contradicting thoughts, individuals rebound with exaggerated value consistency in subsequent thoughts and actions. They also become more hostile toward value-offending others (Tetlock *et al.* 2000). Similarly, Jost, Glaser, Kruglanski, and Sulloway (2003) recently proposed that uncertainty is the driving force behind rigid, black-and-white values that are most often expressed by political conservatives, though no one is fully immune. A perspective that integrates all of these findings is that rigid convictions serve as "cognitive beacons" to draw attention away from troubling thoughts (McGregor 2004).

SUMMARY AND CONCLUSION

Ambivalence is ubiquitous, ranging from the prosaic (e.g., one's conflicted attitude toward fatty foods) to the profound (e.g., one's conflicted attitude toward abortion). Oftentimes, ambivalence is value-based and therefore chronic. Yet we must sometimes act in accord with either our positive or negative inclinations. We have argued that the accessibility of ambivalence is a key determinant of response. When sympathy for a member of a minority is in one's awareness, reactions to that person will be more positive than if hostility is at the forefront of consciousness. The consequences of *simultaneously accessible* ambivalence are different. We have shown that when people are aware of their conflicted cognitions or evaluations, an uncomfortable emotional state results. These uncomfortable emotions are aversive, and lead to efforts to reduce or eliminate them. Sometimes the conflicts themselves can be resolved, yet we suspect that this is not the path of least resistance in the case of value-based ambivalence. Changing one's attitude toward abortion or capital punishment is no light matter. Perhaps we can sometimes trivialize or forget (at least temporarily) about the issue that is causing us discomfort, but self-distraction seems a more likely candidate. Ironically, focusing on other deep values and convictions may serve as the best constant source for distraction from chronic value-based ambivalence.

NOTES

1. In other words, participants' positive or negative evaluations of native people were "primed" by the essays. The effect of priming is to cause associated concepts to become more accessible. In a classic demonstration of priming, Meyer and Schvaneveldt (1971) presented participants with pairs of letter strings on a screen. The letter strings were sometimes both words (e.g., "bread" and "butter"), but other times included pseudowords (e.g., "nurse" and "plame"). If both letter strings were words, participants pressed a "yes" key; otherwise, they pressed

a "no" key. Their response time in making a decision was measured. Also, sometimes the two letter strings were associated words (e.g., "bread" and "butter"), but in other trials the two letter strings were unassociated words (e.g., "bread" and "doctor"). The researchers found that response times were faster for associated words than for unassociated words. For more on priming see McKoon and Ratcliff (1992), and McNamara (1992, 1994).

2. The reverse pattern held for men who were ambivalent about traditional women, i.e., they tended to find traditional women likeable, but not worthy of respect.

3. Manipulation of accessibility was accomplished by first exposing all participants to an audiotape of an interview with a male job candidate. Participants in the admirability prime condition were told that the candidate got the job and were asked to report why the candidate could be thought of as determined, industrious, and intelligent. Participants in the likeability prime condition were told that the candidate did not get the job and were asked to report why the candidate could be thought of as cold, humorless, and irritable. In this way, one of the aspects of ambivalent attitudes toward feminists was rendered accessible (i.e., primed) without any direct mention of feminists (or females for that matter).

4. This is referred to by some scholars as *subjective* ambivalence.

5. This is referred to by some scholars as *objective* (as opposed to subjective; see n. 4) ambivalence.

6. There were six potential ambivalence questions, utilizing the format described earlier. Three questions focused on positive aspects (favorable, positive, beneficial) of the attitude object, and three focused on negative aspects (unfavorable, negative, harmful). Felt ambivalence was measured by asking respondents to agree or disagree with each of the following questions: (a) "I have strong mixed emotions both for and against capital punishment [abortion], all at the same time"; and (b) "I do not find myself feeling torn between the two sides of capital punishment [abortion]; my feelings go in one direction only" (reverse scored).

7. Reaction times were first reciprocally transformed (rendering them as speed scores). Emulating our calculation of potential ambivalence, we squared the slower response time and divided by the faster for each of the three pairs of questions, then averaged the three scores.

8. The affirmative action question was, "Do you think that large companies should have quotas to ensure a fixed percentage of women are hired, or should women get no special treatment?" The value questions were (a) "In selecting a person for a job, the choice should be based on the candidate's qualifications and nothing but these qualifications"; and (b) "It is important to counteract the effects of past discrimination against women by providing special opportunities for their employment" (see Bassili 1998).

9. The mood measure was ostensibly part of an unrelated study on subliminal perception. Participants were led to believe that, on a computer screen, a word would be shown that was hard to detect because it was shown for a brief period of time (20 milliseconds). In fact, a nonsense syllable was shown (but an interval

of 20 milliseconds is so fast that no participant could make it out). After each trial, participants were asked to identify the word that was shown, specifically, to select the word from one of four possible words. In each set of choices, there were three nonemotion words and one emotion word—either a positive emotion word (e.g., "cheerful") or a negative emotion word (e.g., "down"). Participants were told that detection of the word would be difficult but that they were to "go with their feelings" in determining which word had been shown. Selecting an emotion word contributed to an overall mood score.

10. Hass and his colleagues (1992) measured racial ambivalence with their Pro-Black and Anti-Black Attitude Questionnaire (PAAQ). This instrument separately measured positive and negative attitudes toward blacks using agree/disagree questions such as, "Many whites show a real lack of understanding of the problems that blacks face" (positive attitude item); and, "One of the biggest problems for a lot of blacks is their lack of self-respect" (negative attitude item).

11. This was measured in terms of how many condoms they purchased.

12. Disagreement was assumed rather than observed directly, though the pattern of dissonance effects (and the regularity with which similar paradigms are used) makes the assumption a reasonably safe one.

13. Trivialization was measured with such questions as, "How important [on a scale ranging from not at all to extremely important] is the issue of mandatory comprehensive finals in the grand scheme of things?"

4. Ambivalence and Response Instability 🙠

A Panel Study[1]

Stephen C. Craig, Michael D. Martinez, and James G. Kane

Public opinion research has yet to unravel all of the mysteries relating to the stability of attitudes. Instability was once regarded as a reflection either of non-attitudes that were more or less randomly expressed by survey respondents in polite deference to interviewers (Converse 1964, 1970), or of measurement error stemming from vague question wording and other factors having little to do with citizens' cognitive or motivational limitations (Achen 1975). More recently, psychologists and political scientists have embraced the idea that people do not necessarily have a single "true" attitude on issues, but rather a store of multiple and sometimes conflicting attitudes that they might draw upon at any given time (Zaller and Feldman 1992; also see Tesser 1978; Hochschild 1981; Tourangeau and Rasinski 1988; Zaller 1992; Schwartz and Bless 1992; Wilson and Hodges 1992; Hill and Kriesi 2001). While this perspective suggests that the presence of such conflict, or *ambivalence*, has significant effects on attitude stability, the empirical evidence to date is rather mixed. In the following report, we provide a direct examination of the effects of ambivalence on the stability of individuals' attitudes regarding the controversial issue of abortion.

THE CONCEPT OF AMBIVALENCE

Ambivalence exists when "individuals possess multiple and often conflicting opinions toward important issues"; it is a psychological state that can lead people to contradict themselves, that is, "to give temporally unstable responses in the course of a single conversation" (Zaller and Feldman 1992: 584) or, alternatively, at different stages of a multi-wave panel survey. The idea that citizens have competing and even conflicting attitudes is, of course, hardly novel, at least to social psychologists (Allport 1935; Scott 1968, 1969; Kaplan 1972) who have demonstrated on numerous occasions that attitudes can simultaneously have positive and negative components (Klopfer and Madden 1980; Katz, Wackenhut, and Hass 1986; Cacioppo and Berntson 1994; Thompson *et al.* 1995; Priester and Petty 1996, 2001; Lipkus *et al.* 2001; Newby-Clark *et al.* 2002). Thus, just as Hamlet both "loved and loathed" the young Ophelia, it is possible for voters to possess both positive and negative affect for their political leaders (Abelson *et al.* 1982) and other political objects and ideas.

The concept of ambivalence has recently begun to attract the attention of political scientists as well (e.g., Zaller 1992; Zaller and Feldman 1992; Feldman and Zaller 1992; Cantril and Cantril 1999; Meffert *et al.* 2000; Steenbergen and Brewer 2000; Frankovic and McDermott 2001; Lavine 2001; Jacoby 2002; McGraw *et al.* 2003; Haddock 2003; Huckfeldt *et al.* 2004). Alvarez and Brehm (1995; also see 2002 and chapter 2 in this volume), for example, tested a heteroskedastic probit model and reached the conclusion that Americans are somewhat ambivalent about abortion but less so in terms of their racial attitudes.[2] Craig, Kane, and Martinez (2002) likewise found ambivalence on abortion to be fairly common, though results varied according to whether the circumstances under which a woman chose to have an abortion were "elective" or "traumatic" (Cook *et al.* 1992; this distinction is discussed more fully in the next section).

There is, however, surprisingly little research to date that directly examines whether ambivalence reduces attitude stability, and the handful of studies that exist fail to produce a clear answer. Zaller and Feldman (1992) concluded that ambivalence contributes to instability in opinion surveys, but their results are, at best, marginal (and attributed partly to the effects of "coding error"; see p. 598); further, the manner in which that study operationalized ambivalence—for example, whether a person's orientations consistently favored one side or the other of an issue—is arguable (Alvarez and Brehm 1995; Meffert *et al.* 2000; Craig *et al.* 2002). Hill and Kriesi's (2001) analysis of citizens' attitudes toward automobile regulations in Switzerland suggested that unstable responses over a two-year period may have been a function of attitude conflict, though these authors did not directly measure ambivalence in individuals. Some support for the idea that ambivalence reduces attitude stability is found in the psychology literature. In an experimental study of undergraduate psychology students, for example, Bargh, Chaiken, Govender, and Pratto (1992) found ambivalence to be negatively correlated with attitude consistency over a three- to six-week period. But the linkage between ambivalence and attitude instability has not always been evident (e.g., see Bassili 1996b and Armitage and Connor 2000), leaving some doubt about the generalizability of the relationship. It is conceivable that the destabilizing effects of ambivalence, to the extent they exist at all, are either domain-specific or dependent upon the presence of other attitude characteristics. In particular, previous research indicates that *issue salience*, or *attitude importance*, may be a necessary catalyst affecting the relationship between inconsistency and change (Abelson 1959; Zajonc 1968; Tourangeau *et al.* 1989b). Following this reasoning, generally healthy individuals who are ambivalent about low-fat diets might not think about them enough to generate significant attitude change, but ambivalence about political issues (different ones for different people) may be related to instability precisely because of the importance attached to the conflicting considerations.

Accordingly, the argument tested here is, first, that there is a significant link between ambivalence and response instability across surveys; and, second, that the strength of this relationship is amplified by attitude importance. In other words, we anticipate that individuals who are ambivalent about matters they consider to be important will exhibit the greatest degree of change over time.

DATA AND METHODOLOGY

The present study is based on a two-wave telephone panel survey of registered Florida voters, conducted in January/February and June of 1999 by the *Florida Voter* survey organization.[3] From an initial pool of 708 completed interviews in January/February, we base our analysis on 426 individuals (60.2 percent) who participated in both waves.[4] In order to ensure that responses were unaffected by either wording differences or question order (Schuman and Presser 1981), identical question batteries were employed in each instance.

The central theme in the surveys was abortion, an issue of great and perhaps growing importance in American politics (Cook *et al.* 1992, 1994; Smith 1994; Adams 1997; Abramowitz 1995, 1997) and one about which many voters have been shown to be ambivalent (Alvarez and Brehm 1995; Craig *et al.* 2002). Respondents were asked a series of questions that have been included on a more-or-less regular basis in General Social Surveys (GSS) since 1972. The GSS battery is as follows: "Please tell me whether or

not you think it should be possible for a pregnant woman to obtain a legal
abortion if . . ."

- there is a strong chance of serious defect in the baby?
- she is married and does not want any more children?
- the woman's own health is seriously endangered by the pregnancy?
- the family has a very low income and cannot afford any more children?
- she became pregnant as a result of rape?
- she is not married and does not want to marry the man?
- the woman wants it for any reason?

We expect our analysis to show that the likelihood of over-time change in
answers to these questions is greater among respondents who express
ambivalence about the issue of abortion.

In line with prior research (Cook *et al.* 1992; also see Wald 1992), both
confirmatory and principal-components factor analyses revealed that abortion preferences fell into two distinct clusters depending upon whether the
circumstances were regarded as "elective" (too poor, no more children, not
married, any reason) or "traumatic" (woman's health, rape, birth defect),
with levels of support being much higher for the latter than the former.[5]
We also used confirmatory factor analysis to determine that the stability of
preferences from January/February to June was relatively high: correlations
of 0.807 for traumatic and 0.784 for elective.[6] Any empirically demonstra-
ble explanation of the limited instability that does exist should therefore be
all the more impressive.

How, then, should ambivalence, our principal independent variable, be
measured? For reasons outlined elsewhere (Craig *et al.* 2002), we chose not
to follow the approaches recommended by Feldman and Zaller (1992;
also Zaller and Feldman 1992; Zaller 1992; cf. Cantril and Cantril 1999),
who failed to distinguish adequately between "multiple" and "conflicting"
considerations (i.e., people are not ambivalent unless they experience
some degree of genuine psychological conflict); or by Alvarez and Brehm
(1995, 2002), whose heteroskedastic probit model cannot tell us how
much ambivalence exists for a single individual with regard to a given attitude object. Instead, we employed an adaptation of Kaplan's (1972)
method of gauging simultaneously conflicting reactions to a single object.

Recognizing that some attitudes are multipolar rather than bipolar (e.g.,
Abelson *et al.* 1982; Katz and Hass 1988; Cacioppo and Berntson 1994;
Thompson *et al.* 1995; Priester and Petty 1996; Cacioppo *et al.* 1997;
Meffert *et al.* 2000), Kaplan divided the semantic differential scale (Osgood
et al. 1957) at the neutral point and asked subjects to register positive and

negative sentiments separately. Ambivalence is thus measured as a direct function of the "total affect" toward an attitude object (positive plus negative reactions) less the "polarity" of those reactions (the absolute value of positive minus negative responses).

Because this technique was designed for experimental studies, we modified Kaplan's language to accommodate for the limitations of a telephone survey:

> I'm now going to read a series of statements about abortion. After each, I'd like you to consider only your positive feelings for the statement while ignoring any negative feelings you may have for it. Using a 4-point scale, I'd like you to indicate how *positively* you feel toward the statement. If you do not have any positive feelings toward the statement, give the statement the lowest rating of 1; if you have some positive feelings, rate it a 2; if you have generally positive feelings, rate it a 3; and if you have extremely positive feelings, rate it a 4. Please rate each statement based solely on how positively you feel about it, while ignoring or setting aside for the moment any negative feelings you may have for the statement. The first statement is . . . A woman should be able to obtain a legal abortion if there is a strong chance of a serious defect in the baby.[7]

Interviewers read statements covering all seven conditions listed in the GSS battery and asked respondents to rate each one separately.[8] After some filler,[9] the introduction was changed to replace "positive" and "positively" with "negative" and "negatively," and the seven statements were read again. Instructions were repeated if any respondent seemed confused or unsure about what was being asked.

It should be noted that the wording here differs slightly from some prior research which also utilized Kaplan's method of measuring ambivalence. Whereas our questions refer explicitly to an individual's positive and negative *feelings* about these various conditions, other researchers have inquired about the positive and negative qualities of the attitude object. For example, Bassili (1996b: 642; also see Armitage and Connor 2000) asked respondents, "Considering only the positive qualities of a law . . . would you say that the positive qualities of the law are extremely positive, quite positive, slightly positive, or not at all positive?" Conflicting *affective* reactions tapped by our measure could be more salient to the respondent than conflicting *cognitive* assessments, and therefore might be more likely to produce attitude change.

Finally, we employed the similarity–intensity measurement strategy, developed by Thompson and her colleagues and calculated ambivalence as

$$Ambivalence = [(P + N)/2] - |P - N|$$

where P is the positive reaction score and N is the negative reaction score; the range of values for each of our seven ambivalence measures is from -0.5 to $+4.0$, with higher numbers indicating a greater degree of ambivalence.[10] For Thompson et al. (1995; also see Craig et al. 2002), this algorithm proved to be a superior predictor of *subjective* ambivalence, that is, the degree to which individuals report feeling discomfort when asked to evaluate some attitude object.

RESULTS

Dimensions of Preference and Ambivalence

In table 4.1, we show the frequency of ambivalence on these abortion questions, based on a minimal (though admittedly arbitrary) similarity–intensity score greater than zero. From the first column in table 4.1, we can see that nearly 74 percent of our entire sample ($N = 708$) at t_1 had some ambivalent reactions to at least one of the seven abortion statements; almost 59 percent expressed ambivalence on two or more occasions. The mean number of statements about which these voters felt ambivalent was 2.24. Considering only the 426 individuals who participated in both waves of the survey (column 2), the overall pattern at t_1 is very similar, for example, an

Table 4.1   Frequency of ambivalent feelings on seven GSS abortion statements

Number of statements	(Wave one all) Percent Ambivalent	(Wave One Panel) Percent Ambivalent	(Wave Two Panel) Percent Ambivalent
None	26.4	24.9	34.6
One	14.8	16.6	15.4
Two	17.3	17.1	15.4
Three	17.0	15.5	18.4
Four	12.2	12.6	7.4
Five	4.3	3.7	3.5
Six	3.3	4.3	2.4
Seven	4.8	5.3	2.9
Mean	2.24	2.29	1.83

Note: Data are from the January/February ($N = 708$) and June ($N = 426$) waves of the 1999 *Florida Voter* panel survey. Table entries indicate the percentage of respondents (excluding those with missing values) with similarity–intensity ambivalence scores greater than zero (see n.11) on a given number of GSS abortion statements. Column 1 includes all respondents interviewed in the first wave of the panel; columns 2 and 3 include only those who participated in both waves.

average (mean) of 2.29 ambivalent reactions.[11] While ambivalence levels were slightly lower at t_2 (mean of 1.83; see column 3),[12] about two-thirds of all respondents expressed ambivalence on at least one of the statements and half were ambivalent about two or more.

As previously noted, abortion preferences as represented by answers to the GSS battery form two distinct clusters: *elective* and *traumatic.* According to Craig *et al.* (2002), there is a tendency for voters who identify themselves as being pro-choice to exhibit greater ambivalence with regard to elective abortion (too poor, no more children, not married, any reason), while self-professed pro-lifers tend to be more ambivalent about abortion in traumatic circumstances (woman's health, rape, birth defect). In other words, people who usually oppose abortion often feel less comfortable doing so when the pregnancy is involuntary, or when either mother or child faces serious health problems; those who usually support a woman's right to choose often feel less comfortable when the decision to abort is more of an economic or social choice than a medical one. Moreover, factor analysis results show a similar two-dimensional structure of ambivalence (as distinct from preferences): ambivalence scores for the traumatic conditions load highly on one dimension, while ambivalence scores for the elective conditions load on a distinct second dimension (Craig *et al.* 2002: 293–295). In recognition of these patterns, we have created separate indices for each domain: Elective ambivalence is the mean of similarity–intensity scores for the four elective conditions, and traumatic ambivalence is calculated in a similar fashion for the three remaining conditions.

Stability of Preferences

Recall that panel respondents were asked the seven GSS questions regarding approval of a woman's right to a legal abortion in both our January/February and June 1999 surveys. As shown in table 4.2, just 25 percent of those who participated in both waves of our survey exhibited any degree of instability on the three traumatic statements, while 37 percent were inconsistent on one or more of the four elective options—modest figures overall, but hardly insignificant given that abortion is clearly what Carmines and Stimson (1980; also see Adams 1997) called an "easy" issue, and that the questions used to tap preferences on it required only a simple "yes" or "no" answer. A measure of instability was created for each dimension (elective or traumatic) equal to the number of statements on which respondents expressed inconsistent views across the two waves;[13] scores range from 0 (perfectly stable) to 4 (changed answers on "too poor," "no more children," "not married," and "any reason") on elective abortion, and from 0 (perfectly stable) to 3 (changed answers on "woman's health," "rape," and "birth defect") on traumatic abortion.

Table 4.2   Instability of abortion preferences over time

Number of statements	Traumatic abortion percent unstable	Elective abortion percent unstable
None	75.0	63.0
One	13.6	16.0
Two	6.8	9.2
Three	4.6	4.1
Four	n/a	7.6
Number of cases =	363	363

Note: Data are from the 1999 *Florida Voter* panel survey. Table entries indicate the percentage of respondents expressing inconsistent preferences (including shifts to and from "don't know"; see n.13) in January/February and June on a given number of GSS abortion questions, by dimension of preference.

There is little relationship to speak of ($r = 0.11$) between the two attitude change measures, that is, voters with unstable preferences regarding one type of abortion exhibited only a slight tendency to be unstable on the other type as well. Also in line with our expectations, 53 percent of pro-life voters exhibited fixed opinions on the traumatic dimension (compared with 88 percent of pro-choicers), while 55 percent of pro-choice respondents remained stable on elective abortion (compared with 76 percent of pro-lifers). These differences are extremely unlikely to have occurred by chance alone ($\chi^2 < 0.001$) and, unless one wishes to contend (implausibly in our view) that such error is somehow systematic, they do not fit well with the notion (e.g., Zaller and Feldman 1992) that most over-time inconsistencies are due to measurement error.

Bivariate Analyses

Returning to our main theme, we wish to determine whether ambivalence contributes to attitude instability over time. The simple bivariate correlations suggest that it does: Instability with regard to elective abortion is associated with elective ambivalence ($r = 0.226$, $p < 0.001$, $N = 365$), while instability with regard to traumatic abortion is associated with traumatic ambivalence ($r = 0.161$, $p = 0.002$, $N = 364$). Further, in line with our discovery that both preferences and ambivalence about abortion are dimension-specific, elective instability is *unrelated* to traumatic ambivalence ($r = -0.034$, $p = 0.513$, $N = 365$), while traumatic instability is modestly *negatively* correlated with elective ambivalence ($r = -0.114$, $p < 0.05$, $N = 364$). Prior research has shown that people who are ambivalent about elective abortion tend to be more reliably pro-choice on traumatic conditions (Craig *et al.* 2002). The findings here suggest that those preferences also are slightly more stable over time.

Control Variables

It is conceivable, of course, that other aspects of respondents' abortion attitudes could be responsible for a spurious relationship between ambivalence and instability. Other scholars have identified a variety of attitude characteristics that are believed to be associated with instability and, as a result, may serve to weaken the relationship between it and ambivalence. Several of these characteristics were measured in our surveys (see Appendix for question wording):

1. *Importance*: People who feel an issue is personally important to them presumably care deeply about that issue and attach considerable significance to it in their daily lives (Krosnick and Abelson 1992; Krosnick 1988b; Boninger *et al.* 1995b); as a result, attitudes regarding the issue should be resistant to change (Krosnick 1988a; Krosnick and Petty 1995; Schuman and Presser 1981).

2. *Certainty* refers to the confidence that one's views are correct. Individuals possessing a high degree of certainty should be less likely than others to accept opposing arguments (Gross *et al.* 1995; Krosnick and Abelson 1992) and, hence, less likely to alter their views over time (Pelham 1991).

3. *Elaboration* has to do with whether someone has given thoughtful consideration to an idea; if so, it seems likely that the idea will be more persistent and resistant to change (Petty and Cacioppo 1986b; Petty *et al.* 1995). Our measure of elaboration ("how often would you say you think about the issue of abortion?") is similar to that used by Krosnick *et al.* (1993: 1133) to tap "accessibility."

4. *Extremity* is often described (Abelson 1995; Krosnick and Abelson 1992; Krosnick *et al.* 1993) as the extent to which an attitude deviates from the norm or midpoint on some univariate scale. Using a similar logic, the approach here is to count, separately, the number of yes (pro-choice) and no (pro-life) answers given to the seven GSS questions on abortion. Respondents are then scored zero if this number is at or below the overall sample mean (rounded to 4 "yes" and 3 "no"), and either 1 through 3 (pro-choice) or 1 through 4 (pro-life) if it is above the mean. Not surprisingly, there is a fairly strong, though less than perfect, negative correlation between pro-choice extremity and pro-life extremity ($r = -0.58$ in both waves). If prior research is correct, extreme attitudes should be more polarized and

more intense (Abelson 1995; Krosnick *et al.* 1993) and, as a result, more stable (Feldman 1989).

5. *Intensity* refers to the fervor of emotional reaction to an issue or other attitude object (Krosnick and Abelson 1992; Krosnick *et al.* 1993; Krosnick and Schuman 1988; Schuman and Presser 1981). Attitudes buttressed by strong feelings should be particularly resistant to change.

6. *Commitment*, as measured here, combines two items from a battery that seems, according to Abelson (1988: 272) "to capture the raw stuff of emotional conviction." We combine the action component of attitude importance (including the willingness to work on behalf of an issue or cause) with beliefs about whether one's views are likely to change. A stronger commitment, in both senses, implies a greater degree of stability.

7. *Political Knowledge* is not an aspect of abortion attitudes *per se*, but it seems probable that the views of someone who is generally knowledgeable will be less susceptible to change (e.g., because of a greater capacity for counterarguing). Prior research suggests that knowledge contributes to response stability (Feldman 1989).

Most of these measures (importance, certainty, elaboration, intensity, commitment) are negatively correlated with ambivalence about abortion,[14] but only with ambivalence on the elective dimension. Exceptions to this general rule are certainty ($r = -0.11$ with traumatic and -0.18 with elective ambivalence); political knowledge (not correlated with either dimension); and extremity, which is a special case because it is calculated separately for pro-life and pro-choice preferences. The former is correlated positively with traumatic ambivalence (0.17) and negatively (-0.27) with elective ambivalence; the latter is correlated negatively (-0.28) with traumatic ambivalence and uncorrelated with elective ambivalence.[15]

Coefficients in the first column of table 4.3 are bivariate correlations between the variables listed above (as well as ambivalence) and response instability for elective abortion. The overall pattern of these relationships is fairly straightforward: Respondents with lower levels of general knowledge, commitment, elaboration, certainty, importance, and pro-life extremity are more likely to change their answers to the basic GSS questions concerning whether abortions should be legally permitted in elective situations; intensity and pro-choice extremity, on the other hand, are not significantly associated with instability.[16]

We also estimated the relative impact of each of these measures in an ordered logit regression (McCullagh and Nelder 1989) since the upper and lower limits on our dependent variables—a simple count of inconsistent responses between t_1 and t_2 as to whether a legal abortion should be

Table 4.3   A multivariate model of response instability on elective abortion

Variable	Bivariate correlation	Model 1		Model 2	
		b	*s.e.*	*b*	*s.e.*
Elective ambivalence	**0.226**	**0.355**	0.138	**0.514**	0.237
Traumatic ambivalence	−0.034	0.125	0.121	0.172	0.196
Importance	−0.136	0.163	0.210	0.250	0.229
Certainty	−0.107	−0.168	0.101	−0.162	0.101
Elaboration	−0.184	−0.464	0.235	−0.455	0.235
Extremity (pro-life)	−0.295	−1.561	0.282	−1.581	0.282
Extremity (pro-choice)	0.094	−0.456	0.125	−0.450	0.125
Intensity	−0.095	0.045	0.224	0.011	0.227
Commitment	−0.132	0.054	0.067	0.053	0.068
Political knowledge	−0.150	−0.222	0.109	−0.225	0.109
Demographics					
Age		0.018	0.093	0.023	0.093
Gender (female)		0.005	0.260	−0.017	0.262
Education		0.020	0.127	0.012	0.127
Interaction terms					
Traumatic ambivalence ×					
Importance		n/a		−0.027	0.157
Elective ambivalence ×					
Importance		n/a		−0.151	0.191
Pseudo R^2 (Nagelkerke)		0.306		0.308	
−2 Log Likelihood		637.660		636.680	
Number of cases =		333		333	

Note: Data are from the 1999 *Florida Voter* panel survey. Bivariate correlations are Pearson's *r*. Coefficients for models 1 and 2 are ordered logit estimates, with associated standard errors ($p < 0.05$ in bold). The dependent variable is the number of statements (range 0–4) about elective abortion on which respondents expressed inconsistent views in January/February and June.

available under traumatic and elective circumstances—violate classic least squares assumptions.[17] Table 4.3 shows parameter estimates for two models of response instability on elective abortion. The first model includes ambivalence and other characteristics of abortion attitudes, plus demographic variables (age, gender, education). Here again, results suggest that several of the characteristics have an impact; specifically, individuals who think about abortion a great deal, who are convinced their views are correct ($p < 0.10$), who are more knowledgeable about politics (Feldman 1989), and who take an extreme position (either pro-life or pro-choice) tend to have more stable preferences regarding the conditions under which elective abortions should be permitted. Most importantly for our purposes, the relationship between elective ambivalence and response instability is *not* attenuated by other variables included in the model; in other words, the

Table 4.4   A multivariate model of response instability on traumatic abortion

Variable	Bivariate correlation	Model 1		Model 2	
		b	s.e	b	s.e.
Elective ambivalence	**−0.114**	−0.272	0.171	−0.137	0.308
Traumatic ambivalence	**0.161**	**0.390**	0.131	0.091	0.255
Importance	**0.170**	0.489	0.281	0.449	0.301
Certainty	0.040	−0.036	0.128	−0.034	0.129
Elaboration	**0.136**	−0.058	0.269	0.071	0.270
Extremity (pro-life)	**0.322**	0.243	0.141	0.224	0.143
Extremity (pro-choice)	**−0.279**	**−0.612**	0.190	**−0.611**	0.192
Intensity	**0.119**	−0.245	0.286	−0.228	0.293
Commitment	0.049	−0.011	0.078	−0.022	0.079
Political knowledge	−0.040	−0.132	0.129	−0.146	0.129
Demographics					
Age		0.053	0.110	0.041	0.111
Gender (Female)		−0.164	0.298	−0.206	0.300
Education		−0.166	0.141	−0.186	0.143
Interaction terms					
Traumatic ambivalence × importance		n/a		0.252	0.178
Elective ambivalence × importance		n/a		−0.234	0.220
Pseudo R^2 (Nagelkerke)		0.248		0.255	
−2 Log Likelihood		452.787		450.434	
Number of cases =		332		332	

Note: Data are from the 1999 *Florida Voter* panel survey. Bivariate correlations are Pearson's *r*. Coefficients for models 1 and 2 are ordered logit estimates, with associated standard errors ($p < 0.05$ in bold). The dependent variable is the number of statements (range 0–3) about traumatic abortion on which respondents expressed inconsistent views in January/ February and June.

correlation between elective ambivalence and instability does not appear to be spurious.

As noted earlier, we anticipated that voters who were ambivalent about matters they considered to be personally important would exhibit the greatest over-time instability (Tourangeau *et al.* 1989b). This proposition is tested in model 2, which adds two new interaction terms (traumatic ambivalence × importance) and (elective ambivalence × importance), to our list of independent variables. As shown in the last two columns of table 4.3, neither of these has any real effect on stability. In fact, our results are little changed from what we found in model 1: Elective ambivalence, standing alone, remains highly significant, as do elaboration, certainty ($p < 0.10$), knowledge, and extremity in each direction.

The same two models are tested again in table 4.4, with instability regarding traumatic abortion as the dependent variable. Bivariate correlations are quite different than before, and somewhat unexpected as attitude change between t_1 and t_2 appears to be *positively* associated with importance, elaboration, and intensity (plus commitment and certainty, though the latter two correlations are not significant). One possible explanation for this unusual finding is that general questions about the strength of one's abortion views— or at least the ones employed here—tend to elicit people's attitudes toward elective abortion to a greater degree than their attitudes toward traumatic abortion.[18] As a result, when respondents were asked to indicate how important the abortion issue was to them personally, they may have been inclined (for example) to consider the question more in terms of an unmarried woman who does not want to marry the father than in terms of a rape victim.

Model 1 in table 4.4 suggests that the positive effects of traumatic ambivalence and the negative effects of elective ambivalence on traumatic instability persist even when the impacts of other variables are taken into account. Indeed, the multivariate results in Model 1 may tempt some to conclude that ambivalence and extremity are the critical factors in any explanation of response instability with regard to traumatic abortion. However, because most of our control variables (except for extremity) are both (1) general reactions to the abortion issue rather than domain specific, and (2) meta-attitudinal measures based on respondents' self-reports of attitude characteristics (cf. Bassili 1996b), we prefer a more cautious and straightforward interpretation of our evidence: Ambivalence is associated with response instability on traumatic abortion, even when other attitudinal characteristics are held constant.

The addition of interaction terms in model 2 tells us whether the destabilizing effects of ambivalence are greater among individuals who consider abortion to be an important issue. As we saw with elective abortion, there is no support for this hypothesis: Neither of the interaction terms (nor, for that matter, any of the main effects involving ambivalence and importance) are significant; indeed, the only variable left standing is pro-choice extremity. Our data once again fail to support the proposition that attitude stability is greatest among those who combine ambivalence with a sense of issue importance.

CONCLUSION

Results from our 1999 panel survey of Florida voters suggest that ambivalence has a significant impact on the over-time stability of abortion preferences, even when other dimensions of attitude strength are held constant. Ambivalence clearly is a key aspect of public opinion on one of the most emotionally charged and controversial issues of our time.

In light of what we have seen, it does not appear that abortion is such an "easy" issue after all (Carmines and Stimson 1980; Adams 1997). First, opinions about when women should be able to obtain a legal abortion are multi-faceted for many citizens; they depend upon whether the circumstances are traumatic (woman's health, rape, birth defect) or elective (too poor, no more children, not married, any reason)—and, consequently, survey questions designed to gauge the level of public support for abortion rights should be written with these distinctions in mind. Second, ambivalence regarding abortion breaks into the same two dimensions: some people express ambivalent feelings about traumatic abortion, others are ambivalent about elective abortion, and there is only a modest degree of overlap between the two ($r = 0.23$). Third, people with unstable preferences on one type of abortion do not necessarily tend to be unstable on the other type as well, that is, the correlation between the two attitude change indices is positive but weak ($r = 0.11$).

These complexities suggest that many voters do not believe the abortion issue to be as clear-cut as the extreme pro-choice and pro-life factions insist that it is. They also raise doubts about the argument that measurement error is at the root of all, or at least most, of the response instability observed in public opinion surveys. As some researchers in both political science (Hochschild 1981; Zaller and Feldman 1992; Zaller 1992) and social psychology (Katz 1981; Eagly and Chaiken 1993) have argued, ambivalence plays an important role in determining whether or not such instability occurs—certainly on abortion and, almost certainly, on attitudes about many other issues as well. While our results do not call into question the importance of measurement error in surveys, they indicate that people may express varied opinions over time if their psychological conflict with a salient issue remains unresolved.

APPENDIX

Question wordings and coding schemes for the control variables employed in tables 4.3 and 4.4 are as follows:

Importance: How important is the abortion issue to you personally—would you say it is very important, somewhat important, or not very important to you personally? [Scored 0 (not very important) to 2 (very important).]

Certainty: I think my views about abortion are absolutely correct. [Scored 1 (strongly disagree) to 5 (strongly agree).]

Elaboration: How often would you say you think about the issue of abortion—would you say you think about it often, ever once in a while, or hardly at all? [Scored 0 (hardly at all) to 2 (often).]

Extremity (Pro-Life): Calculated as the number of "no" answers to the seven GSS abortion statements, with that number recoded to reflect how many such responses above the sample mean (2.56, rounded up to 3) were given by each individual. [Scored 0 (3 or fewer "no" answers), 1 (4 "no"), 2 (5 "no"), 3 (6 "no"), and 4 (7 "no," the most extreme pro-life position.]

Extremity (Pro-Choice): Calculated as the number of "yes" answers to the seven GSS abortion statements, with that number recoded to reflect how many such responses above the sample mean (3.66 rounded up to 4) were given by each individual. [Scored 0 (4 or fewer "yes" answers), 1 (5 "yes"), 2 (6 "yes"), and 3 (7 "yes").]

Intensity: Compared to how you feel on other issues, are your feelings on abortion extremely strong, fairly strong, or not very strong? [Scored 0 (not very strong) to 2 (extremely strong).]

Commitment: (a) I would be willing to spend a day a month working for a group supporting my abortion views. (b) I can't imagine ever changing my mind about abortion. [Each question scored 1 (strongly disagree) to 5 (strongly agree).]

Political Knowledge: (a) First, do you happen to know what job or political office is now held by Al Gore? (vice president) (b) Whose responsibility is it to determine if a law is constitutional or not? (Supreme Court) (c) Do you happen to know which party has the most members in the House of Representatives in Washington? (Republican) (d) How much of a majority is required for the U.S. Senate and House to override a presidential veto? (two-thirds) (e) Would you say that one of the parties is more conservative than the other at the national level? Which party would you say is more conservative? (Republican) [Additive index scored 0 (none correct) to 5 (all correct).]

NOTES

1. An earlier version of this paper was presented at the 2000 Annual Meeting of the American Political Science Association. We appreciate helpful comments on the paper provided by Jon Krosnick and Laura Stoker.
2. For a different conclusion regarding race, see Katz and Hass (1988).
3. The findings reported here are based upon surveys conducted January 26 through February 9, 1999 (t_1) and June 14–27, 1999 (t_2). The sampling frame was created from a random selection of Florida registered voters (derived from current registration rolls) with working telephone numbers. If needed, a minimum of four callbacks were made in both waves to each working number in an effort to obtain a completed interview. The response rate at t_1 was 54.6 percent of working numbers with voters in the household. Additional information concerning these polls can be obtained from *Florida Voter* directly

(954-584-0204), or from the Graduate Program in Political Campaigning in the Political Science Department at the University of Florida (352-392-0262).

4. The margin of error for this sample was plus or minus 4.8 percentage points. Although attrition can be a problem in panel studies, we were unable to identify any systematic differences (demographic or otherwise, including attitudes about abortion) between voters who participated only in the first wave and those who cooperated in both waves.

5. Overall, Florida voters look very much like the country as a whole in terms of their attitudes about abortion (see Craig *et al.* 2002). In the January/February wave, for example, 89 percent said that a woman should be able to obtain a legal abortion if her health is endangered, 84 percent in the event of rape, 82 percent if there is a chance for serious defect, 44 percent if the family is poor, 41 percent if the woman is not married, 40 percent if she does not want any more children, and 35 percent for any reason at all. Figures were virtually identical for respondents interviewed again in wave two.

6. Correlations *between* the two factors were trivial: 0.049 and 0.063 in January/February and June, respectively.

7. The setup language for this question is slightly different from that described in Craig *et al.* (2002). Also, the GSS preference questions were asked prior to the ambivalence questions in that earlier study, while ambivalence was asked first in both 1999 surveys. The fact that results from the two studies are generally consistent suggests that order effects were not a serious problem.

8. As indicated by the first statement (serious defect), it was necessary to modify the GSS language slightly. For example, "If she is married and does not want any more children" became "A woman should be able to obtain a legal abortion if she is married and does not want any more children."

9. Seven questions, including five that measured political knowledge, separated the positive and negative abortion series. This is in line with the finding by Thompson *et al.* (1995) that more filler questions reduced the correlation between positive and negative responses. In our study, these correlations were negative and in the 0.50–0.60 range—higher than the (roughly) 0.40 reported by Thompson *et al.* based on a paper-and-pencil questionnaire that had numerous filler questions. We believe that the difference is due primarily to the number of questions separating positive and negative statements. Craig, Kane, and Martinez (2002) found negative correlations in the 0.70 range when the two sets of reactions were tapped without *any* filler questions separating them. In other words, the positive and negative components of ambivalence appear to become increasingly independent of one another as consistency effects (due to question placement) decline.

10. Although scores are based on responses in the January/February wave of the panel, our results are substantively similar when ambivalence is measured as a person's mean score across the two waves.

11. Using the similarity–intensity measure, respondents are scored as ambivalent if they have a score greater than zero. Consequently, for purposes of the calculations described in this paragraph, a score of -0.5 is regarded as equivalent to zero.

12. Results here suggest that even though the two surveys were conducted almost six months apart, some voters may have become sensitized to the questions and avoided giving answers that seemed inconsistent (Schuman and Presser 1981). Alternatively, it is possible that ambivalence is not a permanent state of conflict but instead may vary depending upon the moment or the context in which the abortion questions are posed (cf. Zaller and Feldman 1992).

13. We included "don't know" responses in our calculations, since shifting to or from "don't know" could indicate an ambivalent attitude. The inclusion of these responses does not, however, alter the conclusions drawn here or elsewhere in the chapter.

14. Except as noted below, the correlations (Pearson's r) are roughly -0.15 or slightly higher. All of the variables described in the preceding paragraph are derived from responses to wave 1 questions only.

15. For the most part, this follows the simple relationship between abortion preferences and ambivalence reported in Craig *et al.* (2002): Voters having extreme pro-life views tend to be more ambivalent regarding traumatic abortions but less ambivalent regarding elective abortions; those having extreme pro-choice views tend to be ambivalent only about abortions that take place under traumatic circumstances.

16. It is possible that the effects observed here are especially pronounced at the upper ends of our respective scales; if so, squaring respondents' scores might reveal the relationships in table 4.3 (and table 4.4 which follows) to be more robust. We do not, however, find this to be the case.

17. These include the assumption of homoskedasticity of error terms, and the possibility that predicted values could lie outside the actual limits of the dependent variable.

18. In Zaller's (1992) formulation, the strength questions may have triggered a *nonrandom* sample of attitudes (or "considerations") that were used by respondents as the basis for their answers.

5. Meta-Psychological Versus Operative Measures of Ambivalence ᥲ

Differentiating the Consequences of Perceived Intra-Psychic Conflict and Real Intra-Psychic Conflict

Allyson L. Holbrook and Jon A. Krosnick

I n building theories about the inner workings of political actors' minds, political psychologists often posit the existence of latent constructs such as attitudes, beliefs, and personality dispositions. Although no one has ever directly seen an attitude, belief, or personality disposition, assuming that these constructs exist helps scholars to explain political behavior. In this sense, psychological constructs are similar to physical constructs (such as energy) that have been proposed by physicists, chemists, and other scientists to explain the observable phenomena of interest to them.

A variety of methods have been employed over the years to measure psychological constructs, varying in the extent to which they rely on people to describe those constructs themselves. Self-report questions in surveys ask respondents to characterize their own mental states, processes, and structures, whereas other measures (e.g., of reaction time, see Fazio *et al.* 1995; or subtle movements of facial muscles, see Cacioppo and Petty 1979) do not rely on individuals' subjective perceptions of their psychological states at all. Alternatively, some indicators use people's self-reports of one construct to create measures of another; for example, the accuracy of answers to factual quiz questions has been used to build indices of political knowledge (Delli Carpini and Keeter 1996).

Attitudinal ambivalence is a particularly interesting construct in this regard, because it can be measured either by asking people how ambivalent they feel toward an object or by asking people to report how positive and how negative they feel toward an object and mathematically building an index from these reports (Kaplan 1972).[1] These are examples of what we call meta-psychological (MP) and operative (OP) measures, respectively.[2] Political psychologists studying ambivalence have employed both sorts of indicators, seemingly as if they are equivalent vehicles for assessing the same construct.

In this chapter, we describe a program of research comparing MP and OP measures of ambivalence and exploring two questions: (1) Do MP and OP measures of attitude ambivalence assess a single construct or different constructs? (2) Are the effects of MP and OP attitude ambivalence on political cognition and action the same or different? We begin by defining MP and OP measures of ambivalence, reviewing evidence about the relation between the two, and discussing reasons why they might be only moderately positively related to one another. We then propose a set of hypotheses about the distinct consequences that the two types of measures may have for various aspects of political cognition and behavior. This is followed by a review of past research findings regarding the consequences of ambivalence, and a description of results from a new study conducted to test our hypotheses. Finally, we discuss the implications of these findings for research in political psychology.

DEFINING MP AND OP MEASURES OF AMBIVALENCE

Meta-psychological (MP) measures of ambivalence, where people are asked to report the degree to which they feel ambivalent or conflicted, tap the subjective experience of evaluative conflict regarding an object. Priester and Petty (1996), for example, asked respondents to report the extent to which they felt conflict, indecision, and mixed reactions, while Thompson, Zanna, and Griffin (1995) used ten questions developed by Jamieson (1988) to probe whether people were "confused" or "torn" about the attitude object. Similarly, Cacioppo and his colleagues have asked people to report the extent to which their reactions to an object were muddled, divided, tense, contradictory, jumbled, conflicted, consistent, uniform, and harmonious (Cacioppo *et al.* 1997; Cacioppo *et al.* 1996; Gardner 1996).

Operative (OP) measures of ambivalence tap the extent of a person's favorable and unfavorable reactions to an object and then determine whether these reactions are in conflict with one another. Thus, the greatest OP ambivalence occurs when a person feels both very favorable and very unfavorable toward an object. At least six mathematical formulas have been proposed for calculating OP ambivalence using separate measures of positivity and negativity toward an object (Priester and Petty 1996; Thompson *et al.* 1995).[3] These formulas make slightly different assumptions about how conflicting reactions combine to yield ambivalence, but the numbers they yield are typically very strongly correlated with one another (Breckler 1994; Priester and Petty 1996; Riketta 2000; Thompson *et al.* 1995).

THE RELATION BETWEEN MP AND OP AMBIVALENCE

Many studies have assessed the relation between MP and OP measures of ambivalence and found only a modest degree of covariation; Thompson, Zanna, and Griffin (1995) found correlations ranging from 0.21 to 0.40, while Priester and Petty (1996) reported coefficients of similar magnitudes. There are several possible explanations for these results. First, MP and OP measures of ambivalence may assess the same underlying construct but with substantial random measurement error (Bassili 1996b). For example, self-perceptions reported on rating scales certainly entail some error due to ambiguities in people's internal cues and ambiguities in the meanings of the scale points, both of which would attenuate the observed relations. Second, the mathematical formulas used to calculate OP ambivalence may misrepresent the way favorable and unfavorable evaluations combine psychologically to yield operative ambivalence.

Third, discrepancies between MP and OP measures of ambivalence could be due to respondents' intentional choices to distort their MP reports (Bassili 1996b). Being viewed favorably by others often brings more rewards and fewer punishments than being viewed unfavorably, so some individuals are motivated (even if by deceit) to construct favorable images of themselves. A great deal of evidence has been accumulated documenting such systematic and intentional misrepresentation when people respond to questionnaires that tap other constructs (e.g., Paulhus 1984; Sigall and Page 1971; Warner 1965), and this may be true for measures of ambivalence as well.

If ambivalence has social desirability connotations, then MP measures of ambivalence may be biased as a result. A number of psychological theories suggest that individuals strive to be internally consistent, that they are uncomfortable with inconsistencies between their attitudes and behaviors, for example, and that they strive to reduce such inconsistencies (e.g., Festinger 1957; Heider 1958); they also experience social pressure to appear consistent and want others to see them as consistent (Tedeschi *et al.* 1971). Some people may therefore be reluctant to admit that they are ambivalent, particularly those who are concerned about the impressions they make on others. As a result, self-presentational distortions in MP ambivalence reports could lead such reports to diverge from OP measures.

An alternative explanation for the moderate relation between MP and OP measures of ambivalence is that the two types of measures may tap separate constructs that are both meaningful and consequential. For example, OP measures are based only on the extent of conflict between a person's positive and negative evaluative reactions to an object, but MP perceptions of ambivalence may also reflect interpersonal discrepancies such as that between one's own attitude and the attitudes of liked others (Priester and Petty 2001).[4] The latter may be unique variance not present in OP measures. Additionally, people who are high in OP ambivalence may not be aware of or uncomfortable with the conflicting elements of their attitudes, so their perceptions of internal conflict may be much lower (Newby-Clark *et al.* 2002; Thompson and Zanna 1995). Thus, it may make sense to think not of MP and OP measures as tapping a single underlying construct (i.e., ambivalence) but rather of these measures as tapping two distinct constructs: MP ambivalence and OP ambivalence.

If MP and OP ambivalence are separate constructs, it seems likely that the latter is a *cause* of the former. That is, people's subjective experiences of conflict about an object are probably at least somewhat reflections of the co-presence of both positive and negative evaluative reactions toward that object. It is also possible, however, that MP and OP ambivalence will each have unique causes and unique effects on individual thought and action. In fact, prior research suggests that people's subjective experiences can indeed be meaningful and consequential even when they are inaccurate (see Bless and Forgas 2000). For example, people take steps to correct judgments to the extent they *perceive* those judgments to be biased, not to the extent they are *actually* biased (Petty and Wegener 1993; Wegener *et al.* 2000; Wegener and Petty 1995). Similarly, people take steps to resolve inconsistencies among their beliefs, attitudes, and behaviors to the extent they are *perceived* to be inconsistent, not to the extent they *actually* are inconsistent (e.g., Zanna and Cooper 1974). Even if inaccurate, then, perceptions of attitude features can be important for understanding people's cognition and behavior.

Our goal in conducting the research reported here was to investigate the possibility that MP and OP measures of ambivalence might tap distinct constructs. We did so partly by examining the underlying factor structure of these two sorts of ambivalence measures. In particular, we conducted confirmatory factor analyses to determine whether (1) MP and OP measures of ambivalence reflect a single underlying factor, or (2) MP measures of ambivalence reflect one latent factor, and OP measures of ambivalence assess a second.

COGNITIVE AND BEHAVIORAL CONSEQUENCES OF AMBIVALENCE

Even if confirmatory factor analyses were to suggest that MP and OP measures assess different constructs, a single-construct conceptualization may nonetheless be more parsimonious if MP and OP ambivalence have the same effects on cognition and behavior. That is, even if MP and OP ambivalence are not highly related, they may be functionally interchangeable. If treating the two as distinct provides no additional information regarding how and why people think and act as they do, it makes sense to proceed as though they reflect a single construct. We therefore explore whether MP and OP ambivalence have the same or different effects on individual thoughts and action.

Hypothesized Consequences of Ambivalence

If MP and OP ambivalence are separate constructs, they seem likely to have somewhat different impacts by virtue of exerting effects through different mechanisms. In this section, we propose how MP and OP ambivalence might be differently related to a broad range of cognitive and behavioral phenomena: resistance to attitude change, information gathering, the false consensus effect, the hostile media phenomenon, the process of forming evaluations of presidential candidates, and attitude-expressive activism.

Resistance to attitude change. An attitude's ability to withstand attack has been extensively studied, most often by assessing the extent to which an attitude changes in response to a stimulus such as a counter-attitudinal persuasive message (Mutz *et al.* 1996; Petty and Cacioppo 1986a). As people consider a message, they often retrieve relevant considerations from memory that are then used to evaluate the merits of the message. Those ranking higher in OP ambivalence are more likely to generate thoughts consistent with any message, regardless of whether the latter is favorable or unfavorable toward the object. These individuals may therefore be more likely to accept the plausibility of a persuasive message and to change their attitudes in response to it.

MP ambivalence should also be negatively related to resistance, but via a different mechanism. Individuals who feel conflicted about an object may want to reduce that feeling; as a result, when exposed to attitude-relevant information, they may be especially motivated to accept it in the hope of reducing their sense of conflict. These individuals may, consequently, be particularly likely to embrace a persuasive message that attempts to push their attitudes, regardless of the direction of the push.

Information gathering. People are constantly bombarded with information in their environments, but have only limited capacity to attend to and remember that information. It is therefore often necessary to choose what cues one will attend to, though individuals do not always have time to plan their selective attention carefully and deliberately. When cognitively busy or overloaded, the process of choosing which information to "orient to" and remember sometimes happens automatically, without awareness. Accordingly, information-gathering strategies differ depending on whether an individual (1) can choose which pieces of information to attend to, in a manageable information environment; or (2) must choose only some of the available information to attend to, in a complex information environment when they do not have time to plan their selections carefully and deliberately.

MP ambivalence may be related to choices to attend to and learn attitude-relevant information. One possibility is that people who feel conflicted will be motivated to reduce that conflict and attempt to do so by learning new information about the object. It is also possible, however, that individuals high in MP ambivalence will try to avoid situations that make their sense of conflict salient. Thus, MP ambivalence may lead people actively to stay away from object-relevant information in order to avoid ensuing discomfort. If some ambivalent individuals attempt to reduce their feelings of conflict by accumulating attitude-relevant information, while others avoid such information to prevent discomfort, this would yield the appearance of no net association between MP ambivalence and information choices.

OP ambivalence seems unlikely to be associated with attention to information, regardless of the amount of information in the environment or the time and resources required to make decisions about attention. Specifically, we see no reason to expect that having both positive and negative beliefs about an object will affect a person's motivation to learn attitude-relevant information. We also doubt that OP ambivalence will result in an automatic or chronic tendency to acquire attitude-relevant information.

Perceptions of social support. The false consensus effect (FCE) is the tendency for people to overestimate the proportion of others who share their opinions, relative to the judgments made by people who hold different attitudes. This phenomenon may be attributable to a number of social and psychological processes and instigators (see Fabrigar and Krosnick 1995; Marks and Miller 1987; Ross *et al.* 1977), including (1) the salience of one's own attitude; (2) the motivation to maintain one's self-esteem; (3) the need for social support; (4) the presumption that liked others have good qualities (including sharing one's own attitudes); (5) the presumption that one's own attitudes are attributable to situational forces that will affect others equivalently; (6) different people construing objects differently; and (7) selective affiliation with others who have similar attitudes.

There are reasons to anticipate that MP ambivalence will tend to decrease the FCE, and other reasons to expect just the opposite. For example, people who feel conflicted about an object may be less likely to see their attitude as a positive quality if ambivalence is unpleasant. Under these circumstances, people who are meta-psychologically ambivalent presumably would manifest weaker false consensus effects. Alternatively, if people high in MP ambivalence are readily influenced by the opinions of others, high ambivalence could lead them to adopt the attitudes of others they know, thereby yielding a stronger FCE. And if it is true that "misery loves company," people high in MP ambivalence may be motivated to believe that many others share their ambivalence, which also would strengthen the FCE. Finally, if MP ambivalence has different effects for different people in opposite directions, these effects may cancel out in the aggregate, leading to the appearance of no association between MP ambivalence and the magnitude of the FCE.

Considering the possible moderating effect of OP ambivalence suggests another possible mechanism for the FCE. Measures of false consensus ask people to judge how many others share their own opinions. But if a person has a mix of favorable and unfavorable feelings toward an object, then he or she will share, by definition, some views with people who are favorable toward the object and others with people who are unfavorable toward the object. This may lead these ambivalent individuals to experience a frequent sense of commonality with others regarding the object, thus possibly yielding overestimation of the prevalence of one's own views. That is, people high in OP ambivalence may experience an exaggerated sense of the number of others who share their attitudes.

Hostile media phenomenon. The hostile media phenomenon (HMP) is one in which individuals interpret a relatively balanced news media story about an issue as being hostile to their own point of view. Two mechanisms have been proposed to account for this effect (Vallone *et al.* 1985). First, if most of the knowledge a person possesses about the issue is consistent with his or her attitude and very little is inconsistent, a story containing equal amounts of consistent and inconsistent information may appear to be biased. Alternatively, if the neutral attitudinal position implied by a balanced news story is within someone's "latitude of rejection," perceptual contrast may lead that individual to perceive the story as more different from his or her attitudes than its information balance implies (see Sherif and Hovland 1961).

People high in OP ambivalence genuinely have a balance between their favorable and unfavorable evaluations of an object, thus matching balanced news stories' balance to a more substantial degree and yielding a lower likelihood of the HMP. Likewise, if OP ambivalence reduces resistance to change, then a balanced news story should pull operatively ambivalent people's attitudes toward neutrality, yielding more of a match between the story and the person, and less perceived bias in the story. Similarly, if MP ambivalence reduces resistance to change, those high in MP ambivalence may adjust their attitudes to be in line with a balanced news story, thereby yielding a greater perceived match and less perceived bias.

The ingredients of political candidate evaluations. People form evaluations of political candidates on the basis of many considerations, including candidates' positions on policy issues. They like a candidate to the extent that the candidate's attitude on an issue is similar to their own (Krosnick 1988b), consistent with the more general finding that people like similar others more (Byrne 1961, 1971). However, not everyone uses every issue equally to evaluate candidates. Some issues are weighted more heavily than others, and these weights vary across individuals (Anand and Krosnick 2003; Krosnick 1988b, 1990).

A person high in OP ambivalence may be especially likely to perceive resonance between his or her own feelings on an issue and the views of all candidates, no matter what the latter's positions happen to be. This perceived resonance should reduce the weight attached to the issue, because the issue does not offer a useful handle for differentiating among candidates. Likewise, MP ambivalence may lead people to hesitate before using an issue to evaluate a candidate, because these individuals recognize their own inability to settle comfortably into an evaluation of the policy in question. Higher MP ambivalence may therefore be associated with a lower weight attached to an issue.

Activism. People can express their attitudes toward policies to government officials by joining others in signing petitions, attending rallies, and the like. When offered an opportunity to take such an action to express a particular attitude, people may assess the extent to which the proposed activity matches their own views. Individuals higher in OP ambivalence are perhaps more likely to have reasons for agreeing with the position being expressed by any petition or rally, so these individuals should be more inclined to accept such invitations. On the other hand, operatively ambivalent individuals may also be better able to see inconsistencies between their attitudes and the agendas of activist behaviors, and this might reduce the probability that these people will engage in activist behaviors. Operative ambivalence could, of course, make some individuals more likely to act and others less likely, thereby giving the appearance of no relation between OP ambivalence and activism at the aggregate level.

It is possible that MP ambivalence affects the decision to engage in attitude-expressive activism as well. People who feel conflicted about an attitude object may also be conflicted about whether or not a particular act will accurately communicate their attitudes to government leaders, and about whether or not to express their attitude. Under such circumstances, MP ambivalence should lead to less activism.

Evidence from Past Research

Most prior research has examined either OP ambivalence or MP ambivalence, but not both. Many studies have shown that operatively ambivalent attitudes have all the defining characteristics of weak attitudes, including openness to change, instability over time, and little impact on thinking and action. Specifically, people higher in OP ambivalence appear to be more likely to change their attitudes in response to consensus information about the attitudes of their peers (Hodson *et al.* 2001), more likely to change their attitudes in response to a persuasive message (Armitage and Connor 2000), and more likely to manifest attitude instability over time (Bargh *et al.* 1992; Lavine 2001; also see chapter 4 in this volume). On the other hand, Armitage and Connor (2000) and Bassili (1996b) found OP ambivalence to be unrelated to attitude stability.

OP ambivalence has been shown to have effects on cognition and behavior in line with the characterization of this construct offered above. For example, being operatively ambivalent toward a parent is associated with less secure attachment to the parent (Maio *et al.* 2000). OP ambivalence toward a low-status in-group is positively related to out-group favoritism (Jost and Burgess 2000). OP ambivalence toward a stigmatized group is associated with more extreme responses to members of that group (Hass *et al.* 1991). Operatively ambivalent people are more susceptible to priming effects on behavior (MacDonald and Zanna 1998). People higher in operative ambivalence toward political candidates have less extreme attitudes toward those candidates and are less confident in their perceptions of the candidates' stands on policy issues (Guge and Meffert 1998). Operatively ambivalent people tend to decide which presidential candidate to support later in the course of campaigns, and are less likely to use candidates' personalities and issue positions to evaluate them (Lavine 2001). And the impact of attitudes on behavioral intentions and behaviors is weaker among individuals who are more operatively ambivalent (Armitage and Connor 2000; Lavine 2001; Moore 1973, 1980; Priester 2002; Sparks *et al.* 1991).[5]

MP ambivalence has been examined in only a couple of studies in terms of its effects on attitude crystallization and consequentiality. Tourangeau, Rasinski, Bradburn, and D'Andrade (1989b) found that people with attitudes higher in MP ambivalence (and also higher in personal importance) manifested stronger question order effects in attitude measurement than did those lower in MP ambivalence, while Bassili (1996b) found no effect of MP ambivalence on attitude stability and pliability.[6] MP ambivalence is clearly under-studied in this particular domain, and the evidence that does exist raises questions concerning its utility for explaining cognition and action.

We found only one study that estimated the unique effects of MP and OP ambivalence simultaneously. McGraw, Hasecke, and Conger (2003) found that MP ambivalence led to more negative candidate evaluations, but OP ambivalence did not. This divergence is consistent with the notion that OP and MP measures of ambivalence may assess different constructs with distinct consequences. The McGraw study did not, however, address the con-sequences that we outlined earlier. As a result, we know almost nothing about the separate effects of these two types of measures when examined simultaneously.

The Need to Distinguish MP and OP Ambivalence Empirically

If MP and OP ambivalence are distinct but related constructs, it is important to understand how these constructs are different for purposes of theory building, methodology, and the interpretation of results. Rather than assuming that all measures of ambivalence are interchangeable, this perspective suggests that researchers need to consider carefully whether their theory applies to MP or OP ambivalence (or both), to make appropriate decisions when measuring ambivalence, and to interpret results accordingly. Furthermore, because MP and OP ambivalence are likely to be related, controlling for one is a critical step in identifying the unique consequences of the other.

If MP and OP ambivalence are distinct constructs, a failure to treat them as such could result in researchers employing measures that do not match their theories, the illusory appearance of inconsistent results (reflecting differences in the indicators used in different studies), and the overgeneralization of results. Researchers who think of MP and OP measures of ambivalence as interchangeable also may combine both types into a single index (e.g., Hanze 2001) and, in so doing, run the risk of masking dissimilar effects of MP and OP ambivalence.

A NEW STUDY OF ATTITUDES ABOUT ABORTION AND CAPITAL PUNISHMENT

Our investigation is the first to use confirmatory factor analysis to test whether OP and MP measures of ambivalence reflect different constructs, and to examine the unique effects of MP and OP ambivalence on a wide range of cognitions and behaviors. Respondents visited a laboratory and completed an extensive questionnaire about a policy issue that included indicators of both OP and MP ambivalence, in addition to measures of resistance, information gathering, perceptions of social support for one's own attitude, perceptions of media bias, the ingredients of political candidate evaluations, and activism.[7]

Method

A total of 654 undergraduates at Ohio State University participated in this study during the fall of 2000 to partially fulfill an introductory psychology course requirement. Three hundred and twenty-five respondents were assigned to answer questions about one target issue (abortion), while the remaining 329 answered questions about a second target issue (capital punishment). Each person completed a questionnaire alone on a computer for approximately one hour.

The questionnaire included items assessing both OP and MP ambivalence regarding the target issue. MP ambivalence was measured via three questions that asked respondents how mixed their feelings were about the issue, how much conflict they felt about it, and how decisive their feelings about the issue were. OP ambivalence was measured by asking respondents to report their positivity and negativity toward the target policy. Two calculation methods were used to estimate ambivalence: the gradual threshold model (Priester and Petty 1996), and the negative acceleration model (Scott 1966). These two measures were chosen because they are based on slightly different conceptual ideas about how positivity and negativity combine to form ambivalence, and because a model using these variables as indicators of OP ambivalence fit the data well.[8] Coding was such that higher numbers indicated greater ambivalence.

Resistance to attitude change was measured in two ways. First, respondents were asked three questions about how easy it would be for someone to change their attitudes, how firm their attitudes were, and how firm their attitudes were relative to their other attitudes (MP measures). Second, resistance was assessed operatively by measuring attitude change in response to a persuasive message. Participants answered four questions assessing their attitudes on the issue, read a counter-attitudinal essay, and then reported their attitudes a second time.[9] Attitude change was coded such that less change in the direction of the message (greater resistance) is indicated by higher numbers. The pre-message attitude measures yield an assessment of attitude extremity.

Deliberate gathering of attitude-relevant information was assessed via two meta-psychological measures. First, respondents rank-ordered pieces of information about a variety of topics, indicating which of these they would most and least like to learn; each list contained one piece of information about the target issue, and responses were coded such that larger numbers reflect a greater preference for information regarding that issue. In addition, respondents were asked three direct questions designed to gauge their interest in learning more about the target issue.

We also implemented an operative measure of information gathering, tapping automatic attention to attitude-relevant information and referred to as "orienting" (Roskos-Ewoldson and Fazio 1992). Respondents were briefly shown four lists of words, then asked to recall as many of these words as they could. Each list contained one word related to the target issue. Because the exposure time was brief, recalling attitude-relevant information from these lists is a measure of how quickly and automatically people noticed and paid attention to that information. For each of the four lists, respondents who recalled the information about the target issue were coded 1, while those who did not were coded 0. Recall scores from the first two lists were averaged to create one index of orienting; recall scores from the third and fourth lists were averaged to create a second index.

Respondents answered a series of questions about the opinions of others on the target issue to gauge the false consensus effect. These questions assessed the extent to which people thought they were in the majority on the issue, their beliefs about the proportions of others who agreed with them, and their perceptions of the attitudes of "most" Americans. All these variables were coded so that greater perceived consensus is indicated by larger numbers.

To assess perceptions of media bias, respondents were asked about the extent to which they thought media coverage of the target issue was biased; those who said they perceived any bias were then asked the direction of the bias. This variable was coded to range from 1 to −1. For respondents asked about legalized abortion, positive numbers indicate a bias in media coverage toward endorsing the view that abortions should be easy to obtain; negative numbers indicate a bias in favor of the view that abortions should be difficult to obtain. For respondents asked about capital punishment, positive numbers indicate a bias in media coverage toward endorsing the view that capital punishment should be used more often; negative numbers indicate a bias in favor of the view that capital punishment should be used less often. In both cases, a negative association between this measure and attitudes reflects perceived hostile media bias.

To assess the extent to which they used candidates' policy stands as a basis for evaluation, respondents were asked to specify then-Texas Governor George W. Bush's and Vice President Al Gore's positions on the target issue. Respondents also reported their own attitudes toward each of these candidates. Two variables were created from the answers to these questions. First, candidate preferences were calculated by subtracting respondents' attitudes toward Gore from their attitudes toward Bush; positive numbers indicate a preference for the former, negative numbers a preference for the latter. Second, an issue discrepancy variable was calculated by subtracting the absolute value of the difference between the respondent's position and Bush's position from the absolute value of the difference between his or her position and Gore's position. Positive values mean that a person's attitude was more similar to Bush's than to Gore's, while negative numbers indicate that a respondent's attitude was more similar to Gore's than to Bush's.[10] Issue discrepancy and candidate preference should be positively correlated if people tended to prefer candidates with attitudes similar to their own.

Activism was measured in two ways. Respondents were asked general questions about how involved they were in activities related to the target issue, and also whether they had performed a series of specific activist behaviors to express their attitudes on the issue. Both sets of questions were aggregated to yield separate measures of activism, which were coded so that larger numbers indicated more activism.

Analysis Strategy

To examine the relation between MP and OP ambivalence, parameters of two structural equation models were estimated. The first model posited that all five measures of ambivalence (three MP and two OP; see appendix) are indicators of a single latent construct (figure 5.1). In the second model, MP measures were posited as indicators of one latent construct and OP measures as indicators of a second latent construct, with the two being allowed to covary (figure 5.2). We evaluated these models by examining their goodness-of-fit statistics. The second model also yielded an estimate of the relation between MP and OP measures of ambivalence, disattenuated to correct for measurement error.

To assess the impact of MP and OP measures on cognition and behavior, we estimated the parameters of structural equation models positing that OP and MP ambivalence influenced resistance, information gathering, perceptions of social support, and activism. In these models, each thought and behavior was predicted by three latent variables, indicated by (1) the three MP measures of ambivalence, (2) the two OP measures, and (3) attitude

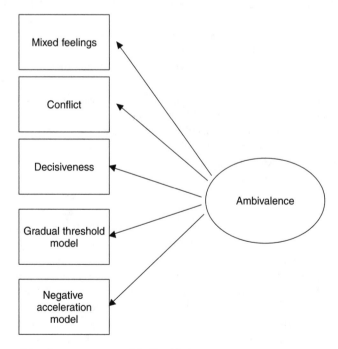

Figure 5.1   One-construct model of ambivalence

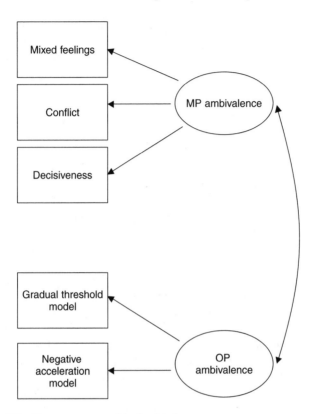

Figure 5.2   Two-construct model of ambivalence

extremity. Each dependent variable was also a latent variable with multiple indicators, in order to allow for disattenuating the parameter estimates to correct for measurement error.

Two of the hypothesized effects of MP and OP ambivalence (moderation of the hostile media phenomenon, use of candidates' issues positions to evaluate them) were tested by interactions. In order to test these interactions, we used a procedure described by Jöreskog *et al.* (2001) and based upon a model first proposed by Kenny and Judd (1984). All measured variables were centered (see Cohen *et al.* 2003 for a discussion of centering), and LISREL 8.51 and PRELIS were used to estimate factor scores for all latent variables (MP ambivalence, OP ambivalence, attitude extremity, and in the case of the hostile media phenomenon, attitudes toward the target policy). Data for manifest variables and factor scores for the latent variables were then imported into SPSS, where OLS regressions were estimated. Using this approach, we tested whether MP ambivalence, OP ambivalence, and extremity moderated the relation between attitudes and perceived media bias, and the impact of issue discrepancies on candidate preferences.

RESULTS

Factor Structure

For the factor analyses, three goodness-of-fit statistics were examined: the ratio of the χ^2 statistic to degrees of freedom (df), RMSEA, and GFI. χ^2/df ratios smaller than 3.0 indicate acceptable fit (Gefen *et al.* 2000). RMSEAs of 0.05 or less represent good fit, RMSEAs of 0.05 to 0.07 represent adequate fit, and RMSEAs of 0.08 or greater represent poor fit (Browne and Cudeck 1992; Byrne 1998). GFIs of 0.90 or higher indicate acceptable fit (Byrne 1998; Hair *et al.* 1998).

Abortion. For abortion, the model treating all five measures of ambivalence as indicators of a single latent factor fit the data very poorly: χ^2/df = 29.46, RMSEA = 0.30, and GFI = 0.85, suggesting that the five measures of ambivalence do *not* reflect a single latent factor. The model with two correlated factors representing MP and OP ambivalence fit the data well: χ^2/df = 1.41, RMSEA = 0.04, GFI = 0.99, and a relation between MP and OP ambivalence significantly larger than zero but moderate in size ($\beta = 0.49$, $p < 0.01$). The pattern here suggests that MP ambivalence and OP ambivalence are two separate but related constructs.

Capital punishment. Similar results were obtained for capital punishment. The model in which all five measures of ambivalence regarding capital punishment were indicators of a single latent factor fit the data very poorly: χ^2/df = 36.82, RMSEA = 0.34, GFI = 0.81. Again, the model with separate MP and OP factors fit the data much better: χ^2/df = 0.98, RMSEA = 0.00, GFI = 1.00. The relation between MP and OP ambivalence was significantly larger than zero but only moderate in size ($\beta = 0.43$, $p < 0.01$).

Differences across issues. To test whether the factor structure of ambivalence was consistent across both issues, multiple group analyses were conducted comparing unconstrained models for the two respondent groups with models that constrained the factor loadings, variances, and covariances to be equal across issues. The fit of the one-factor model did not differ across issues ($\Delta\chi^2(5) = 6.11$, n.s.), nor did that of the two-factor model ($\Delta\chi^2(6) = 8.92$, n.s.). We therefore concluded that the structure of MP and OP ambivalence seems equivalent for abortion and capital punishment.

Consequences of Ambivalence

Next, we examined the effects of MP and OP ambivalence on resistance, information gathering, the magnitude of the false consensus effect, perceptions of media bias, the ingredients of candidate evaluations, and activism. Data for the two target issues were combined for these analyses because our results were consistent when they were analyzed separately.

Resistance. Individuals higher in MP ambivalence tended to manifest less OP resistance ($\beta = -0.32$, $p < 0.01$, see row 1 of column 1 in table 5.1). Consistent with past research, resistance was lower among respondents higher in OP ambivalence as well ($\beta = -0.12$, $p < 0.05$; see row 2 of column 1 in table 5.1). A regression predicting MP resistance manifested the same effects (see column 2 of table 5.1): Greater MP ambivalence ($\beta = -0.57$, $p < 0.01$; see row 1 of column 2 in table 5.1) and greater OP ambivalence ($\beta = -0.10$, $p < 0.05$; see row 2 of column 2 in table 5.1) were both associated with less MP resistance.

Information gathering. Respondents scoring higher on MP ambivalence tended to report less interest in learning information about the issue measured meta-psychologically ($\beta = -0.17$, $p < 0.01$; see row 1 of column 3 in table 5.1). However, OP ambivalence was not associated with MP interest ($\beta = -0.03$, n.s.; see row 2 of column 3 in table 5.1). Neither MP ambivalence nor OP ambivalence significantly predicted information choices ($\beta = -0.07$ and -0.00, respectively; see rows 1 and 2 of column 4 in table 5.1). Likewise, neither was related to the operative measure of information gathering, that is, orienting ($\beta = -0.04$ for MP ambivalence and -0.07 for OP ambivalence; see rows 1 and 2 of column 5 in table 5.1).

The false consensus effect. Greater MP ambivalence predicted a stronger false consensus effect ($\beta = 0.12$, $p < 0.05$; see row 1 of column 6 in table 5.1). In contrast, OP ambivalence was not associated with the magnitude of the false consensus effect ($\beta = 0.06$, n.s.; see row 2 of column 6 in table 5.1).

Perceptions of media bias. Replicating Vallone et al.'s (1985) finding, attitudes predicted perceived media bias ($\beta = -0.20$, $p < 0.01$; see column 1 of table 5.2): respondents more favorable toward abortion or capital

Table 5.1 Effects of ambivalence on resistance, information gathering, false consensus, and activism

Predictor	OP resistance	MP resistance	Reported interest in learning attitude-relevant information	Choices to learn attitude-relevant information	Orienting to attitude-relevant information	Magnitude of false consensus effect	General activism	Specific activist behaviors
				Consequence				
MP ambivalence	-0.32**	-0.57**	-0.17**	-0.07	-0.04	0.12*	0.03	0.05
OP ambivalence	-0.12*	-0.10*	-0.03	-0.00	-0.07	0.06	0.11*	-0.04
Extremity	-0.43**	0.04	0.15	0.21*	0.08	-0.32**	0.24**	0.16*
χ^2	267.82	146.69	110.39	89.06	81.26	261.30	111.97	152.01
df	59	48	48	48	38	48	48	59
χ^2/df	4.54	3.06	2.30	1.86	2.14	5.44	2.33	2.58
RMSEA	0.08	0.06	0.05	0.04	0.04	0.09	0.05	0.05
GFI	0.94	0.96	0.97	0.98	0.98	0.93	0.97	0.96
Squared multiple correlation	0.13	0.41	0.09	0.06	0.02	0.19	0.04	0.02
N =	593	601	602	624	621	613	602	602

Note: ** $p \leq 0.01$; * $p \leq 0.05$. Data are from a 2000 study of undergraduate students at Ohio State University. Table entries are standardized LISREL parameter estimates. Note that OP Resistance is coded so that higher numbers indicate less attitude change.

Table 5.2 Effects of ambivalence on hostile media bias and ingredients of candidate evaluation

Predictor	Consequence			
	Hostile media bias		Candidate preferences	
	Main effects model	Moderation model	Main effects model	Moderation model
Attitude	−0.20**	−0.14*	n/a	n/a
Issue discrepancy	n/a	n/a	0.27**	0.23**
MP ambivalence	n/a	−0.05	n/a	0.00
OP ambivalence	n/a	0.02	n/a	0.10*
Attitude extremity	n/a	0.00	n/a	0.14**
MP ambivalence × attitude	n/a	0.09†	n/a	n/a
MP ambivalence × issue discrepancy	n/a	n/a	n/a	−0.11*
OP ambivalence × attitude	n/a	0.01	n/a	n/a
OP ambivalence × issue discrepancy	n/a	n/a	n/a	−0.08†
Attitude extremity × attitude	n/a	−0.02	n/a	n/a
Attitude extremity × issue discrepancy	n/a	n/a	n/a	0.00
R^2 =	0.04	0.05	0.07	0.11
Number of cases =	606	606	606	606

Note: ** $p \leq 0.01$; * $p \leq 0.05$; † $p \leq 0.10$. Data are from a 2000 study of undergraduate students at Ohio State University ($N = 654$). Table entries are standardized OLS coefficients from regressions using latent variable factor scores.

punishment perceived media coverage to be more biased against these views. The interaction between MP ambivalence and attitudes indicates, however, that individuals higher in ambivalence were less likely to perceive media bias against their position ($\beta = 0.09$, $p < 0.10$; see row 6 of column 2 in table 5.2). The impact of attitudes on perceived media bias among individuals who reported high levels of MP ambivalence (above the median) was nonsignificant ($\beta = -0.06$, n.s.), whereas the impact of attitudes on perceived media bias was strong and significant among individuals who reported low levels of MP ambivalence (below the median, $\beta = -0.23$, $p < 0.001$). The interaction between OP ambivalence and attitudes was not significant ($\beta = 0.01$, n.s.; see row 8 of column 2 in table 5.2), meaning OP ambivalence did not moderate this effect.

Candidate evaluations. As expected, respondents who agreed more with President Bush on the target issue were more likely to support him

(β = 0.27, p < 0.01; see column 3 of table 5.2). MP ambivalence moderated the impact of issue positions on candidate preferences (β = -0.11, p < 0.05; see row 7 of column 4 in table 5.2). Respondents low in MP ambivalence (below the median) used the issue to evaluate candidates a great deal (β = 0.72, p < 0.001), whereas respondents high in MP ambivalence used the issue much less (β = 0.27, p < 0.05). OP ambivalence also was a marginally significant moderator of the impact of issues on candidate preferences (β = -0.08, p < 0.10; see row 9 of column 4 in table 5.2). Respondents low in OP ambivalence (below the median) used the issue to evaluate candidates more (β = 0.33, p < 0.001) than did respondents high in OP ambivalence (β = 0.25, p < 0.001).[11]

Activism. MP ambivalence did not predict involvement in activities related to the target issue (β = 0.03, n.s.; see row 1 of column 7 in table 5.1), but OP ambivalence was positively associated with participation in such activities (β = 0.11, p < 0.05; see row 2 of column 7 in table 5.1). Neither MP nor OP ambivalence affected the likelihood of performing specific attitude-expressive activist behaviors (β = 0.05 and -0.04, respectively; see rows 1 and 2 of column 8 in table 5.1).

DISCUSSION

Confirmatory factor analyses suggested that MP and OP ambivalence measures represent distinct constructs, while subsequent analyses indicated that the two have different impacts on cognition and behavior.

Effects of Meta-Psychological (MP) Ambivalence

High MP ambivalence was found to be associated with less resistance, less reported interest in learning issue-relevant information, a stronger false consensus effect, less perceived hostile media bias, and a reduced tendency to use candidates' issue positions to evaluate them. We hypothesized that individuals high in MP ambivalence would feel discomfort when exposed to information that brings to mind their sense of conflict about the issue, and that they might use either of two strategies to deal with this discomfort. First, when possible, they might avoid any stimuli that brings their discomfort to mind. Consistent with this reasoning, our data showed MP ambivalence to be negatively associated with interest in attitude-relevant information (though not with choices to learn attitude-relevant information). Furthermore, we saw that people high in MP ambivalence were less likely to use candidates' issue positions as a basis for evaluation. This may reflect an attempt to avoid discomfort by not thinking about the issue.

Even if people who are high in MP ambivalence about an issue try to avoid thinking about their ambivalent attitudes, this may not always be possible; thus, when issue-relevant information cannot be avoided, these individuals may be particularly influenced by such information. Indeed, we found people scoring high in MP ambivalence to be less resistant to change when exposed to a counter-attitudinal essay they could not choose to avoid. Two other observed effects of MP ambivalence also may reflect a lack of resistance. First, respondents higher in MP ambivalence perceived that greater proportions of others agreed with their opinion on the target issue and, second, perceived that media coverage of the issue was less biased. If the false consensus effect occurs because people are persuaded to adopt the attitudes they perceive most others to hold, then we would expect high-ambivalence individuals to manifest a stronger false consensus effect. And if those high in MP ambivalence are more persuaded by the news media stories they encounter, these individuals would presumably be less likely to perceive those stories to be biased against their own positions.

Effects of Operative (OP) Ambivalence

The effects of OP ambivalence on thoughts and behaviors distinguish this construct from its MP counterpart. Our data showed OP ambivalence to be negatively related to resistance, which is consistent with past research (Armitage and Connor 2000; Hodson *et al.* 2001). We also found two new effects: greater OP ambivalence was associated with less use of candidates' issue positions to evaluate them, and with increased reports of general activism (though not reports of specific activist behaviors).

We hypothesized that OP ambivalence will primarily influence how people perceive attitude-relevant information around them. Individuals with a great deal of OP ambivalence feel both positivity and negativity toward the attitude object, so they may be likely to see a broad range of information as consistent with their own attitudes. The diversity of information about the attitude object thus leads them to see elements of their own position in a persuasive message (resulting in less resistance), and in candidates' issue positions (leading respondents to perceive smaller differences between the candidates and using their positions less to evaluate them).

Greater OP ambivalence also was found to be associated with reports of more general involvement in activities related to the issue. This may occur because people high in OP are biased toward thinking of reasons why a possible activist behavior is consistent rather than inconsistent with their attitudes (reflecting a general bias towards confirmatory thinking that has been observed in other contexts; see Hoch 1984; Klayman and Ha 1987; Koriat *et al.* 1980; Tschirgi 1980; Wason and Johnson-Laird 1972; Yzerbyt and Leyens 1991).

Mediation

It is possible that OP ambivalence is a cause of MP ambivalence, in which case the latter would be expected to mediate any observed effects of the former. If this were so, then OP ambivalence alone would have significant effects that all but disappear when controlling for MP ambivalence. Our evidence that OP ambivalence had unique effects on cognition and behavior challenges a complete mediation hypothesis. Furthermore, in models predicting resistance, activism, information gathering, perceived consensus, perceived media bias, and the ingredients of candidate evaluations, the effect of OP ambivalence changed in only one instance when MP ambivalence was excluded as a predictor: Higher OP ambivalence was associated with a modest false consensus effect ($\beta = 0.09$, $p < 0.05$) when MP ambivalence was not included as a predictor, and had a slightly weaker effect ($\beta = 0.06$, n.s.) when MP ambivalence was added to the equation. A Sobel test of mediation (Baron and Kenny 1986) disconfirmed the hypothesis that this drop indicated significant mediation (Sobel test statistic = 1.48, n.s.). Therefore, our analyses produced no evidence that the effects of OP ambivalence were suppressed due to mediation via MP ambivalence.

Consistency with Prior Findings

Although most of the hypotheses set forth here have not been tested before, a few of them have; as noted, our results are generally consistent with past findings. There is, however, one exception: Our analysis found that high MP ambivalence predicted less resistance to persuasion, but Bassili (1996b) did not. We examined MP ambivalence while controlling for OP ambivalence and attitude extremity, whereas Bassili looked only at the single order correlation of MP ambivalence and resistance. Yet when we examined the relation of MP ambivalence to resistance without controlling for OP ambivalence or extremity, MP ambivalence was associated with both the OP measure of resistance ($\beta = -0.13$, $p < 0.05$) and the MP measure ($\beta = -0.63$, $p < 0.01$) in our data; consequently, different control variables do not explain the discrepancy.

We also measured MP ambivalence with multiple indicators and thus were able to correct for measurement error, whereas Bassili used a single measure. It is possible, then, that the relation we observed may have been attenuated in Bassili's data. However, when the single-order correlations between each of our three measures of MP ambivalence and the three measures of MP resistance were examined, all were highly significant; this suggests that measurement error alone cannot account for the discrepancy between our results and Bassili's.

Finally, our measures of resistance were also somewhat different from Bassili's measure of pliability. The latter involved asking respondents whether they would change their attitudes if particular consequences occurred. For example, those who said that large companies should have quotas to ensure that a fixed percentage of women are hired were asked, "Would you feel the same even if this means not hiring the best person for the job?" Respondents who said they would not feel the same were coded as pliable. There is, however, no evidence that these individuals actually changed their minds or believed they were likely to. Specifically, a person could say that he or she would feel differently if quotas meant not hiring the best person for the job, but not believe that this would be a consequence of quotas. It is therefore unclear how Bassili's measure of pliability would be related to our measures of OP and MP resistance, so the difference in measurement may explain the discrepancy in our findings. Our measure of attitude change is the more conventional one, so our finding that MP ambivalence predicts resistance seems compelling.

CONCLUSION

Meta-psychological (MP) ambivalence reflects individuals' subjective experience of conflict about an object, whereas operative (OP) ambivalence reflects the extent to which people have both favorable and unfavorable orientations toward an object. Thus, the terms "MP ambivalence" and "OP ambivalence" seem more appropriate than MP and OP "measures" of a single ambivalence construct. This insight has important implications for the way that ambivalence is conceptualized in theory building and for interpretation of empirical findings: Researchers studying ambivalence should choose their measures carefully, based on theory rather than simply convenience. A theory about perceptions of ambivalence should be tested using measures of MP ambivalence, and the findings of such research should not be generalized to OP ambivalence. Likewise, a theory concerning the mixture of favorable and unfavorable reactions to an object stored in memory should be tested using OP ambivalence measures. Furthermore, combining measures of OP and MP ambivalence into a single index may lead to illusory conclusions. We therefore suggest that political psychologists assess both MP and OP ambivalence as often as possible and explore their causes and effects side by side in order to build richer and more accurate theories.

APPENDIX

Question wordings and codings for questions employed in our analysis are shown here. For some constructs, everyone was asked the same questions; for others, questions were asked either about abortion or about capital punishment, with respondents being randomly assigned to the particular target issue.

MP ambivalence: (1) "People's thoughts and feelings about an issue can be all one-sided or very mixed. How mixed are your thoughts and feelings about *[legalized abortion/capital punishment]*—extremely mixed, very mixed, somewhat mixed, a little mixed, or not at all mixed?" (2) "How much conflict do you feel about your opinion about *[legalized abortion/capital punishment]*—none at all, a little, a moderate amount, quite a bit, or a great deal?" (3) "People can be very decisive or very indecisive in their thoughts and feelings about an issue. How indecisive are your thoughts and feelings about *[legalized abortion/capital punishment]*—extremely indecisive, very indecisive, somewhat indecisive, a little indecisive, or not at all indecisive?" [Scores range from 0 to 1, with higher numbers indicating more ambivalence.]

OP ambivalence: (1) "Please ignore any unfavorable thoughts or feelings you might have about *[legalized abortion/capital punishment]* and just think about the favorable thoughts and feelings you have about *[legalized abortion/capital punishment]*. How many favorable thoughts and feelings do you have about *[legalized abortion/capital punishment]*—none at all, a few, some, a lot, or many?" (2) "Please ignore any favorable thoughts or feelings you might have about *[legalized abortion/capital punishment]* and just think about the unfavorable thoughts and feelings you have about *[legalized abortion/capital punishment]*. How many unfavorable thoughts and feelings do you have about *[legalized abortion/capital punishment]*—none at all, a few, some, a lot, or many?" [See n. 8 for calculation formulas; scores range from 0 to 1, with higher numbers representing a greater number of favorable or unfavorable thoughts.]

MP resistance: (1) "How easy do you think it would be for someone to change your opinion about the issue of *[legalized abortion/capital punishment]*—extremely easy, very easy, somewhat easy, somewhat difficult, very difficult, or extremely difficult?" (2) "How firm is your opinion about *[legalized abortion/capital punishment]*—not at all firm, slightly firm, somewhat firm, very firm, or extremely firm?" (3) "Compared to other issues, how firm is your opinion about *[legalized abortion/capital punishment]*—less firm than other opinions, more firm than other opinions, or about as firm as other opinions? (If Less): Much less firm or somewhat less firm? (If More): Much more firm or somewhat more firm? (If About As Much): Do you lean toward thinking your attitude about *[legalized abortion/capital punishment]* is less firm than your attitudes about other issues, lean toward thinking it is more firm, or don't you lean either way?" [Scores range from 0 to 1, with higher numbers indicating more resistance.]

Attitudes: (1) "Do you favor *[legalized abortion/capital punishment]*, oppose it, or neither favor nor oppose it? (If Favor): Do you strongly favor it or somewhat favor it? (If Oppose): Do you strongly oppose it or somewhat oppose it? (If Neither): Do you lean toward favoring *[legalized abortion/capital punishment]*, lean toward opposing it, or don't you lean either way?" (2) "Do you think *[legalized abortion/capital punishment]* is good, do you think it is bad, or do you think it is neither good nor bad? (If Good): Do you think it is very good, or somewhat good? (If Bad): Do you think it is very bad, or somewhat bad? (If Neither): Do you lean toward thinking *[legalized abortion/capital punishment]* is good, lean toward thinking it is bad, or don't you lean either way?" (3) "Do you think *[legalized abortion/capital punishment]* is wise, do you think it is foolish, or do you think it is neither wise nor foolish? (If Wise): Do you think it is very wise, or somewhat wise? (If Foolish): Do you think it is very foolish, or somewhat foolish? (If Neither): Do you lean toward thinking *[legalized abortion/capital punishment]* is wise, lean toward thinking it is foolish, or don't you lean either way?" (4) "Do you think *[legalized abortion/capital punishment]* is beneficial, do you think it is harmful, or do you think it is neither beneficial nor harmful? (If Beneficial): Do you think it is very beneficial, or somewhat beneficial? (If Harmful): Do you think it is very harmful, or somewhat harmful? (If Neither): Do you lean toward thinking *[legalized abortion/capital punishment]* is beneficial, lean toward thinking it is harmful, or don't you lean either way?" [Scores ranged from 0 to 1, with higher numbers indicating more positive attitudes.] Note: These questions were asked before and after a persuasive message in order to assess resistance operatively. Attitude change was coded so that greater resistance (i.e., less change) was represented by higher numbers. Pre-message answers to the first attitude question were used to calculate issue discrepancies for assessing the ingredients of candidate evaluations.

Choices of information to acquire: Respondents were shown a list of descriptions of information and asked to report which they most and least wanted to learn. (1) Editorials published in the *New York Times*—List 1 (death penalty errors, how taxes trickle down, school vouchers' flaw); List 2 (the fuzzy abortion debate, taking action on hate crimes, jobs and inflation); (2) Pieces of information about people in the United States—List 3 (percent of convicted murderers who are eventually put to death, number of Americans without health insurance, current rate of unemployment); List 4 (average age at which most smokers begin to smoke, number of abortions conducted in the United States each day, number of homeless people in the United States); (3) Candidates' opinions about the following issues—List 5 (school vouchers, capital punishment, campaign finance reform); List 6 (legalized abortion, education reform, pollution). [Each piece of information was coded 1 if the respondent wanted to learn it the most, 0 if s/he wanted to learn it least, and 0.5 otherwise. For those in the abortion target issue condition, the first editorial from List 2, the second piece of information from List 4, and the first issue on List 6 were treated as attitude-relevant pieces of information. For respondents in the capital punishment target issue condition, the first editorial from List 1, the first piece of information from List 3, and the second issue on List 5 were treated as attitude-relevant pieces of information.]

Interest in information: (1) "How interested are you in learning more about the issue of *[legalized abortion/capital punishment]*—not at all interested, slightly interested, somewhat interested, very interested, or extremely interested?" (2) "How likely are you to seek out information about the issue of *[legalized abortion/capital punishment]*—not at all likely, a little likely, somewhat likely, very likely, or extremely likely?" (3) "Compared to other issues, how interested are you in learning more about the issue of *[legalized abortion/capital punishment]*—less than about other issues, more than about other issues, or about as much as about other issues? (If Less): Much less interested or somewhat less interested? (If More): Much more interested or somewhat more interested? (If About As Much): Do you lean toward thinking you are less interested in learning about the issue of *[legalized abortion/capital punishment]* than about other issues, lean toward thinking you are more interested in learning about it than about other issues, or don't you lean either way?" [Scores range from 0 to 1, with higher numbers indicating more interest.]

Orienting to attitude-relevant information: "In the next task, you will very briefly be shown a list of words. After you see each list, you will have one minute to list all the words you remember seeing." Each of the following four lists was shown to respondents for 2 seconds; the latter then had one minute to list all the words they remembered seeing.

List #1	*List #2*	*List #3*	*List #4*
Justice Department	Abortion	Senate	National Security
Education	School Vouchers	Interest Group	Social Spending
Death Penalty	Taxes	Fetus	Pro-Choice
Liberal	Capital Punishment	Electric Chair	Health Care
Government Services	Crime	NAFTA	Democrats
Defense Spending	Global Warming	International Peace	Lethal Injection
Pro-Life	Pollution	Weapons Development	Capitol Hill
Smog	Military Costs	Republicans	Utility Deregulation
Environment	Conservative	Defense Spending	President

[The number of correctly recalled attitude-relevant words from the first two lists was one indicator of orientation, and the number of correctly recalled attitude-relevant words from the second two lists was a second indicator of orientation. For respondents in the abortion target issue condition, the words "pro-life," "abortion," "fetus," and "pro-choice" were used as target words; for those in the capital punishment target issue condition, the words "death penalty," "capital punishment," "electric chair," and "lethal injection" were used.]

False consensus effect: (1) "In your opinion, what percent of Americans do you think have the same opinion as you about the issue of *[legalized abortion/capital punishment]*?" (2) "Do you think most Americans strongly favor *[legalized abortion/capital punishment]*, somewhat favor it, slightly favor it, neither favor nor oppose it, slightly oppose it, somewhat oppose it, or strongly oppose it?" (3) "If someone conducted a survey of all U.S. adults, do you think most people would be on the same side of the *[legalized abortion/capital punishment]* issue as you, or would most people be on the other side?" (4) "Do you think you are in the minority when it comes to your opinion about *[legalized abortion/capital punishment]*, or in the majority?" (5) "Do you think most people agree with your position on *[legalized abortion/capital punishment]*, or disagree with it?" [Scores for the first question range from 0 to 1, with higher numbers indicating a stronger false consensus effect. Scores for the second question range from 0 to 1, with higher numbers indicating more favorable attitudes. The absolute value of the difference between these two scores was calculated and recoded to range from 0 to 1, with higher numbers indicating a stronger false consensus effect. Responses to the last three questions were coded so that 1 indicated the respondent thought s/he was in the majority, and 0 indicated the respondent thought that s/he was in the minority. These scores were then averaged to yield a measure of majority perceptions.]

Hostile media bias: "Some people feel that the news media have been biased in their coverage of *[legalized abortion/capital punishment]*. Other people feel that the news media have been fair and objective in their coverage of this issue. Do you think the news media have been not at all biased, a little biased, somewhat biased, very biased, or extremely biased in their stories about *[legalized abortion/capital punishment]*?" (If the respondent said something other than "Not At All Biased"): (a) For abortion, "What kind of bias have you noticed? Have the news media been biased toward saying that abortions should be easy to obtain, or have they been biased toward saying that abortions should be difficult to obtain?" (b) For capital punishment, "What kind of bias have you noticed? Have the news media been biased toward saying that capital punishment should be used more often, or have they been biased toward saying that capital punishment should be used less often?" [Scores range from -1 to $+1$, with higher numbers indicating greater bias toward saying that abortion should be easy to obtain or capital punishment should be used more often.]

Presidential candidates' policy attitudes: (1) "What is George W. Bush's opinion about *[legalized abortion/capital punishment]*? Does he favor *[legalized abortion/capital punishment]*, oppose it, or neither favor nor oppose it? (If Favor): Does he strongly favor it or somewhat favor it? (If Oppose): Does he strongly oppose it or somewhat oppose it? (If Neither): Do you think he leans toward favoring *[legalized abortion/capital punishment]*, leans toward opposing it, or don't you think he leans either way?" (2) "What is Al Gore's opinion about *[legalized abortion/capital punishment]*? Does he favor *[legalized abortion/capital punishment]*, oppose it, or neither favor nor oppose it? (If Favor): Does he strongly favor it or somewhat favor it? (If Oppose): Does he strongly oppose it or somewhat oppose it? (If Neither): Do you think he leans toward favoring *[legalized abortion/capital punishment]*, leans toward opposing it, or don't you think he leans either way?" [Scores range from 0 to 1, with higher numbers indicating more favorable attitudes toward the policy.]

Evaluations of presidential candidates: (1) "Is your opinion of George W. Bush favorable, unfavorable, or neither favorable nor unfavorable? (If Favorable): Is it very favorable or somewhat favorable? (If Unfavorable): Is it very unfavorable or somewhat unfavorable? (If Neither): Do you lean towards being favorable towards George W. Bush, or do you lean towards being unfavorable about him?" (2) "Is your opinion of Al Gore favorable, unfavorable, or neither favorable nor unfavorable? (If Favorable): Is it very favorable or somewhat favorable? (If Unfavorable): Is it very unfavorable or somewhat unfavorable? (If Neither): Do you lean towards being favorable towards Al Gore, or do you lean towards being unfavorable about him?" [Scores range from 0 to 1, with higher numbers indicating more positive attitudes.]

General involvement in activities: (1) "How involved are you in activities related to the issue of *[legalized abortion/capital punishment]*—not at all involved, a little involved, somewhat involved, very involved, or extremely involved?" (2) "How often do you engage in activities related to the issue of *[legalized abortion/capital punishment]*—never, occasionally, often, very often, or extremely often?" (3) "Compared to other issues, how involved are you in activities related to the issue of *[legalized abortion/capital punishment]*—less than other issues, more than other issues, or about as much as other issues? (If Less): Much less involved or somewhat less involved? (If More): Much more involved or somewhat more involved? (If About As Much): Do you lean toward thinking you are less involved in activities related to the issue of *[legalized abortion/capital punishment]*, lean toward thinking you are more involved in activities related to the issue of *[legalized abortion/capital punishment]*, or don't you lean either way?" [Scores range from 0 to 1, with higher numbers indicating more activism.]

Specific activist behaviors: "Have you ever . . . (1) written a letter to a public official about the issue of *[legalized abortion/capital punishment]*? (2) given money to an organization concerned with the issue of *[legalized abortion/capital punishment]*? (3) joined an organization concerned with the issue of *[legalized abortion/capital punishment]*? (4) participated in a protest march or rally on the issue of *[legalized abortion/capital punishment]*? (5) attended a group meeting to discuss the issue of *[legalized abortion/capital punishment]*? (6) made a telephone call to a government official to express your opinion on the issue of *[legalized abortion/capital punishment]*? (7) written a letter to a newspaper or magazine to express your opinion on the issue of *[legalized abortion/capital punishment]*? (8) called a talk radio program to express your opinion on the issue of *[legalized abortion/capital punishment]*? [Responses to each question were coded 1 for yes, 0 for no. Scores for the first two behaviors were averaged together to form one measure of activism, scores for the next two were averaged to form a second, scores for the fifth and sixth to form a third, and scores for the final two to form a fourth.]

NOTES

1. Ambivalence has also been gauged by other methods: (1) examining individual-level error variance in models predicting respondents' answers to specific policy questions, on the assumption that greater variance reflects greater conflict between relevant values (Alvarez and Brehm 1995, 1997, 1998); (2) coding responses to open-ended questions asking respondents to report their thoughts (researchers looking for mentions of conflicting values and direct mentions of feelings of ambivalence; Feldman and Zaller 1992); and (3) gauging inconsistencies between attitudes toward specific attitude objects (e.g., abortion or capital punishment) and ideology (Huckfeldt and Sprague 1998a,b). All of these seem to us to be relatively indirect.

2. We borrowed the term "operative" from Bassili (1996b), and generalized his "meta-attitudinal" into "meta-psychological."

3. Also see chapter 4 in this volume for an example.

4. Priester and Petty (2001) found that interpersonal discrepancies predicted unique variance in MP ambivalence, even when controlling for the effect of OP ambivalence. Interpersonal discrepancies primarily influenced MP ambivalence for issues that were important, and when the discrepancies were with the attitudes of liked others. Furthermore, the impact of interpersonal discrepancies on MP ambivalence appeared to be greater when OP ambivalence was high. These findings indicate that interpersonal discrepancies cause MP ambivalence. It is also possible, however, that such discrepancies may influence OP ambivalence. The discovery that a liked other holds an attitude discrepant from one's own may lead to the incorporation of reactions to the attitude object that are similar to those of the liked other, thereby increasing OP ambivalence.

5. Jonas, Diehl, and Bromer (1997) manipulated the consistency of information provided to respondents and found that ambivalence led to *more* attitude–intention consistency. However, this finding has only been demonstrated with attitudes toward newly formed objects and has not been found with existing attitudes toward familiar objects.

6. Although Schuman, Presser, and Ludwig (1981) claimed to show that question order effects were stronger among more ambivalent respondents, these investigators actually were measuring certainty rather than ambivalence.
7. Question wordings and codings are detailed in the Appendix to this chapter.
8. All the proposed formulas for calculating ambivalence yield numbers that are highly correlated with one another (Priester and Petty 1996; Thompson *et al.* 1995), and our own tests of the consequences of OP ambivalence using alternative calculations yielded results comparable to those reported here. The formulas we employed are as follows (see the Appendix for question wording):

Gradual Threshold Model:
If negativity (N) is greater than positivity (P),
Ambivalence = $(5 \times (P + 1)^{.4}) - ((N + 1)^{(1/(P + 1))})$.
If P is greater than or equal to N,
Ambivalence = $(5 \times (N + 1)^{.4}) - ((P + 1)^{(1/(N + 1))})$.

Negative Acceleration Model:
If positivity (P) is greater than negativity (N),
Ambivalence = $(2 \times N + 1)/(P + N + 2)$.
If N is greater than or equal to P,
Ambivalence = $(2 \times P + 1)/(P + N + 2)$.

9. Some respondents read strong arguments, others read weak arguments. Because this manipulation did not affect the amount of attitude change observed, the two groups were combined for the analyses reported below. Attitudes toward abortion manifested significant change in the direction of the persuasive message (mean change = 0.02, $t(294) = 6.41$, $p < 0.001$), as did attitudes toward capital punishment (mean change = 0.03, $t(299) = 8.09$, $p < 0.001$).
10. Mean placement of each candidate on the target issue was used to estimate the candidate's actual attitude when calculating this variable. Alternatively, we might have content-analyzed speeches and other public statements by the candidate to gauge his or her position on the attitude continuum. This is difficult to do, however, because candidates often do not clearly and consistently state their positions on issues (Page 1978), and the news media do not always report candidates' positions to the public (Graber 1980; Patterson 1980; Patterson and McClure 1976). Yet another approach would be to treat each respondent's placement of a candidate as a measure of his or her perception of the candidate's position. Yet analyses using this measure may be distorted by projection, whereby people adjust their perceptions so that candidates they like appear to have attitudes more similar to their own, and candidates they dislike appear to have attitudes more different from their own (Krosnick 2002; Page and Brody 1972). We chose to use average perceived candidate positions in our analyses to eliminate this potential confound.

11. Also consistent with our hypotheses about the effects of operative ambivalence on perceptions of candidates' attitudes, greater OP ambivalence was associated with smaller perceived differences between the candidates' positions ($\beta = 0.10$, $p < 0.05$); MP ambivalence was not associated with the magnitude of perceived differences ($\beta = 0.08$, n.s.).

6. Ambivalence Toward American Political Institutions

Sources and Consequences

Kathleen M. McGraw and Brandon Bartels

The characterization of attitudes as lying along a single bipolar (negative to positive) continuum has widely been rejected as inadequate in social and political psychology. Instead, scholars recognize that attitudes can have separate positive and negative components—a two-dimensional view which contends that ambivalence is fundamental to our understanding of attitudes. As the contributions to this volume illustrate, within a relatively short period of time scholars have made important advances in demonstrating the role that ambivalence plays in the expression of attitudes about social and political policies, individuals, and social groups.[1] However, there has been no consideration of ambivalence toward another object of tremendous importance to the political system, namely, the institutions of American government.

Our starting point is a simple one: Although Congress, the Supreme Court and the presidency are at the center of the U.S. governmental system, there has been remarkably little consideration of public opinion about those institutions from a cross-institutional, comparative perspective. Hibbing and Theiss-Morse (1995) provide a commendable exception to this general rule, but their analysis is best regarded as a starting point. In *Congress as Public Enemy*, the authors demonstrated that public attitudes and views about Congress, the Supreme Court and the president are distinct from one another; they also persuasively made the case that it is important to understand why those distinctions exist, and why they matter for democratic governance. Yet their analysis is incapable of shedding light on the micro-foundations of citizens' institutional attitudes. Our goal is to extend Hibbing and Theiss-Morse's arguments for studying and comparing public opinion regarding the three branches of government. We will do this by examining the extent to which attitudes about those institutions are characterized by ambivalence, exploring the sources of ambivalence, and considering its consequences.

To place our investigation in proper context, we start with an overview of how ambivalence has been conceptualized in previous scholarship. We then briefly describe what might be construed as the "two faces of ambivalence," namely, that ambivalence may promote both normatively desirable *and* undesirable outcomes in political judgment and decision-making. The subsequent analysis involves an exploration of (1) the extent of Americans' ambivalence about Congress, the president, and the Supreme Court; (2) the relationships between ambivalence and basic political orientations of trust, efficacy, and support for democratic processes, and (3) the consequences of ambivalence for the mass public's evaluations of the institutions of government. We close by summarizing our results and discussing their implications.

CONCEPTUALIZATION AND OPERATIONALIZATION OF AMBIVALENCE

Ambivalence has been conceptualized in a variety of ways, and there is little doubt that diverging conclusions about its incidence and consequences are tied to specific conceptual and measurement decisions. Let us therefore consider some of the different approaches taken by scholars in earlier studies. Hochschild (1981), for example, wrote that she used ambivalence "as a generic term to indicate a wide range of views" and argued that various expressions of ambivalence—including helplessness, anger, inconsistency, confusion—are critical (pp. 239–242) for understanding the concept. In Hochschild's analysis, it is these overt manifestations that really define ambivalence. In contrast, Zaller and Feldman (1992) defined ambivalence (axiomatically): "Most people possess opposing considerations on most issues, that is, considerations that might lead them to decide the issue either way" (p. 585). In this view, it is the mental elements that define ambivalence. The Zaller and Feldman (1992) position corresponds to most social psychological treatments, which conceive of ambivalence as a structural property of attitudes (e.g., Cacioppo and Berntson 1994; Cacioppo *et al.* 1997; Thompson *et al.* 1995). Our treatment follows from this tradition, as we conceive of ambivalence as a structural property of the mental representation of an attitude, reflecting the coexistence of both positive and negative evaluations of the attitude object.

Three general procedures have been used in previous scholarship to measure ambivalence. In the first, the researcher infers its existence, for example, Hochschild's (1981) intensive interviews, as well as Chong's (1993) and Feldman and Zaller's (1992) analyses of open-ended survey data. Although more complex in application, Alvarez and Brehm (2002; cf. Steenbergen and Ellis, 2003) also use an inferential approach, inferring ambivalence from patterns of error variance in heteroskedastic probit models of binary choice. A second approach requires the self-report of subjective experiences, for example, by asking individuals their agreement with statements such as "I have both positive and negative feelings about——" or "I find myself feeling torn between the two sides of——" (McGraw *et al.* 2003; Priester and Petty 1996, 2001; Thompson *et al.* 1995; Tourangeau *et al.* 1989a).

The third type of measurement strategy involves two steps. First, positive and negative reactions to some target are assessed separately. This is done either holistically, that is, by asking individuals to rate, in an overall fashion, the positivity and negativity of their reactions to the target (e.g., Craig *et al.* 2002; Thompson *et al.* 1995), or by soliciting specific positive and negative reactions (e.g., Lavine 2001; McGraw *et al.* 2003). In the second step, positive and negative reactions are combined to yield a continuous measure of ambivalence (for reviews of various computational formulas, see Breckler 1994; Priester and Petty 1996; Thompson *et al.* 1995). With this third strategy, some researchers have made use of indicators of ambivalence that might be considered primarily *cognitive* in content, that is, tapping positive and negative beliefs about the target (Alvarez and Brehm 2002; Feldman and Zaller 1992; Lavine 2001; McGraw *et al.* 2003; Meffert *et al.* 2000; Steenbergen and Brewer 2000), while others have employed indicators that are more *affective* or emotional (Lavine *et al.* 1998b; Meffert *et al.* 2000; Steenbergen and Ellis 2003).

There are many important unanswered questions regarding the relationships among these various indicators, as well as questions as to which is the superior measure of the construct. Some of these questions are addressed by other contributors to this volume, but they are beyond the scope of the present chapter. Rather, our measurement approach is dictated by the data available to us for exploring institutional ambivalence (described more fully below). Specifically, we make use of the third measurement strategy described above in assessing both positive and negative beliefs about Congress, the Supreme Court, and the president.

The Two Faces of Ambivalence

Ambivalence has been linked to a variety of attitudinal and behavioral consequences, though we postpone detailing expectations about the specific consequences of institutional ambivalence that motivate our analyses until the relevant results are presented. Rather, at this juncture, we simply note that the literature presents two very different portraits of the role ambivalence plays in the political system, and its attendant normative implications. These two portraits emerge from Hochschild's (1981) analysis, where she notes that some people have the ability to cope with conflicting reactions but that "most respondents lack this happy ability to maintain and draw strength from distinctions among beliefs and domains. Most make the distinctions, but react to them with uncertainty and distress, not contentment and 'health' " (p. 240). According to Hochschild, then, the consequences of ambivalence for most people are negative, and this is a view that largely characterizes the public opinion literature. Ambivalence has been linked to response instability and is said to decrease the predictability of public opinion responses, weaken the relationship between intentions and behavior, result in more negative general evaluations, and lead to a variety of negative subjective experiences (in Hochschild's analysis, helplessness, anger, inconsistency, and confusion). From this perspective, ambivalence clearly has negative normative implications for the functioning of the political system: It leads to a polity characterized by negativity and confusion, lacking stable opinions, and therefore subject to manipulation by the media and political elites.

On the other hand, as Hochschild describes, ambivalence does not inevitably lead to negative outcomes, and there is a more modest research tradition demonstrating that ambivalence is associated with deeper and more systematic information processing, the searching out of new information, open-mindedness and a willingness to evaluate evidence in an even-handed fashion, and improved coping with severe health stressors. From this perspective, ambivalence produces a better-informed, more engaged, and more open-minded polity, and thus should have positive normative implications for the functioning of the political system.

Most likely, of course, is that ambivalence manifests itself in a variety of ways that have both positive and negative normative impacts. In the service of truth in advertising, we want to point out that it is not our goal to provide any sort of definitive statement regarding when, why, or how ambivalence produces desirable and undesirable outcomes. However, it is important to be sensitive to the "two faces of ambivalence," and so we proceed in the analyses that follow by being cognizant of each of these two possibilities.

DATA, MEASURES, AND THE INCIDENCE OF
INSTITUTIONAL AMBIVALENCE

The data used to explore ambivalence toward U.S. political institutions are drawn from the 1997 American National Election Study (ANES) Pilot Study, which was a telephone re-interview of 551 randomly selected respondents from the 1996 ANES election-year survey. Since Pilot Study respondents were interviewed in both the pre- and post-election waves of the 1996 survey, data are available for each respondent from three points in time (1996$_{pre}$, 1996$_{post}$, and 1997).

The 1997 Pilot Study included new instrumentation designed to explore a number of topic areas, including nonelectoral participation, group conflict, religion, and evaluations of President Clinton, the Supreme Court, and Congress. It is this last battery of questions that form the core of our analysis.[2] Respondents were asked how well a series of six traits described Congress, President Clinton, and the Supreme Court. These traits were (1) doesn't get much accomplished; (2) too involved in partisan politics; (3) doesn't care what ordinary people think; (4) corrupt; (5) too conservative; and (6) too liberal, with response options of "extremely well," "quite well," "not so well," and "not well at all." Responses to four of these trait questions were used to create measures of ambivalence toward each of the three targets. We decided to drop the "too conservative" and "too liberal" measures because it is difficult to classify those responses as reflecting clearly positive or negative beliefs. In contrast, the remaining four traits are all phrased so that *agreement* (responses of "extremely well" and "quite well") reflects a *negative* assessment of the target on that trait. We then infer that *disagreement* (responses of "not so well" and "not well at all") reflect more *positive* assessments of the target on a particular trait dimension.

To our knowledge, these are the only existing available data suitable for a comparative analysis of institutional ambivalence. Their value is that they allow us to compare the incidence, sources, and consequences of ambivalence, based on identical indicators, across the three institutional targets. Of course, "President Clinton" is not an institution, but rather a specific individual who inhabited the office; the institution of the presidency clearly is more than just the officeholder. However, there has been virtually no work on public opinion about the institution of the presidency *per se*, and so our focus on a sitting president is consistent with the existing literature (Hibbing and Theiss-Morse 1995). To avoid excessive verbiage, we thus refer to the three "institutional targets" in the analysis and discussion that follows.

By categorizing the four trait attributions into positive and negative responses, we can examine the extent to which opinions about these targets are characterized by ambivalence. Given four traits, three patterns of responses are possible: (1) *nonambivalence*, or a 4–0 mix, where the respondent's beliefs are either all positive or all negative; (2) *weak ambivalence*, or a 3–1 mix, where beliefs are either three positive and one negative, or three negative and one positive; and (3) *ambivalence*, or a 2–2 mix, where beliefs are characterized by two positive and two negatives. Although this tripartite classification scheme is straightforward and does not require any complex statistical estimation, it should be noted that computing ambivalence scores by applying the widely used Thompson *et al.* (1995; see chapter 4 in this volume) algorithm yields exactly the same three categories and incidence rates.

Descriptive data are provided in table 6.1. The top panel summarizes the full distribution of responses to the trait questions. The basic pattern we see is consistent with long-standing differences in evaluations of the three branches of government (see Hibbing and Theiss-Morse 1995). Beliefs about Congress tend to be the most negative, with 43.9 percent of respondents providing either all or three out of four negative responses. In contrast, beliefs about Clinton and the Supreme Court are predominantly positive, with 56.5 percent and 70.1 percent, respectively, providing either all or three out of four positive responses. A similar pattern is evident in general evaluations of the institutions, as reflected by the thermometer ratings displayed in the middle panel of table 6.1.

There is a mini-debate in the literature concerning the incidence of ambivalence in the American public. Some scholars conclude that it is widespread (Hochschild 1981; Zaller 1992), others that it is a relatively rare phenomenon (Alvarez and Brehm 2002; Jacoby 2002; Steenbergen and Brewer 2000), while still others take a moderate position that the incidence of ambivalence is "nontrivial" (Craig *et al.* 2002; Lavine 2001; Meffert *et al.* 2000). In our view, these debates are premature given a lack of consensus on how ambivalence is most suitably measured, and secondary to the more important questions regarding how variations in levels of ambivalence are systematically related to important political outcomes. The bottom panel of table 6.1 reveals that at least some Americans are ambivalent about the three central institutions of U.S. government. The question of the incidence rate—how much ambivalence is there?—depends on whether we focus on the fully ambivalent, in which case the incidence rate is clearly a sizable minority of the public (14–25 percent, depending on the target), or whether the weakly ambivalent are included (in which case, we are looking at a much larger 50–70 percent). Regardless, ambivalence is most

Table 6.1   Distribution of trait beliefs and level of ambivalence

	Congress	Supreme Court	President Clinton
Trait belief response patterns			
0 Positive–4 Negative	19.3%	6.5%	13.0%
1 Positive–3 Negative	24.6	9.3	16.4
2 Positive–2 Negative	25.0	14.1	14.0
3 Positive–1 Negative	20.5	27.1	20.9
4 Positive–0 Negative	10.6	43.0	35.6
Feeling thermometers			
Mean score	54.7	62.9	58.5
Standard deviation	(17.6)	(17.1)	(26.8)
Distribution of ambivalence			
Nonambivalent	29.9%	49.5%	48.6
Weakly ambivalent	45.1	36.4	37.4
Ambivalent	25.0	14.1	14.0
Number of cases (1996) =	508	495	506
Number of cases (1997) =	544	538	545

Note: Data are from the 1996 American National Election Study (trait beliefs and distribution of ambivalence) and 1997 ANES Pilot Study (feeling thermometers).

pronounced for Congress, but also present in beliefs about the Supreme Court and the president.

Relationships among Institutional Ambivalence Measures

We next consider relationships among the three institutional ambivalence measures, to determine whether they are independent or representative of a more fundamental individual difference or political orientation. There are two competing perspectives here. On the one hand, Thompson, Zanna, and Griffin (1995) concluded that there is a sizable individual difference component to ambivalence about policy issues; people who are ambivalent about an issue like AIDS testing, for example, also tend to be ambivalent about an issue like euthanasia. Similarly, Dennis (1966: 608) speculated that "a general ambivalence to politics" colors public opinion about a variety of political issues. Other scholars have argued that the experience of ambivalence and related phenomena, such as value conflict, are largely target-specific, not rooted in fundamental individual differences (Alvarez and Brehm 2002; Lavine 2001; Tetlock 1986). In order to determine which of these perspectives characterizes ambivalence about political institutions, we examined the correlations among the three ambivalence measures (which

Table 6.2   Institutional ambivalence and evaluation correlations

	Congressional ambivalence	Supreme Court ambivalence	Clinton ambivalence	Congressional evaluations	Supreme Court evaluations	Clinton evaluations
Congressional ambivalence	—					
Supreme Court ambivalence	0.068	—				
Clinton ambivalence	0.060	0.148***	—			
Congressional evaluations	0.120**	− 0.099*	−0.010	—		
Supreme Court evaluations	0.077	− 0.206***	−0.001	0.500***	—	
Clinton evaluations	0.063	− 0.073	−0.112*	0.343***	0.259***	—

Note: *** $p \leq 0.001$; ** $p \leq 0.01$; * $p \leq 0.05$. Data are from the 1996 American National Election Study and 1997 ANES Pilot Study. Table entries are Pearson's correlation coefficients ($N = 460$, listwise deletion of missing data).

were recoded to a three-point scale, taking values of 0 [nonambivalent], 0.5 [weakly ambivalent], and 1.0 [ambivalent]). For purposes of comparison, we also include evaluations of the three targets, namely, thermometer ratings of institutions from the 1997 wave of the survey. The correlations are summarized in table 6.2.

There are three noteworthy patterns evident in this table. First, whereas ambivalence toward the Supreme Court and Clinton are modestly and positively related, ambivalence toward Congress is independent of the other two. Second, there is considerably less overlap among the ambivalence measures (mean $r = 0.092$) than among the general evaluation indicators, where the typical finding of strong positive relationships is evident (mean $r = 0.367$; cf. Wilcox *et al.* 1989). The fact that institutional ambivalence measures have very little overlap supports the position that these reactions are largely target-specific, rather than being primarily rooted in a chronic component on which people consistently vary. Finally, we see the first bit of evidence suggesting that the consequences of ambivalence may vary with the institutional target: Ambivalence toward the Supreme Court and Clinton are associated with more *negative* evaluations, whereas ambivalence toward Congress is associated with more *positive* evaluations.

SOURCES OF INSTITUTIONAL AMBIVALENCE

Despite an increasing amount of research on the topic, there has been relatively little consideration of the sources of ambivalence. Hochschild

(1981) and Zaller (1992) imply that ambivalence is nearly ubiquitous and· invariant, a claim that would suggest that a search for systematic sources rooted in individual differences is futile. However, the data presented in table 6.1 work against the Hochschild/Zaller perspective, as it is clear that the incidence of ambivalence toward political institutions is neither ubiquitous nor invariant. There has been some consideration of the factors that predict the subjective experience of ambivalence, including the impact of information and the objective mental elements that comprise attitudinal ambivalence (McGraw *et al.* 2003; Priester and Petty 1996), interpersonal attitudinal discrepancies (Priester and Petty 2001), and personality characteristics such as need for cognition and fear of invalidity (Thompson *et al.* 1995). More relevant to our purposes, given the data available to us, there are some hints in the literature that ambivalence about political issues varies as a function of core demographic characteristics and attitudinal characteristics (Craig *et al.* 2002; Steenbergen and Brewer 2000), as well as core political values (Craig *et al.* 2002; Mulligan and McGraw 2002).

We explored the impact of a variety of such factors on ambivalence toward the three institutional targets. We underscore that this exercise is largely exploratory and only loosely guided by theoretical expectations. Our model includes key demographics (sex, race, age, political sophistication), core political attitudes (partisanship, ideology), and a set of more general political and moral orientations (trust, efficacy,[3] support for democratic processes, moral conservatism, religiosity).[4] Question wordings for all variables, recoded to scales with scores ranging between 0 and 1, are provided in the Appendix. Table 6.3 reports both bivariate correlations and the results from a multivariate ordinary least squares regression.

Given the low adjusted R^2s evident in the table, it is clear that these models do not do an especially good job of explaining the variance in institutional ambivalence. This pessimistic observation can be tempered somewhat by taking into consideration the explanatory power of the same set of variables for predicting respondents' evaluations (i.e., thermometer ratings) of the targets (not reported in tabular form). The discrepancy in R^2s is enormous for the Clinton models (adjusted $R^2 = 0.042$ versus 0.478 for ambivalence and evaluations, respectively), and so it is clearly the case that the model does a very poor job of explaining ambivalence toward Clinton. By the same token, the models using the same set of variables to predict evaluations of Congress and the Supreme Court are not nearly as robust as for the Clinton evaluation models (adjusted $R^2 = 0.203$ and 0.108, respectively, for the thermometer ratings), and so the discrepancy between the evaluation and ambivalence models is not nearly so great for those two targets.

Table 6.3 Sources of institutional ambivalence

	Congress		Supreme Court		Clinton	
	r	b (s.e.)	r	b (s.e.)	r	b (s.e.)
Female$_{1996pre}$	−0.055	−0.079 (.037)*	−0.009	0.006 (.036)	−0.004	−0.019 (0.036)
Black$_{1996pre}$	0.129**	0.104 (.067)	0.040	0.050 (.067)	−0.106*	−0.150 (0.066)*
Age$_{1996pre}$	0.049	0.001 (.001)	0.098*	0.001 (.001)	0.123**	0.003 (0.001)**
Sophistication$_{1996mixed}$	0.033	−0.013 (.025)	0.063	0.077 (.025)**	−0.087†	−0.021 (0.024)
Partisanship$_{1997}$ (Democrat)	0.071	−0.050 (.058)	0.002	0.066 (.058)	−0.084†	−0.023 (0.057)
Partisan Strength$_{1997}$	0.128**	0.096 (.046)*	0.046	0.040 (.045)	−0.069	−0.064 (0.045)
Ideology$_{1997}$ (Liberal)	0.060	0.039 (.042)	−0.048	−0.030 (.041)	−0.098*	−0.032 (0.041)
Trust$_{1996post}$	0.228***	0.257 (.098)**	−0.158***	−0.112 (.096)	−0.018	0.140 (0.095)
Efficacy$_{1996post}$	0.191***	0.157 (.101)†	−0.204***	−0.392 (.100)***	−0.128**	−0.166 (0.099)†
Democratic Processes$_{1996post}$	0.142***	0.080 (.094)	−0.031	0.038 (.095)	−0.068	−0.114 (0.093)
Moral Conservatism$_{1996post}$	−0.109*	−0.269 (.103)**	−0.066	0.035 (.100)	−0.083†	0.018 (0.099)
Religiosity$_{1996pre}$	0.094*	0.199 (.077)**	0.030	0.014 (.075)	0.097*	0.136 (0.074)†
Intercept	n/a	−0.035 (.103)	n/a	0.415 (.103)***	n/a	0.333 (0.102)***
Adjusted R^2	n/a	0.090***	n/a	0.054***	n/a	0.042**
Number of cases =	444	444	433	433	447	447

Note: *** $p \leq 0.001$; ** $p \leq 0.01$; * $p \leq 0.05$; † $p \leq 0.10$. Data are from the 1996 American National Election Study and 1997 ANES Pilot Study. Entries in columns 1, 3, and 6 are Pearson's correlation coefficients (listwise deletion of missing data). Entries in columns 2, 4, and 6 are unstandardized regression coefficients, with standard errors in parentheses. Postscripts for independent variables indicate the wave of the survey in which each variable was measured.

There are three patterns, and non-patterns, in table 6.3 that strike us as noteworthy. First, we find two sources of ambivalence that are constant across the three targets. One is respondent age: All else equal, older citizens tend to be more ambivalent, a conclusion consistent with prior research (Steenbergen and Brewer 2000). In addition, religiosity and ambivalence are positively related, although the magnitude of that positive effect clearly varies. While such a result may seem surprising, it should be noted that our measure of religiosity does not tap religious fundamentalism, which has been linked to close-mindedness and dogmatism (Saroglou 2002); we would expect these latter characteristics to be associated with less ambivalence rather than more. Ambivalence, however, is often linked with the ability or willingness to be open-minded, and the positive religiosity–ambivalence relationship shown in table 6.3 is consistent with recent evidence (Saroglou 2002) indicating that religiosity is associated with greater openness to experience, one of the "Big Five" dimensions of personality (McCrae and Costa, 2003).[5] Along the same lines, the strong inverse relationship between congressional ambivalence and moral conservatism may reflect the impact of dogmatism or closed-mindedness, given the substantial overlap among these constructs (Jost *et al.* 2003).

Second, there is a series of variables for which no systematic effects emerged. Other than the positive impact of partisan strength on congressional ambivalence, it seems clear that ambivalence toward the three branches of government is not rooted in the core political cleavages of ideology or partisanship. Further, though scattered effects emerged from our multivariate analyses (sex in the case of Congress, sophistication for the Supreme Court, and race for President Clinton), we can see no consistent effects attributable to key demographic variables.

The third pattern, involving relationships between ambivalence and the basic political orientations of trust, efficacy, and support for democratic processes, strikes us as the most provocative. Consider the effects of this cluster of variables on ambivalence toward the Supreme Court and Clinton. While these effects vary in magnitude, the general pattern is that more *negative* orientations (less trust, efficacy, and support) are associated with greater ambivalence; all the bivariate correlations, and the only significant coefficients in the multivariate analyses, reveal this relationship. The pattern for congressional ambivalence is markedly different, indicating that more *positive* orientations are associated with greater ambivalence; all three bivariate relationships are positive and significant, and two of the relationships (for trust and efficacy) hold even with the multivariate controls. In short, citizens' fundamental levels of affection and disaffection for the political system push them in different directions when it comes to ambivalence toward the three institutions.

Reconciling the implications of this unexpected set of results requires taking into account the sociohistorical context within which opinions about the three institutions are situated (i.e., negative for Congress, variable but positive in the aggregate for President Clinton,[6] and positive for the Supreme Court). These might be considered default, or baseline opinions. Consider again the top panel of table 6.1, where the modal response pattern for both Clinton and the Supreme Court was "four positive–zero negative." Respondents who expressed positive orientations toward the political system—that is, scoring higher in trust, efficacy and support for democracy—were particularly likely to hold positive beliefs about these two targets. For example, zero-order correlations between trust in government and the number of positive trait beliefs are $r = 0.28$, $p < 0.001$ for Clinton, and $r = 0.14$, $p < 0.01$ for the Supreme Court; results are similar for efficacy and support for democratic processes. It is the disaffected who are more likely to hold negative beliefs, and as a consequence exhibit more ambivalence because the holding of both positive and negative beliefs about these two targets means moving away from a default position of *positivity*.

In contrast, although there is no clear modal response in the trait belief patterns for Congress (table 6.1), it is evident that negativity predominates over positivity. Here, too, we would expect that a more positive orientation toward politics should be associated with granting Congress more positive traits, and this is the case ($r = 0.30$, $p < 0.001$, for trust and the number of positive trait beliefs; results again are similar for efficacy and support for democratic processes). Accordingly, it is individuals with more positive orientations toward the political system who exhibit greater congressional ambivalence because holding both positive and negative beliefs about Congress means moving away from a default position of *negativity*.

THE IMPACT OF AMBIVALENCE ON INSTITUTIONAL EVALUATIONS

Cacioppo's asymmetric nonlinear model of attitude formation (Cacioppo *et al.* 1997) predicts that ambivalence will be associated with more negative evaluations because negative information receives greater weight in the judgment process. Evidence in the realm of candidate evaluations generally supports this prediction (Holbrook *et al.* 2001; McGraw *et al.* 2003). In order to examine whether ambivalence is associated with negative evaluations of the institutions, we re-estimated the table 6.3 models using thermometer ratings of the institutions as dependent variables and adding the institution-appropriate measure of ambivalence as a predictor—the latter to determine the independent impact of ambivalence on evaluations above and beyond the effects of other variables. For the sake of brevity, we summarize our results rather than reporting them in tabular form. First, although the bivariate relationship between congressional ambivalence and evaluations is weakly positive (see table 6.2), that relationship does not survive the multivariate analysis; in fact, ambivalence appears to have no independent impact on evaluations of Congress ($b = -0.007$, n.s.). In contrast, and in line with expectations, ambivalence toward the Supreme Court and Clinton (especially the former) are associated with more negative evaluations (for the Supreme Court, $b = -0.064$ [0.024], $p < 0.01$; and for Clinton, $b = -0.037$ [0.027], $p = 0.16$).

Meffert, Guge, and Lodge (2000) demonstrated that ambivalence is related to more moderate evaluations of political candidates. Those authors did not consider the negativity hypothesis and, in fact, it is entirely possible for ambivalence to produce both negativity and moderation if the two are correlated with each other. To examine the relationship between ambivalence and the extremity of institutional evaluations, we re-estimated the evaluation models using the folded (at the scale midpoint of 50) thermometer scores as dependent variables. Results are consistent with both Meffert *et al.* conclusions and our own negativity results: Ambivalence toward Congress has no impact on the extremity of the congressional evaluations ($b = -0.001$, n.s.), whereas ambivalence toward President Clinton and the Supreme Court are linked to more moderate evaluations of those targets ($b = -0.051$ [0.019], $p = 0.008$ for Clinton; and $b = -0.061$ [0.018], $p = 0.001$ for the Supreme Court).

FURTHER CONSEQUENCES OF INSTITUTIONAL AMBIVALENCE

Instability

In light of evidence from previous research linking ambivalence to attitudinal instability (Lavine 2001; Zaller and Feldman 1992; also see chapter 4 in the present volume), we wished to assess the extent to which ambivalence leads to unstable opinions about political institutions. Unfortunately, the 1996–97 ANES data are ill-suited for investigating this question because ambivalence was measured in the final wave (ideally, ambivalence would be used to predict *future* instability). Given this caveat, we nonetheless examined the stability of thermometer ratings between the 1996 post-election and 1997 waves. Overall, evaluations of President Clinton were substantially more stable than evaluations of Congress and the Supreme Court ($r = 0.83, 0.55$, and 0.45, respectively, all $p < 0.001$). However, a comparison of the stability coefficients computed separately for ambivalent, weakly ambivalent and non-ambivalent respondents revealed that the stability of the evaluations do not vary as a function of institutional ambivalence.

Uncertainty

A variety of often contradictory arguments have been put forth regarding the relationship between uncertainty and ambivalence. Alvarez and Brehm's (1997) theoretical framework presumes that the two are independent of one another. This appears to be the case for the *subjective*, or self-reported experiences of ambivalence and uncertainty (McGraw *et al.* 2003), but there is evidence indicating that *objective* ambivalence, of the sort we focus on in this chapter, is associated with a greater degree of self-reported uncertainty about candidates' policy stands (Meffert *et al.* 2000) and opinions about candidates (McGraw *et al.* 2003).

There also is little consensus in the public opinion literature regarding the measurement of uncertainty. One strategy relies on explicit "don't know" responses to survey questions (Alvarez and Franklin 1994; Bartels 1986; McGraw *et al.* 2002), and that is the approach taken here.[7] Specifically, we make use of a series of questions asking respondents to place the three institutional targets on a scale measuring ideology. The respondents were asked, in the 1997 wave, "We hear a lot of talk these days about liberals and conservatives. In your booklet is a seven-point scale on which the political views that people might hold are arranged from extremely liberal to extremely conservative. Where would you place Bill Clinton/the U.S. Congress/the Supreme Court on this scale?" Those who responded "haven't thought much about it" or who said they "don't know" are treated as being uncertain about the ideological leanings of the three institutions.

By and large, very few respondents are uncertain about Clinton's ideology (6.7 percent), whereas more are uncertain about the ideological leanings of Congress (20.7 percent) and the Supreme Court (21.4 percent). Given the lack of variance in the Clinton ideological uncertainty measure, it is not surprising that no systematic relationship between ambivalence toward Clinton and uncertainty about his ideology was detected. On the other hand, the results for the other two institutions are suggestive (albeit weak), and counter to the hypothesis that ambivalence is linked to greater uncertainty. That is, ambivalence toward Congress is associated with *less* uncertainty about its ideological leanings, with 19.7 percent, 20.1 percent, and 26.3 percent of ambivalent, weakly ambivalent and nonambivalent respondents, respectively, providing a "don't know" answer to the question. Likewise, ambivalence toward the Supreme Court is associated with *less* uncertainty about its ideology, with 15.7 percent, 24.4 percent, and 25.9 percent of the ambivalent, weakly ambivalent, and nonambivalent providing a "don't know" response. Generally, these findings support maintaining a distinction between ambivalence and uncertainty in theoretical and empirical work (Alvarez and Brehm 2002; McGraw *et al.* 2003).

Information Seeking

The inverse relationship between ambivalence and uncertainty makes sense, once the role ambivalence plays in information processing and search is taken into account. Specifically, ambivalence has been linked to more systematic information processing and an increased search for information, presumably motivated by a desire to reduce the negative feelings and discomfort that accompanies ambivalence (Jonas *et al.* 1997; Maio *et al.* 1996; Meffert *et al.* 2000; Steenbergen and Ellis 2003). Researchers have recently identified the neurological mechanisms associated with ambivalence that support this logic, as ambivalence has been linked to greater ventrolateral prefrontal cortex activity, the area of the brain implicated in controlled, systematic processing (Cunningham *et al.* 2003).

Although we lack functional neuroimaging data or direct evidence of systematic processing, we can consider the relationship between institutional ambivalence and seeking out information about political matters. The dependent variable in this analysis is based on the responses to a question asked in both the 1996 and 1997 waves: "Some people seem to follow what's going on in government and public affairs most of the time, whether there's an election going on or not. Others aren't that interested. Would you say that you follow what's going on in government and public affairs most of the time, some of the time, only now and then, or hardly at all?" The two responses were highly correlated ($r = 0.66$), and so they were averaged to create a summary "attention to government" variable. We examined the impact of the three institutional ambivalence indicators on this measure, controlling for more general levels of political sophistication (see appendix). Our results are summarized in table 6.4.

Not surprisingly, the propensity to pay attention to political matters is most strongly predicted by political sophistication. More importantly, and consistent with the hypothesis that ambivalence promotes information seeking, ambivalence toward Congress in particular, and to a lesser extent President Clinton, are associated with a person's paying greater attention to politics. This helps to clarify the inverse relationship between ambivalence

Table 6.4   Ambivalence and information seeking

	OLS coefficient estimate	Standard error
Sophistication	0.171***	0.014
Congressional ambivalence	0.068*	0.030
Presidential ambivalence	0.045†	0.032
Supreme Court ambivalence	0.010	0.031
Intercept	0.546***	0.022
Adjusted R^2 =	0.237***	
Number of cases =	470	

Note: *** $p \leq 0.001$; * $p \leq 0.05$; † $p = 0.15$. Data are from the 1996 American National Election Study and 1997 ANES Pilot Study. Attention to government is the dependent variable. Table entries are unstandardized OLS regression coefficients.

and uncertainty: If the ambivalent tend to be more attentive, they should accumulate more information and so be *less*, rather than *more*, uncertain about political matters.[8]

Differentiation between Congress and Own Representative

The results in table 6.4 indicate that ambivalence toward Congress is linked to attention to political matters. This suggests one final consequence of ambivalence, namely, producing differentiation between categorical opinions (in this case, evaluations of Congress as an institution) and opinions about a specific member of that category (evaluations of one's own elected representative in Congress). Although Fenno's (1975) famous paradox, itself arguably a statement of ambivalence (i.e., hate Congress/love my own member), suggests an independence between the two judgments, they are positively related in the aggregate (Born 1990; Hibbing and Theiss-Morse 1995). Born also demonstrated that evaluations of Congress and of one's own member tend to be more distinct for the politically sophisticated, presumably because their greater store of political knowledge and willingness to invest cognitive resources lead them to form and maintain separate cognitive representations of the two targets.

The link between ambivalence toward Congress and greater attention to politics suggests that ambivalence may exert an influence similar to that of sophistication on the propensity to differentiate between Congress as an institution and one's own representative. For the sample as a whole, the correlation between thermometer ratings of the respondent's representative and Congress as a whole is significant and positive ($r = 0.34$, $p < 0.001$), consistent with previous investigations (Born 1990; Hibbing and Theiss-Morse 1995). We also computed partial correlations between the two thermometer ratings, controlling for the effects of sophistication, for each of the three levels of congressional ambivalence. As predicted, the relationship between evaluations of Congress and one's own member varied as a function of ambivalence. The relationship is strongest for the nonambivalent (partial $r = 0.46$, $p < 0.001$), slightly weaker for the weakly ambivalent (partial $r = 0.35$, $p < 0.001$) and weakest for the fully ambivalent (partial $r = 0.18$, $p < 0.05$). The difference between nonambivalent and ambivalent is highly significant (following Fisher r to z conversions, $z = 2.45$, $p < 0.01$), though the difference between weakly ambivalent and ambivalent is not as strong ($z = 1.56$, $p = 0.12$).

DISCUSSION

Because a large amount of data has been presented, let us summarize the major findings before discussing their implications. First, it is clear that the institutional attitudes of some Americans can be characterized as ambivalent, that institutional ambivalence tends to be distinct (rather than characterized by cross-institutional overlap), and that the largest amount of ambivalence is evident in attitudes about Congress. Second, there are sources of ambivalence that are unique to each institution, and sources that are relatively constant, including age, religiosity, and more general evaluative orientations toward the political system (although the impact of the latter cluster of variables varies for the institutions; we elaborate on this below).

Third, we identified both evaluative and what might be considered cognitive consequences of holding ambivalent attitudes. Consistent with the Cacioppo model (Cacioppo *et al.* 1997), and the existing literature linking ambivalence to evaluations of political candidates (Holbrook *et al.* 2001; McGraw *et al.* 2003; Meffert *et al.* 2000), ambivalence toward the president and Supreme Court are associated with more negative and more moderate evaluations of those targets. However, ambivalence toward Congress has no detectable consequences for evaluations of that institution. The reverse pattern is evident in the impact of ambivalence on a set of cognitive consequences, where the effects of congressional ambivalence are more pronounced and robust, and the effects of presidential and Supreme Court ambivalence are weak or nonexistent. In particular, congressional ambivalence is linked to less uncertainty about the ideological orientation of Congress, a greater propensity to seek out political information, and differentiation between evaluations of Congress as an institution and of one's own representative. Arguably, these three consequences reflect a connected underlying dynamic: Ambivalence promotes more attention and learning, which in turn reduces uncertainty and results in separate cognitive representations of the two targets.

In sum, ambivalence toward the core institutions of American government exists, and it has systematic and theoretically meaningful links to important political outcomes. Some of these links are largely consistent with the existing literature on ambivalence in public opinion, whereas others were not anticipated by prior theorizing and scholarship. Most notably, there is a striking divergence between the patterns of relationships that were observed for the Supreme Court and President Clinton, and those observed for Congress. Of course, the conclusion that "Congress is different" should come as no surprise to students of American politics (Hibbing and Theiss-Morse 1995). What needs to be addressed are the reasons that these particular inter-institutional differences were observed in regard to ambivalence.

Specifically, there are two key sets of findings where the results for congressional ambivalence diverge from those observed for ambivalence toward the other institutions. First, ambivalence toward Congress is linked to more *positive* general political orientations, whereas ambivalence toward the Supreme Court and the president is linked to more *negative* political orientations. As we argued earlier, these patterns can be understood by taking into account the default, or baseline, opinions about these institutions. If the starting point is largely negative, as in the case of Congress, it is the addition of positive beliefs that creates ambivalence, and the general orientations of trust, efficacy, and support for democratic processes help to produce those positive beliefs. In contrast, if the starting point is largely positive as in the case of the Supreme Court and president, it is the addition of negative beliefs that creates ambivalence, and the source of those negative beliefs can be traced in part to disaffection for the political system.

There are two larger implications that follow from this line of reasoning. The first is that micro-psychological theories of ambivalence have failed to take into account perceptual "figure-ground" mechanisms that might shape substantially the expression and dynamics of ambivalence. In *gestalt* terms, current information that can produce ambivalence is figural against a positive or negative background, and a fuller understanding of how, why, and when ambivalence matters will need to take into account both the background and contemporary information. Second, in terms of macro-political and normative implications, it is clear that ambivalence is neither a uniformly positive nor uniformly negative political phenomenon. Both "faces" of ambivalence are evident in these data. Ambivalence toward the

Supreme Court and the president are linked to political disaffection and more negative opinions, and so ambivalence toward those institutions can be implicated in a larger pattern of dissatisfaction toward the political system. But because ambivalence toward Congress is rooted in positive political orientations, it appears that some forms of ambivalence are part of a more general web of public support for the system.

The same point is implicated in a second area where Congress was found to be "different," that is, in the positive cognitive consequences associated with congressional ambivalence (less uncertainty, more attention to politics, and greater differentiation in evaluative judgments). The observed pattern is consistent with prior research linking ambivalence to more systematic information processing and an increased search for information (Jonas *et al.* 1997; Maio *et al.* 1996; Meffert *et al.* 2000; Steenbergen and Ellis 2003). While this is typically assumed to result from a negative affective state produced by ambivalence, there is to our knowledge no strong evidence supporting the existence of a mediating link and we are not able to bring to bear relevant data for evaluating the hypothesis. The mediating mechanisms are important, and worth understanding. If ambivalence produces negative emotions and discomfort, the enhanced attention to political matters can be understood as a manifestation of the well-known principle that negative affective states produce more effortful and systematic information processing (Marcus *et al.* 2000; Pratto and John 1991; Taylor 1991). It is possible, however, that the relationship between ambivalence and attention is not mediated by negative feelings, and instead is the result of a greater open-mindedness and willingness to engage in cognitive differentiation (Tetlock 1986), which in turn promotes a heightened involvement in the world of politics.

As noted earlier, the literature on ambivalence has been characterized by a variety of measurement approaches; and many unanswered questions regarding the relationships among different measurement strategies remain. We have made use of the best—in fact, the only—existing survey data available for a systematic cross-institutional comparison of ambivalence. Nevertheless, because of the limited nature of the data and because this is a preliminary investigation, we are unable and unwilling to draw any conclusions about whether these same patterns would emerge if different measurement techniques were employed.

Its limitations notwithstanding, we hope that our work here contributes to an improved understanding of attitudinal ambivalence and its importance for understanding a host of political outcomes. In closing, we would echo Hibbing and Theiss-Morse's (1995: 28) assessment that "there comes a point when we must roll up our sleeves, recognize that in the United States both the separation of powers and the federal structure provide numerous, distinct elements of 'government,' and try to sort through people's attitudes toward these distinct institutions." By ignoring attitudes toward governmental institutions—their structure, how they evolve over time, and why they matter for political judgment, choice, and involvement—scholars miss out on fully understanding a fundamental component of the relationship between the mass public and the political system.

APPENDIX

Question wording and coding schemes for scaled variables used in our analyses are as follows:

Trust in government ($1996_{post,}$ $\alpha = 0.57$): (1) Would you say the government is pretty much run by a few big interests looking out for themselves, or that it is run for the benefit of all the people? (2) Do you think that people in the government waste a lot of the money we pay in taxes, waste some of it, or don't waste very much of it? (3) Do you think that quite a few of the people running the government are crooked, not very many are, or do you think hardly any of them are crooked at all? (4) How much of the time do you think you can trust the government in Washington to do what is right—just about always, most of the time, or only some of the time?

Political efficacy ($1996_{post,}$ $\alpha = 0.72$): (1) Sometimes politics and government seem so complicated that a person like me can't really understand what's going on. [strongly agree to strongly disagree] (2) People like me don't have any say about what the government does. [strongly agree to strongly disagree] (3) Public officials don't care much what people like me think. [strongly agree to strongly disagree] (4) Over the years, how much attention do you feel the government pays to what the people think when it decides what to do—a good deal, some, or not much? (5) How much do you feel that having elections makes the government pay attention to what the people think—a good deal, some, or not much?

Satisfaction with democratic processes ($1996_{post,}$ $r = 0.29$): (1) On the whole, are you satisfied, fairly satisfied, not very satisfied, or not at all satisfied with the way democracy works in the United States? (2) Thinking of the last election in the United States, where would you place it on this scale of one to five, where one means that the last election was conducted fairly and five means that the last election was conducted unfairly?

Moral conservatism ($1996_{post,}$ $\alpha = 0.65$): (1) The world is always changing and we should adjust our view of moral behavior to those changes. (2) The newer lifestyles are contributing to the breakdown of our society. (3) This country would have many fewer problems if there were more emphasis on traditional family ties. (4) We should be more tolerant of people who choose to live according to their own moral standards, even if they are very different from our own. [responses to all questions range from strongly agree to strongly disagree]

Sophistication: Average of standardized scores from six component measures ($\alpha = 0.88$): (1) political knowledge [sum of correct responses to questions tapping knowledge of which party controlled the U.S. House and U.S. Senate, and positions held by Newt Gingrich, Al Gore, William Rehnquist, and Boris Yeltsin, all 1996_{post}]; (2) respondent's education; (3) interviewer's pre- and (4) post-election assessment of respondent's knowledge about politics; (5) interviewer's pre- and (6) post-election assessment of respondent's intelligence.

Religiosity ($1996_{pre,}$ $\alpha = 0.77$): (1) Do you consider religion to be an important part of your life, or not? (2) Which of these statements comes closest to describing your feelings about the Bible? One, the Bible is the actual Word of God and is to be taken literally, word for word. Two, the Bible is the Word of God but not everything in it should be taken literally, word for word. Three, the Bible is a book written by men and is not the Word of God. (3) Lots of things come up that keep people from attending religious services even if they want to. Thinking about your life these days, do you ever attend religious services, apart from occasional weddings, baptisms, or funerals? (If yes) Do you go to religious services every week, almost every week, once or twice a month, a few times a year, or never? (4) Outside of attending religious services, do you read the Bible several times a day, once a day, a few times a week, once a week or less, or never? (5) Outside of attending religious services, do you pray several times a day, once a day, a few times a week, once a week or less, or never?

NOTES

1. For recent contributions in political science and political psychology, see Alvarez and Brehm (2002); Cantril and Cantril (1999); Craig *et al.* (2002); Chong (1993); Feldman and Zaller (1992); Hochschild (1981); Holbrook *et al.* (2001); Huckfeldt *et al.* (2004); Huckfeldt and Sprague (1998a, b); Jacoby (2002); Lavine (2001); Lavine *et al.* (1998b, 2000); McGraw *et al.* (2003); Meffert *et al.* (2000); Nelson (1999); Steenbergen and Brewer (2000); Tourangeau *et al.* (1989a); Zaller and Feldman (1992); Zaller (1992). For prominent social psychological treatments, see Breckler (1994); Cacioppo and Berntson (1994); Cacioppo *et al.* (1997); Kaplan (1972); Priester and Petty (1996, 2001); Scott (1966); Thompson *et al.* (1995).
2. The only other analysis of these items of which we are aware is Burden and Box-Steffensmeier (1998).

3. Our five-item measure of efficacy is somewhat unorthodox in that it includes elements of both internal and external efficacy (see Craig *et al.* 1990). Its psychometric properties are adequate, however, and a principle components factor analysis yields a single-factor solution on which all five indicators load.

4. In preliminary statistical tests, we also explored the impact of egalitarian and humanitarian values; no systematic relationships were evident.

5. There is strong, though not complete, consensus among personality theorists that the fundamental dimensions of personality can be reduced to five factors. In addition to Openness to Experience, these include Extraversion, Agreeableness, Conscientiousness, and Neuroticism.

6. Keep in mind that these data were collected prior to the Monica Lewinsky scandal and the president's subsequent impeachment.

7. There are two principal alternatives used to measure uncertainty. One assesses uncertainty subjectively, in response to a question such as, "How certain are you of [the judgment just provided]?" (Alvarez 1997; Gross *et al.* 1995). The other makes use of deviations from scale midpoints, for example, the discrepancy between a respondent's perception of a candidate's issue position or other attribute and the candidate's "true" position, defined as the sample mean (Alvarez 1997).

8. This causal interpretation, which posits that ambivalence produces more information seeking, is consistent with psychological theory and some experimental evidence (e.g., Maio and Esses 1996). Of course, the alternative causal model, namely, that the seeking of political information produces ambivalence, cannot be ruled out with these data.

7. Patriotic to the Core? ⟿

American Ambivalence About America

Jack Citrin and Samantha Luks

In the last scene of Some Like It Hot, *Tony Curtis, still in drag, finally tells his ardent suitor, "But I'm a man." Joe E. Brown's reply is, "Nobody's perfect."*

Patriotism refers to the love of one's country. The image of the nation as an extended family, expressed by the pervasive use of terms like "mother country," "fatherland," and "band of brothers," makes such love seem natural. Yet the emotions evoked by family frequently are both intense and ambivalent. Some people love their families to a fault, while others do so despite or even because of those faults. Using the same logic, is patriotism blind or can it take the form of a love–hate relationship, with the emotional anguish and erratic behavior that often accompanies a conflicted state of mind?

This chapter explores the phenomenon of ambivalence toward a political love object: the American nation. In the modern world, according to Ernest Gellner (1983), a national identity is a quasi-physical attribute of the self, like one's nose or ears. Having a national identity means being situated, emotionally as well as legally, within a homeland (Billig 1995). In established nations, the meaning and significance of nationality is typically taken for granted. This occurs because, beginning in early socialization, daily life and political events are "flagged" or "framed" in national terms (Billig 1995; Reicher and Hopkins 2001). Transmitting a positive sense of national identity is manifest in the United States, where one pledges allegiance to the flag and sings the national anthem at most sporting events, and where national unity is based on a common civic religion rather than shared ancestry (Huntington 1981). A cross-national study conducted by the National Opinion Research Center in 1996 found, for example, a higher level of national pride in the United States than in virtually all other countries surveyed.[1] The unique slogan, "America, Love It or Leave It," serves as warning to those who might possess conflicting feelings about nationhood.

DANGLING QUESTIONS ABOUT THE CONCEPT OF AMBIVALENCE

Attitudes are people's evaluations of "objects," that is, their overall assessments of objects on a continuum from positive to negative, or favorable to unfavorable (Eagly and Chaiken 1993). An attitude develops on the basis of affective, cognitive, and behavioral responses to a particular attitude object (and the person's position on the continuum), and represents a weighted summary of the evaluative implications of these responses (Chaiken *et al.* 1995). In the case of political attitudes, evaluative implications generally reflect connections to one's interests, social identifications, and values (Boninger *et al.* 1995a).

This conception implies that three types of consistency are structural properties of attitudes: evaluative-cognitive, evaluative-affective, and affective-cognitive. The first two properties refer to the degree of consistency between the person's overall, abstract assessment of an object and the meanings of his or her beliefs about, or emotional reactions to, that object. Affective-cognitive consistency refers to the degree of similarity in the meaning of emotional responses to an object and beliefs about it (Chaiken *et al.* 1995). The relationship between feelings and belief, or passion and reason, has long interested both psychologists and political philosophers (Marcus 2003), and new developments in theory and measurement have served to renew interest in how emotions influence political judgment and behavior (Marcus 2003; Lavine 2001). One important issue is how to treat the relationship between negative and positive emotions (Osgood *et al.* 1957; Abelson *et al.* 1982; Green and Salovey 1999), something addressed here in the treatment of American attitudes toward the nation.

Given that both logic and "psycho-logic" dictate consistency, one interpretation of a discrepancy between an overall evaluation of an object and its emotional or cognitive foundations is that the attitude is not genuine (Converse 1964; Rosenberg 1968). In the case of non-attitudes, responses to the attitude object fluctuate almost randomly over time, vary with minor changes in question wording or order, and have no stable relationship to behaviors toward the object (Converse 1964). An alternative possibility, however, is that inconsistency is a sign of ambivalence rather than vacuity. The dictionary defines ambivalence as the possession of "simultaneous conflicting feelings toward a person or thing, like love or hate" (*New World Dictionary of the American Language, Second College Edition* 1974: 43). While this definition refers to conflicting emotions, in public opinion research the term is more commonly used to refer to a situation in which the evaluative implications of beliefs about an object are in conflict. The presumed root of this *cognitive* form of ambivalence is the collision of two or more deeply held values (Craig *et al.* 2005; Alvarez and Brehm 1995).

So, for example, ambivalence about affirmative action policies arises when a person's commitment to social equality conflicts with his or her support for the principle of rewarding individual merit. In this circumstance, forming a policy preference involves making a trade-off, and choices may vary according to which value or principle is made most salient through question wording in survey research and framing efforts in political campaigns or the media. Ambivalence about one attitude object, then, is a function of a lack of ambivalence about others that are associated with it. McGraw, Hasecke, and Conger (2003) cite David Mamet's witty definition of ambivalence as "watching your mother-in-law drive over a cliff in your new Cadillac." In this example, however, there is no ambivalence about either the mother-in-law or the car, just regret that getting rid of one costs you the other.

On the assumption that there is no such thing as a free lunch, one might conclude that on most issues ambivalence is pervasive. Yet there is substantial evidence that ordinary citizens do not always recognize that one can't have something for nothing (Sears and Citrin 1985). It may be the case, as Zaller and Feldman (1992: 585) maintain, that most people possess opposing beliefs on most issues. Indeed, it seems certain that when attitude objects are represented in diffuse or highly abstract terms, they are more likely to elicit multiple and inconsistent considerations. In the same vein, when an attitude object is encountered frequently and in varied contexts over the life span, the considerations stored in memory are likely to be both numerous and diverse in their evaluative meaning. However, one cannot assume that ordinary citizens are aware of their own ambivalence about an object or experience it as troubling (also see chapters 3 and 5 in this volume).

"Nation," "country," and "America" are highly generalized terms whose subjective meaning may vary from one individual to the next. A patriotic symbol like the flag may represent democracy and equality to some who salute it and military victories to others who do the same. "America" refers to a people, but also to a government acting on their behalf and this distinction is a common source of divided feelings and loyalties. Applying the concept of ambivalence to the domain of American nationalism therefore raises the following empirical questions:

- Do Americans simultaneously hold conflicting feelings about their country, reporting feelings of shame as well as pride, despair as well as hope, and so forth? In other words, how pervasive is ambivalence in this attitudinal domain?

- Are positive and negative components of attitudes toward the American nation separate? This claim is fundamental to the idea of ambivalence, and some scholars maintain that evidence supports the proposition, for example, in the case of attitudes toward racial groups and other political objects (Katz and Haas 1988). Yet others suggest that any observed orthogonality between positive and negative responses to the same object is largely attributable to the effect of nonrandom measurement error (Citrin and Green 1994). Accordingly, the presence of ambivalence needs to be addressed on a case-by-case basis rather than simply assumed.

- Is ambivalence distinguishable from being located in the middle of the range of an attitudinal continuum; in other words, is there a strong negative relationship between ambivalence and extremity of opinion? Introspection will confirm that knowing a great deal about political issues, and understanding that any choice involves making trade-offs between important values, does not prevent one from consistently adopting the same partisan or ideological position. Evidence that behavioral responses to an attitude object can vary with the salience, and accessibility, of a specific "consideration" associated with it is consistent with the idea that ambivalence is not the same as taking middle position. Determining the presence of these framing effects, however, requires prior knowledge of the foundations of ambivalence, that is, of what attributes of an attitude object give rise to conflicting evaluations.

This chapter relies on national survey data to develop a measure of *emotional* ambivalence about America. We will then use that measure to assess the number of *ambivalent patriots* among the general public, investigate the structure of popular feelings about the United States, and describe the social and political correlates of ambivalent patriotism and its relationship to several measures of national identity, attitudes toward other countries, and confidence in domestic political institutions.

NATIONAL IDENTITY AND PATRIOTISM

A nation is a group of people with a shared sense of identity who are seeking a homeland. From the standpoint of macropolitics, the concept of national identity refers to the quality that distinguishes one nation from all others. Yet history shows that no objective trait—not language, religion, race, or culture—is a necessary condition of nationhood. The characteristics that unite members of a nation and differentiate them, *in their own minds*, from others are both varied and malleable. Recognizing this, Rupert Emerson (1960: 102) wrote that a nation "is a body of people who feel they are a nation." From the standpoint of the individual, then, national identity refers to one of many group memberships that potentially define one's self-concept. As a doctrine, nationalism implies that membership in the nation should be critical in defining one's overall social identity. In other words, when the chips are down, a person's national identity should affect political opinions and behavior independent of alternative foci of affiliation such as kinship, religion, language, or class.

Self-categorization is the first step in the formation of a national identity. Through the processes of social learning and social comparison, people come to describe themselves as American, British, French, and so forth. Identifying "as" is not the same as identifying "with," however. Put another way, formal citizenship does not automatically mean a positive emotional bond with the nation. The value and emotional significance of nationality may vary across individuals, with a strong national identity implying a psychological merger of self and nation. To capture Americans' sense of national identity, therefore, we develop a measure based on questions about the subjective importance of being an American and feelings of closeness to America. A strong sense of national identity implies a positive overall evaluation of the nation and should promote supportive behavior toward the nation, its official representatives, and fellow-nationals. If patriotism means a love of country and a willingness to sacrifice for it, then it is an expression or consequence of a strong sense of national identity.

Yet patriotism itself is an analytically and normatively ambiguous concept (Sullivan *et al.* 1992; Kateb 2000). Analytically, the problem is that people have different conceptions about what qualities define their nation and, therefore, what it means to defend it. The moral dilemma is whether the patriot's identification with fellow-nationals implies a sense of superiority toward outsiders that leads to prejudice or overt hostility. In an empirical analysis of how ordinary people think, Sullivan, Fried, and Dietz (1992) distinguished between patriotism as an emotional response to the flag, anthem, and other symbols of nationhood, and patriotism as a defense of political principles and policies. The second, more ideological version of patriotism, they argue, accepts—and even demands—the coexistence of a strong emotional attachment to the country combined with criticism of some of its behaviors. Schatz and Staub (1997) made a similar distinction between "constructive" patriotism, in which love of country is based on humanitarian national values, and "blind" patriotism, manifested by an uncritical perspective as expressed in the slogan, "my country, right or wrong."[2] Kosterman and Feshbach (1989) accepted the contrast between a balanced and idealized attitude toward the nation, although they labeled the former "patriotism" and the latter "nationalism." In all of these formulations, though, ambivalence is compatible with one type of manifestation of a strong national identity: ideological patriotism (Sullivan *et al.*), constructive patriotism (Schatz and Staub) or "patriotism" (Kosterman and Feshbach). We ourselves have developed measures of *patriotism* to capture feelings of pride in one's own country, and *chauvinism* to assess the belief that America is superior to all other nations.

RESULTS

The evidence for this chapter comes from the 1996 General Social Survey (GSS) conducted by the National Opinion Research Center. The GSS reports results from face-to-face interviews administered to nationally representative samples of adults. The data presented here are derived principally from two modules in the 1996 survey; one of these included questions about national identity and patriotism, while the other dealt with emotions.

Americans in the mid-1990s overwhelmingly indicated that membership in the national community had great significance for their overall sense of identity. At a time of low confidence in *government* (Nye *et al.* 1997), over 90 percent of the GSS sample said that they would rather be a citizen of the United States than of any other country in the world, and 81 percent described themselves as feeling either "very close" or "close" to America. When asked to assess the importance of being an American on a scale from one to ten (the latter being "the most important thing in my life"), 45 percent gave their national identity the highest possible rating while just 6 percent awarded it a score less than five. We combined the answers to these three questions, each weighted equally, into an overall *American National Identity* (ANI) index. Because of the different number of response options, scores were first standardized and then summed to create a continuum of 1 to 4. The median ANI score is 3.57, with an interquartile range from 3.18 to 3.80.

The 1996 GSS also contained several questions that tapped people's emotional responses to America. The root question was, "When you think of the United States, how often do you feel" satisfied, enthusiastic, and hopeful on the positive side, or worried, frustrated, angry, and upset on the negative side. Respondents could say they felt this way always, most of the time, some of the time, rarely, or never. Following Thompson *et al.* (1995), we created an *Emotional Ambivalence* (EA) index that takes into account both the intensity of responses and the numerical balance of positive and negative feelings. The formula is

$$Ambivalence = [(P + N)/2] - |P - N|$$

where P is the sum of positive responses, each weighted by intensity (in our case, the frequency of feeling a particular way), and N is the sum of negative reactions.[3] Because of the uneven numbers of positive and negative items, utilizing all the information required a method of calculating ambivalence that was somewhat different from the approach used by Thompson and her colleagues. We first created separate indices for the positive and negative set of items and then rescaled each to have a range of 1 to 4; the resultant ambivalence index can be numerically interpreted as one constructed by treating each item individually. For example, a minimum score of -0.5 indicates that the respondent answered "all of the time" for all of the questions in *either* the positive or negative component of the index and "none of the time" for all questions in the other component. At the opposite end of the scale, an ambivalence score of $+4$ indicates that the respondent answered "all of the time" to all seven items.

How Much Ambivalence?

Given the pervasiveness of strong feelings of national identity among Americans, it is not surprising that when asked about the United States, positive emotional responses predominate. The distribution of responses to each of our seven emotion items is shown in table 7.1, where we can see that "always" or "most of the time" responses are consistently more widespread for positive emotions (Satisfied, Enthusiastic, Hopeful) than for negative ones (Frustrated, Angry, Upset, Worried). For example, 38 percent say they feel enthusiastic about the United States always or most of the time, compared to just 19 percent who report being frustrated that often and 7 percent who generally feel angry.

Still, the evidence that most Americans feel negatively about their country at least some of the time suggests that ambivalence, in the sense of

Table 7.1   Distribution of responses to GSS emotional patriotism items

	Positive items			Negative items			
	Satisfied	Enthusiastic	Hopeful	Worried	Frustrated	Angry	Upset
Always	8	11	21	5	4	1	2
Most of the time	39	27	34	14	15	6	7
Some of the time	41	42	35	51	53	43	49
Rarely	9	16	7	22	20	35	31
Never	2	4	2	9	7	14	11
Number of cases =	697	692	692	700	696	695	699

Question: "When you think of the United States, how often do you feel . . . ?"
Note: Data are from the 1996 General Social Survey. Table entries indicate the percentage of respondents who give the indicated response for each of the seven emotion items.

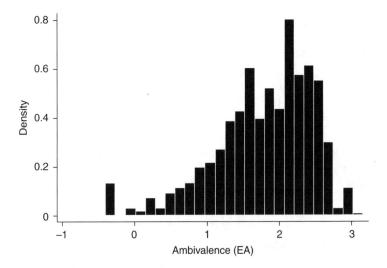

Figure 7.1   Distribution of ambivalence toward the United States
Source: 1996 General Social Survey.

the same person experiencing both favorable and unfavorable reactions to the United States, does exist. Indeed, figure 7.1 shows a good deal of variation in the EA index described earlier. The modal EA score is slightly greater than 2, while the mean is 1.78 (roughly equivalent to having a score of 2 on one emotional component index and a score of 2.25 on the oppositely valenced one); in addition, nearly half (49 percent) of our sample displays what we would describe as a moderate level of ambivalence toward America (scores between 1.25 and 2.15). Extreme ambivalence, or the equivalent of an intense love–hate relationship, is rare, however; the maximum ambivalence score observed is 3.16 out of a theoretical maximum of 4, and only 8 percent have a score greater than 2.5. Finally, as the preceding discussion suggests, the overall attitude of a large majority of those who exhibit little or no ambivalence toward the United States is favorable rather than unfavorable.

Are Feelings About the United States Bipolar?

The idea of ambivalence presumes that positive and negative responses to an attitude object are ontologically distinct. The normal expectation is that evaluations tend to be consistent; for example, perceptions of a group as honest would seem unlikely to be associated with evaluations of the same group as lazy or unintelligent. We therefore need to consider empirically the degree of independence among positive and negative clusters of feelings toward the United States. One reason to expect the coexistence of these opposing reactions is that respondents are not asked about responses to a particular event at a given moment in time. Instead, what is being assessed is a *memory* of past reactions to a global object. It may well be that the foundations of positive and negative emotions are different, with hope and enthusiasm associated with exposure to ceremonious displays of national symbols, while anger and worry are more likely to be based on criticisms of specific actions by national leaders.

As previously noted, before creating the EA index we constructed separate scales of positive and negative emotions. The correlation (Pearson's r) between these two scales is -0.35, which is statistically significant ($p < 0.001$) but not sufficiently high to indicate that the two scales measure the same thing. Nevertheless, because the seven emotion items were asked sequentially and because their format and response options were identical, it is possible that the correlation between positive and negative dimensions is attenuated by the operation of nonrandom measurement error. In other words, to the extent that some respondents reflexively gave the same "always" or "most of the time" answer to each question, the extent of ambivalence could have been artificially inflated (Green and Citrin 1994).

An exploratory factor analysis of the seven emotion items does, in fact, generate a solution with separate positive and negative factors (data not shown). However, we can test for the role of nonrandom error through a confirmatory factor analysis using LISREL. Here we proceeded by comparing the fit of (1) a one-factor confirmatory factor analysis model to

(2) an alternative model having both a "positive" and a "negative" factor, and to (3) a one-factor model with a nonrandom measurement error factor added. In the first model, let the observed variables be a function of the following equation:

$$\chi_{ki} = \lambda_{k1}\xi_{1i} + \delta_{ki}, \quad \text{where}$$
$$\text{cov}(\xi_1, \delta_k) = 0 \quad \text{and} \quad \text{cov}(\delta_j, \delta_k) = 0, \quad j \neq k.$$

By comparison, the second model tests the fit of a confirmatory factor analysis where the positively worded items load on one factor, and the negatively worded items on another which is correlated with the first:

(2a) for Satisfied, Enthusiastic, and Hopeful
$\chi_{ki} = \lambda_{k1}\xi_{1i} + \delta_{ki}$, and

(2b) for, Worried, Frustrated, Angry, and Upset
$\chi_{ji} = \lambda_{j2}\xi_{2i} + \delta_{ji}$, where
$\text{cov}(\xi_1, \delta_k) = 0, \qquad \text{cov}(\xi_2, \delta_k) = 0,$
$\text{cov}(\xi_1, \xi_2) \neq 0,$
and $\text{cov}(\delta_j, \delta_k) = 0, \quad j \neq k.$

Finally, our third model explores the possibility that the attenuation in the correlation between positive and negative items is due to nonrandom measurement error. In this model, each item loads both on one "substantive" factor and one nonrandom error factor, as follows:

$$\chi_{ki} = \lambda_{k1}\xi_{1i} + \lambda_3\xi_{3i} + \delta_{ki}, \quad \text{where}$$
$$\text{cov}(\xi_1, \delta_k) = 0, \qquad \text{cov}(\xi_3, \delta_k) = 0,$$
$$\text{cov}(\xi_1, \xi_3) = 0, \quad \text{and} \quad \text{cov}(\delta_j, \delta_k) = 0, \quad j \neq k.$$

Notice that in this last model, the loading for the nonrandom error factor is assigned the same value for all of the observed variables, implying that we expect the method-associated measurement error to be equivalent across all items.

The first column in table 7.2 shows the results of a single factor model, with the loading for Satisfied being fixed at 1 to allow for identification. Results indicate that all seven items have significant loadings on the factor, though their magnitudes are unequal: The two remaining items that tap positive emotions about the United States (Enthusiastic and Hopeful) have relatively small loadings, with values of 0.68 and 0.66, respectively while, conversely, the four items measuring negative emotions have factor loadings about twice as large, ranging from −1.14 for Worried to −1.53 for

Table 7.2 Confirmatory factor analysis of emotional patriotism items

	Random error model	*Random error 2-factor model*		*Nonrandom error model*
		Positive	*Negative*	
Factor loadings				
Satisfied	1.00	1.00	n/a	1.00
Enthusiastic	0.68 (0.10)	1.34 (0.12)	n/a	0.84 (0.07)
Hopeful	0.66 (0.10)	1.19 (0.11)	n/a	0.78 (0.07)
Worried	−1.14 (0.11)	n/a	1.00	−0.79 (0.08)
Frustrated	−1.53 (0.12)	n/a	1.34 (0.10)	−1.08 (0.08)
Angry	−1.44 (0.11)	n/a	1.28 (0.10)	−1.01 (0.08)
Upset	−1.38 (0.11)	n/a	1.23 (0.09)	−0.96 (0.07)
Factor variances	0.20 (0.03)	0.27 (0.04)	0.26 (0.01)	0.33 (0.04)
Nonrandom error factor variance	n/a	n/a	n/a	0.09 (0.01)
Factor covariances	n/a	−0.12 (0.02)		n/a
Factor correlations	n/a	−0.43		n/a
Measurement error variances				
Satisfied	0.51(0.03)	0.43(0.03)		0.33 (0.03)
Enthusiastic	0.88 (0.05)	0.48 (0.05)		0.60 (0.04)
Hopeful	0.83 (0.05)	0.53 (0.04)		0.61 (0.04)
Worried	0.60 (0.04)	0.60 (0.04)		0.59 (0.04)
Frustrated	0.32 (0.03)	0.31 (0.03)		0.31 (0.02)
Angry	0.31 (0.02)	0.30 (0.02)		0.31 (0.02)
Upset	0.33 (0.02)	0.32 (0.02)		0.32 (0.02)
Chi-square	304.5	105.2		105.9
Degrees of freedom	14	13		13
Probability	0.000	0.000		0.000
Chi-square/df	21.68	8.093		8.15
GFI	0.88	0.96		0.96
AGFI	0.76	0.91		0.91
Root mean squared error	0.095	0.054		0.048
Number of cases = 681				

Note: Data are from the 1996 General Social Survey. Table entries are maximum likelihood estimates, with standard errors in parentheses.

Frustrated. At face value, it would appear that the underlying factor does not fit all of the indicators equally well. Also interesting is that the divide between the goodness of fit of the items isn't necessarily according to whether the items were positively or negatively worded. The factor loading for Worried is only slightly larger than the fixed coefficient for Satisfied; further, the error variances for Enthusiastic, Hopeful, and Worried are considerably larger than those for the other items. Finally, the overall fit of this model is rather poor. The adjusted goodness-of-fit index is only 0.76 and the root mean squared error is 0.095, both well outside of the realm for an acceptable model.

In the second model (see column 2), which estimates loadings for separate positive and negative factors, the fit is substantially improved. The adjusted goodness-of-fit index increases to 0.91 and the root mean squared error decreases to 0.054. While these measures of fit are not excellent, they are acceptable. Further, the measurement error variances of the positive items are reduced considerably, though the magnitudes of the factor loadings do have a fairly wide range (from 1.00 to 1.34). The covariance between the two factors is modest (−0.12) and reflects a correlation of −0.43. In general, these results indicate that a two-factor model fits the data considerably better than a one-factor model does, thereby suggesting that positive and negative emotions about the United States may be substantially independent of one another.

The third model tested in table 7.2 explores a different possibility, namely, that the poor fit of the first model is due to nonrandom measurement error in the battery of survey items. Column 3 shows the results of adding to that model a nonrandom error factor that is uncorrelated with the original factor. In fact, making this adjustment causes the magnitude of loadings on the substantive factor to even out considerably (though not completely). Comparing Models 1 and 3, we see the loadings for Enthusiastic and Hopeful increase to 0.84 and 0.78, respectively, while loadings for Worried and Frustrated shrink to −0.79 and −1.08, respectively. The degree of fit also is considerably superior to the first model: The adjusted goodness-of-fit index increases to 0.91, placing it over the threshold for acceptance, and the root mean squared error is roughly halved to 0.048.

The question remains as to whether Model 2 or Model 3 is a better representation of the underlying structure of emotions about the United States. Because the models are not nested, there is no simple way to compare them with each other and, as a result, neither model comes out a clear winner. The goodness-of fit indices are nearly identical and both models have the same number of degrees of freedom, implying that we cannot accept one model simply because it is more parsimonious than the other.[4] Even though Models 2 and 3 fit the data equally well, they tell rather different stories about the structure of emotional evaluations about the United States: Model 2 points to separate attitudinal bases for positive and negative evaluations, while Model 3 points to only a single attitude. Because Model 3 is conceptually more parsimonious, there is no compelling reason to prefer Model 2 over it.

Bipolarity in emotional responses to an attitude object is one indicator of the presence of ambivalence. The confirmatory factor analysis reported here gives some support to the idea that Americans harbor ambivalent feelings about their country, but this conclusion must be tempered by the evidence that measurement processes are implicated in generating distinctive positive and negative emotional dimensions. We therefore posit the presence of ambivalence as a hypothesis that additional research needs to confirm.

Which Groups Express Ambivalent Feelings?

We have reported evidence of substantial variation in feelings of ambivalence toward the United States. What factors explain these individual differences? In the context of generally positive attitudes toward the national community, one hypothesis is that disadvantaged groups would be more likely to report negative feelings like frustration or anger. Yet figure 7.2 shows that there are no significant differences between whites and blacks, or between men and women. And when we compare income groups, the wealthy are slightly more likely than Americans with low incomes to score high on our measure of emotional ambivalence toward the United States ($r = 0.09$, $p < 0.05$). By contrast, age is negatively related to ambivalence ($r = -0.11$, $p < 0.01$), a reflection of the positive relationship between age and patriotism found in previous research (Citrin *et al.* 2001).

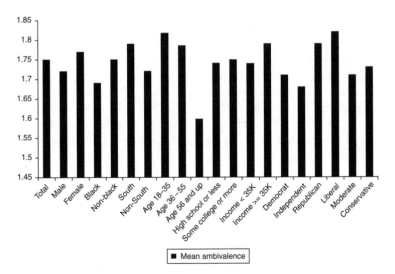

Figure 7.2   Emotional ambivalence (EA) by social and demographic characteristics
Source: 1996 General Social Survey, see fig 7.1.

A second plausible supposition is that political interest and engagement should boost ambivalence because paying more attention to political events, over time, inevitably exposes one to a mixture of good and bad news about the nation and its conduct. In other words, the more you know and think about an object, the more likely you are to possess numerous and varied considerations about it. Unfortunately, the GSS does not include direct measures of political knowledge, interest, or engagement. Using level of formal education as a crude proxy, however, we again find no relationship to ambivalence about the United States ($r = 0.00$). Similarly, self-identified Independents and ideological moderates, who generally have relatively low levels of political involvement, are *not* more ambivalent than party identifiers or respondents with either a liberal or conservative ideological identification. Figure 7.2 also shows that the direction of one's partisan or ideological identification is unrelated to ambivalence. The microfoundations of ambivalent *feelings* about the United States apparently lie more in the domain of individual psychology rather than social background.

Ambivalence About America and Strength of National Identity

A strong sense of national identity, typically established early in life and enduring thereafter (Jahoda 1963; Dawson and Prewitt 1969; Dennis *et al.* 1971; Sears and Levy 2003), indicates that membership in the nation has value and emotional significance, that is, that nationality is fundamental to one's self-concept. Earlier we reported that a positive sense of national identity is pervasive among the American public. Here we ask whether a favorable overall evaluation can coexist with emotional ambivalence. Looking first at the three items that comprise our ANI index ("How important is being an American to you," "How close do you feel to America," and "I would rather be a citizen of America than of any other country in the world"), we find that emotional ambivalence about the United States has a significant relationship to only one: As ambivalence increases, expressed feelings of closeness to America diminish ($r = -0.147$, $p < 0.001$). This result seems plausible, since "closeness to America" is itself more similar to the positive emotional items than are the questions asking about the significance of belonging to America.[5]

Ambivalence and scores on the combined index are also weakly related, with a Pearson's r that is small (-0.087) but statistically significant ($p < 0.05$). There is, if anything, the hint of a small curvilinear relationship between ambivalence and ANI. When the latter is collapsed into three categories, ambivalence (EA) mean scores for Low, Middle, and High ANI respondents are 1.80, 1.89, and 1.69, respectively. Still, even those with a very strong sense of national identity often report negative as well as positive feelings about their country.

Ambivalence and Patriotism

At the beginning of this chapter, we distinguished between the emotional (or affective) and cognitive foundations of attitudes. Clearly, it would be instructive to develop a measure of cognitive ambivalence toward America based on the evaluative implications of beliefs about the country's values and achievements, and then to examine the connections between this property of patriotism and the measure of emotional ambivalence we developed. Pride in the achievements of one's country is a common definition of patriotism. Thus, to the extent that such pride implies approval or satisfaction, pride in specific features of national life might be considered as the cognitive foundations of one's overall evaluation of the United States. Feelings of shame, by contrast, imply "contra-identification" (Tajfel 1981) or dislike of one's country.

The 1996 GSS asked respondents whether they felt very, somewhat, not very, or not at all proud about ten aspects of America:

The way its democracy works (Democracy).
Its political influence in the world (Influence).
America's economic achievements (Economics).
Its social security system (Socsec).
Its scientific and technological achievements (Scitech).
Its achievements in sports (Sports).
Its achievements in the arts and literature (Artlit).
Its armed forces (Military).
Its history (History).
Its fair and equal treatment of all groups in society (Groups).

Because these items refer to a specific object, they have an initial appeal for exploring the extent of cognitive ambivalence about America. However, the absence of a positive evaluation does not imply the presence of a negative one. To say that one is not very or not at all proud about American achievements in sports, for example, may indicate indifference rather than shame or disapproval. And the 1996 GSS did not ask directly about unfavorable evaluations of these specific aspects of national life; rather, it included only a general question about whether the respondent agreed or disagreed that "there are some things about America today that make me ashamed of America" (Ashamed).

Nevertheless, the array of pride items provides an opportunity to probe the evaluative beliefs associated with emotional ambivalence toward America. A broad range of considerations is represented: liberal values (Groups, Socsec), conservative symbols (Military, Influence), consensual symbols (Democracy, History, Economics), and nonpolitical achievements (Scitech, Sports, Artlit). Although pride is the dominant outlook, with a sample mean of 8.1 (out of 10) either very or somewhat proud responses, there is variation across items. For example, fully 95 percent said they were very or somewhat proud of America's scientific and technological achievements, compared to just 50 percent who felt this way about the country's social security system. In addition, 65 percent either agreed or strongly agreed that there were some things in America that made them feel ashamed—another indication that a strong sense of patriotism does not mean a wholly uncritical view of one's country.

Ambivalent feelings about the United States are, predictably, associated with less pride in the country's accomplishments. Bivariate correlations between emotional ambivalence (EA) and the various pride items are negative, albeit modest in size (ranging from -0.18 for social security to -0.06 for pride in the military). Going further, table 7.3 reports regression coefficients from an analysis estimating the effects of ambivalence and national identity on each of the pride items, and on the question asking about feelings of shame in "some things about America today."[6] The equations here also included controls for party identification, ideology, age, education, income, region, and race, although for clarity of presentation we do not report the coefficients for these variables.

In this model, EA has statistically significant, negative relationships with Groups, Social Security, Influence, Democracy, History, and Economics, as well as Ashamed.[7] Looking just at the pride items, the strongest effects are evident for the liberal considerations of fair treatment of groups ($b = -0.165$) and the social security system ($b = -0.155$). Equality is, of course, a fundamental American value and we speculate that it is the perceived failure to realize the egalitarian ideal that promotes much of the ambivalence that exists about America. More generally, these results suggest that the roots of ambivalent feelings are largely political in nature. Hence, we constructed a Political Patriotism (PP) index with a balance of consensual, liberal, and conservative considerations; the index (Cronbach's alpha $= 0.74$) summed answers to the Groups, Social Security, Influence, Military, Democracy, and History pride items. This measure correlates at $r = -0.21$ with emotional ambivalence. Additionally, the mean EA score of 1.92 for intermediate scorers on PP is not significantly higher than the 1.72 mean for those classified as low on patriotism, although it is significantly different from

Table 7.3 Impact of emotional ambivalence on pride in America

	Emotional ambivalence (EA)	*American national identity (ANI)*	*Adjusted R-squared*
Democracy	−0.118**	0.430**	0.22
	(0.042)	(0.060)	
Political influence	−0.114*	0.401**	0.12
	(0.045)	(0.062)	
Economic achievements	−0.091†	0.382**	0.13
	(0.047)	(0.064)	
Social security	−0.155**	0.143†	0.14
	(0.055)	(0.078)	
Science and technology	−0.040	0.286**	0.13
	(0.038)	(0.053)	
Sports	−0.083†	0.371**	0.11
	(0.047)	(0.066)	
Arts and literature	−0.039	0.272**	0.06
	(0.045)	(0.063)	
Military	−0.056	0.487**	0.23
	(0.042)	(0.059)	
History	−0.126**	0.442**	0.19
	(0.047)	(0.066)	
Equal treatment of groups	−0.165**	0.547**	0.18
	(0.056)	(0.076)	
Ashamed	0.358**	−0.431**	0.09
	(0.069)	(0.095)	

Notes: ** $p \leq 0.01$; * $p \leq 0.05$; † $p \leq 0.10$. Data are from the 1996 General Social Survey. Table entries are OLS regression coefficients, with standard errors in parentheses. Estimates include controls for party identification, ideology, gender, race, age, education, income, and region (South). Number of cases varies between 469 and 492.

the 1.60 mean for the larger group of individuals who rank high on Political Patriotism.

Ambivalence and Chauvinism

In a series of ingenious experiments, Tajfel and Turner (1986) showed that mere categorization as a group member leads to in-group favoritism. This effect is more pronounced when social identities are potent, that is, when the group one belongs to has enduring value and emotional significance. An important question for social identity theorists remains the conditions under which ethnocentrism (or pride in one's own group) fuels hostility toward outsiders. In the case of national identity, the debate centers on the relationship between patriotism and chauvinism. That is, does a fundamental allegiance to one's own country and identification with fellow-nationals breed prejudice and aggressiveness toward other nations (Spinner-Halev and Theiss-Morse 2003)? The empirical evidence from American and European publics is mixed (Citrin *et al.* 2001; Blank and Schmidt 2003; De Figueiredo and Elkins 2003), with results varying according to the definition and measurement of the main constructs. Whatever the strength of the underlying relationship, however, we expect that ambivalence about one's own nation will moderate the tendency to regard other countries as less worthy.

The 1996 GSS asked respondents whether they agreed with four questions that we combined into an index of Chauvinism (alpha = 0.65): (1) "The world would be a better place if people from other countries were more like Americans." (2) "Generally speaking, America is a better country than most other countries." (3) "People should support their country even if the country is in the wrong." (4) "America should follow its own interests, even if this leads to conflicts with other nations." The combined index correlates 0.46 with American National Identity and 0.42 with the Political Patriotism index built from responses to the Democracy, Influence, History, Groups, Military, and Social Security pride questions. Surprisingly, though, chauvinism was unrelated to ambivalent feelings about the United States ($r = -0.07$, n.s.), and there was no significant difference in ambivalence between those with the lowest chauvinism score (mean EA = 1.78) and those in the middle of this attitudinal continuum (mean EA = 1.81); mean ambivalence for those ranking highest on chauvinism was 1.65. Thus, as we found to be the case with feelings of national identity and patriotism, emotional ambivalence is slightly higher among middle scorers; this curvilinear pattern is not nearly strong enough, however, to warrant treating ambivalence as being equivalent to the middle position on a directional attitude scale.

Finally, the 1996 GSS included several questions about specific policies that arguably engage nationalistic attitudes. Respondents were asked whether the current level of immigration should be decreased, remain the same, or be increased, and whether they agreed that foreign imports should be limited, foreigners should be prohibited from buying land in America, and television should give preference to American programs. Contrary to expectations, emotional ambivalence was not associated with opposition to these restrictionist and protectionist measures. It seems that conflicting emotional responses to the United States need not reduce either feelings of superiority regarding other countries or chauvinistic positions on specific policy questions.

Institutional Performance and Ambivalent Patriotism

David Easton (1953) identified three levels of a political system: the community, regime, and incumbent authorities. National identity and patriotism are attitudes referring to the political community (i.e., the people who belong to a particular system) and thus far we have been investigating ambivalence toward the country as a whole. A natural question is whether citizens' conflicting feelings arise from their mixed evaluations of the conduct of other levels of the political system. We explore this possibility by considering how support for the country's leading governmental institutions—the federal executive, Congress, and Supreme Court—are related to attitudes toward objects at the community level. The 1996 GSS included questions asking respondents how much confidence they had in "the people running" the aforementioned institutions. While there is some debate as to how much people interpret these questions as referring to current leadership versus enduring characteristics of the institutions themselves (Nye *et al.* 1997), here we are concerned only with an overall evaluation of political objects outside the community level. For this reason, we simply interpret our summary index (alpha = 0.67) as a measure of confidence in government (CG).

The correlations between this measure of institutional support and measures of American national identity (ANI), ambivalence (EA), and patriotism (PA) are 0.11 (p < 0.05), −0.16 (p < 0.001) and 0.23 (p < 0.001), respectively. As results of the multivariate regression analyses reported in table 7.4 show, the negative relationship between CG and EA remains statistically significant (b = −0.065) even after we control for ANI, social background, party identification, and political ideology. Perceptions about how well the regime's main political institutions are performing appear to be reflected, to some extent, in the degree to which one expresses conflicting emotional reactions to the country as a whole.

Table 7.4   Impact of confidence in government on emotional ambivalence

	Emotional ambivalence (EA)
Confidence in government (CG)	−0.065*
	(0.027)
American national identity (ANI)	−0.065
	(0.073)
Constant	2.589**
	(0.322)
Adjusted R-squared	0.02
Number of cases =	319

Notes: ** $p \leq 0.01$; * $p \leq 0.05$. Data are from the 1996 General Social Survey. Table entries are OLS regression coefficients, with standard errors in parentheses. Estimates include controls for party identification, ideology, gender, race, age, education, income, and region (South).

DISCUSSION

As a structural property of attitudes, ambivalence refers to the presence of conflicting feelings or beliefs about an object. Due to data limitations, this chapter could only examine Americans' emotional reactions toward their country. We found that even within a context of pervasive patriotism, self-reports of mixed emotional responses to the United States were widespread. Surprisingly, emotional ambivalence was only weakly related to feelings of national identity; it sometimes was present even among those who said that being an American was one of the "most important things" in their life. It also appears that ambivalent feelings are an across-the-board phenomenon, present among all ethnicities, educational levels, and partisan groups.

In public opinion research (Feldman and Zaller 1992; Zaller 1992), the concept of attitudinal ambivalence originally was invoked to explain (or perhaps explain away) seeming inconsistencies in individuals' responses to the same object. Specifically, it is argued that the foundations of any over-all evaluation are distinguishable clusters of valenced associations that sometimes tug people in opposite directions. Put another way, attitudes toward certain objects (such as abortion, blacks, the presidency, or America) are the outcome of attitudes toward their constituent parts, that is, the beliefs and feelings about objects associated with them. Hence, inconsistent responses toward these objects could be interpreted as a function of which sub-attitudes were salient at the time of the interview and how they were weighed in specific situations requiring trade-offs among competing values or considerations.

In our view, the idea of attitudinal ambivalence implies that positive and negative responses to an attitude object are empirically distinct; in the language of factor analysis, they comprise separate dimensions. In the present example of feelings toward the United States, however, data analysis that takes account of nonrandom measurement error fails to confirm unequivocally this neat partitioning of emotional reactions. Positive and negative reactions, although often harbored by the same individual, remain associated in predictable ways to an overall evaluative orientation toward the attitude object. The general lesson we draw is that the assumption of bipolarity in emotion (or affect) must be tested case by case, using statistical techniques that recognize the corrosive effects of method variance. Put somewhat differently, we need multiple indicators of attitude ambivalence.

Our analysis revealed relatively restricted substantive effects of the observed emotional ambivalence toward the United States. As expected, ambivalence was negatively related to patriotism, the latter measured in terms of pride in the nation's institutions and achievements. Yet the strength of this relationship was quite modest, and ambivalence toward the United States did not mitigate either in-group favoritism or chauvinistic attitudes toward foreigners. One possible explanation for this finding of emotional-evaluative inconsistency is, again, methodological. The objects of the survey questions used in these several measures of attitudes toward the national community are not identical. For example, a strong sense of national identity captures an enduring aspect of one's self-concept, whereas self-reported feelings about "the United States" may reflect past and present reactions to specific actors and actions.

In fact, one inference to draw from the pattern of results presented here is that emotional ambivalence about the United States may be rooted in a perceived gap between values and performance. This conclusion dovetails with prior research linking attitudinal ambivalence to the collision of political principles in a choice situation (Alvarez and Brehm 1995; Sniderman *et al.* 1991). The implication is that the utility of the concept of ambivalence depends upon knowledge about the cognitive foundations of attitudes, that is, the nature of valenced beliefs linked to an object. In the case of patriotism, that would mean investigating more fully the normative content of national identity (or what it means to be an American) and the reasons for loving one's country. With such information in hand, the relationship between emotional and cognitive ambivalence, their developmental trajectories, and their influences on specific judgments can be assessed.

NOTES

1. These other nations included Australia, Bulgaria, Canada, Cyprus, Czech Republic, France, Germany, Great Britain, Hungary, Ireland, Israel, Italy, Japan, Latvia, New Zealand, Norway, Phillipines, Poland, Russia, Slovenia, Spain, Sweden, and Switzerland.
2. The liberal bias here is palpable, since it is hard to envisage a manifestation of "constructive" patriotism in an "ethnic" nation or one with an authoritarian political system.
3. For further discussion of this measure, employed in a slightly different context, see chapter 4 in this volume as well as Craig *et al.* (2002).
4. We attempted to estimate a model containing both positive and negative factors and the nonrandom error factor, but it produced a nonrandom error factor with negative variance.
5. These results do not change when we conduct a multivariate analysis including controls for social background, party identification, and political ideology.
6. We make no assumption about the causal direction of these relationships.
7. As is evident from the table, ANI (American National Identity) has a strong *positive* relationship to all the pride items.

8. Is It Really Ambivalence? ∽

Public Opinion Toward Government Spending

William G. Jacoby

A mbivalence within citizens' political orientations is currently an important topic for scholars interested in American public opinion. The very existence of the volume within which this chapter appears is telling evidence of that fact. The usual conception of ambivalence stresses that individuals feel pulled in conflicting directions by the beliefs that enter into the development of their own attitudes. Empirically, ambivalence is manifested by the expression of contradictory opinions. However, I believe that a note of caution would be useful. We should not be too eager and always assume that contradictory opinions signal the presence of attitudinal ambivalence. There are, of course, many other potential sources for conflicting feelings about government, politics, and policy.

In this chapter, I will show why such caution is necessary by examining a set of contradictory opinions that have been widely noticed in the research literature: general feelings about governmental size and specific attitudes toward policy-based spending. Although there does, at first glance, appear to be some conflict in citizens' orientations on these matters, the contradictions become far less troublesome as soon as one recognizes the subjective nature of public reactions toward various forms of government spending. In fact, one of the most striking results in the empirical analysis to be presented below is the *consistency* with which beliefs about the scope of government help to shape spending attitudes, regardless of policy area. Such a high level of correspondence between individual reactions toward these different attitude objects simply could not occur if there were widespread ambivalence about them within public opinion.

BACKGROUND

While government spending is clearly an important policy issue (Jacoby 2000), public opinion on this topic is a bit "messy," to say the least. Americans show highly variegated preferences toward spending in different policy areas. However, differences of opinion do not always conform to traditional lines of ideology (Free and Cantril 1967), partisanship (Sears and Citrin 1985), or feelings about the size of government (Bennett and Bennett 1990). That is, conservatives, Republicans, and others who express reservations about expansive governmental power are not necessarily more likely than their liberal, Democratic, and pro-government counterparts to oppose spending in all areas. Such findings often lead to rather pessimistic conclusions regarding the quality of mass attitudes and citizen capacities for logical, realistic thinking about the political system. But, there is another perspective that provides a more benevolent interpretation based upon the existence of relatively widespread ambivalence among the general public.

In a recent study of this topic, Cantril and Cantril (1999) characterized ambivalence as a situation in which individuals possess contradictory orientations toward the size of government and the government's specific policy responsibilities. They asked:

> How many Americans are ambivalent when they think about government? On the one hand, how many worry about government's scope and power as a general matter *even* as they think many of its specific activities should be continued or expanded? On the other hand, how many are comfortable with government's scope and power as a general matter *even* as they think some of what it does should be scaled back? (Cantril and Cantril 1999: 5)

These questions were addressed using data from a 1996 *New York Times/* CBS News opinion survey, in which (1) general feelings were operationalized by combining individual responses across three questions (whether government does too many things that people could do better for themselves, whether the federal government has about the right amount of power, and whether government regulation of business is needed to make sure corporations act responsibly); and (2) feelings about specific activities were measured by reactions toward federal spending across ten different policy areas (e.g., enforcing clean air standards, job training for low-income people, programs to help finance college education, keeping dangerous consumer products off the market, etc.; see pp. 11–14).

Cantril and Cantril demonstrated that roughly one-third of the American public display contradictory stands on these two facets of public opinion: *Ambivalent critics* (estimated at 20 percent of the population) are people who have generally negative views of government but still believe that it should maintain spending in at least nine of the ten areas; *ambivalent supporters* (12 percent), in contrast, are those who take a positive stand toward the government while supporting continued or increased spending in eight or fewer policy domains. The authors assumed that attitudinal patterns such as these reflect ambivalence. Focusing especially on the ambivalent critics (who, in their view, constitute "the truly competitive arena" of American politics; Cantril and Cantril 1999: 137), they argued that conflicting feelings about the scope of government and its specific policy responsibilities are a fundamental component of American public opinion, having a variety of consequences for the political system as a whole.

I contend that this interpretation may be premature. As we shall see, the seemingly contradictory stands that some people take regarding government and its activities are not necessarily in conflict at all—and our tendency to believe otherwise stems from a failure to recognize an important distinction that citizens themselves make when they think about government spending. Once subjective interpretations of the term "government spending" are taken into account, it becomes obvious that there is a great deal of *consistency* between people's feelings about government in general and their attitudes toward specific types of spending.

DATA AND BASIC RESULTS

The data for this analysis are taken from the 1992 American National Election Study (ANES). This source is used because recent ANES interview schedules contain survey questions that are nearly ideal for present purposes. Further, I employ the 1992 study in particular because it contains additional information (to be explained below) that is relevant to my analysis. I want to emphasize, however, that the overall results are highly robust and replicable at several other time points.[1]

Citizens' Beliefs About the Size of Government

General attitudes toward the size and power of the federal government are measured here by combining individuals' answers to three separate survey items. Specifically, 1992 ANES respondents were asked the following series of questions: "Next, I am going to ask you to choose which of two statements I read comes closer to your own opinion. You might agree to some extent with both, but we want to know which one is closer to your views. . . ."

- One, the less government the better; or two, there are more things that government should be doing.
- One, we need a strong government to handle today's complex economic problems; or two, the free market can handle these problems without government being involved.
- One, the main reason government has become bigger over the years is because it has gotten involved in things that people should do for themselves; or two, government has become bigger because the problems we face have become bigger.

Responses to these questions were coded on a three-point scale that includes a middle category indicating indifference or an inability to choose between the two statements. Agreement with the first statement in a pair was coded as a zero, the middle category assigned a value of one, and agreement with the second statement coded as a two. Scores for the second pair of statements were reversed, so that larger values always correspond to a pro-government response. Finally, a summary index was created by taking the sum of response scores across the three items; the reliability coefficient (Cronbach's alpha) for this index is quite high, at 0.72. It therefore seems reasonable to interpret its values as a general measure of individual beliefs about the size and power of the federal government.

Summary statistics for the index provide a revealing first look at how Americans think about the role of government. Individual scores range from zero (maximal hostility and concern about government size/power) to six (maximal support for large, powerful government). The mean (based upon 2,132 observations) is 3.92, which is significantly larger than the index midpoint (a value of 3.00); at the same time, it is smaller than the median (4.00), indicating that the mean is being "pulled" toward the lower end of the scale by an asymmetric distribution. It is also worth noting that the standard deviation (2.21) is only about half the size of the interquartile range (4.00)—the size of the interval that contains the central 50 percent of the observations. This latter fact, combined with the difference between the mean and median, suggests that the distribution of opinion is not only centered closer to the right-hand end of the index; it also is negatively skewed, with the longer tail extending toward the left side. In substantive terms, based upon their answers to these questions, one might reasonably conclude that Americans tend to be more favorable than hostile toward a large federal government.

Public Attitudes Toward Government Spending

Citizens' government spending preferences are operationalized using another battery of survey items from the 1992 ANES. Respondents were asked, "If you had a say in making up the federal budget this year, for which of the following programs would you like to see spending increased and for which would you like to see spending decreased? Should federal spending on——be increased, decreased, or kept about the same?" The latter question was repeated for 16 policy areas: food stamps, welfare programs, AIDS research, financial aid for college students, programs that assist blacks, solving the problem of the homeless, aid to countries of the former Soviet Union, social security, science and technology, child care, dealing with crime, improving and protecting the environment, government assistance to the unemployed, poor people, public schools, and aid to big cities.

Frequency distributions for responses to the 16 spending questions are shown in table 8.1. Clearly, the public's preferences vary widely by policy area. For example, more than two-thirds of the NES respondents believe federal spending on crime and the homeless should be increased (70 percent and 73 percent, respectively), while less than one-fifth believe spending should be increased for food stamps, welfare and helping the countries of the former Soviet Union (18 percent, 17 percent, and 16 percent, respectively). Despite this sizable variation in support for further spending, Americans generally do *not* believe that government spending should be reduced. There is no policy area for which a majority of the respondents say that expenditures should be cut, and there are only two policies where pluralities give that response: welfare programs and helping the former Soviet Union, with 43 percent wanting to reduce spending in each case. Thus, the overall pattern is for Americans to favor current or increased spending levels in a wide variety of distinct policy areas.

Contradictory Attitudes and Ambivalence

The univariate results presented so far tell us little about ambivalence *per se*. For that purpose, the distributions of the separate variables are far less important than is the relationship between them. Specifically, ambivalence should *attenuate the correlation between individuals' general feelings about government and their spending attitudes.* This would occur if there were (1) substantial numbers of ambivalent opponents of large government who favor increased spending, simultaneously with consistent opponents who prefer decreased spending; and/or (2) substantial numbers of ambivalent supporters of large government who favor decreased spending levels, alongside consistent supporters who prefer increased spending. In short, ambivalence is signaled most clearly by the existence of seemingly contradictory patterns of opinion.

Let us start with the same basic strategy employed by Cantril and Cantril (1999). In their analysis, citizens' feelings about government were

Table 8.1 Frequency distributions for policy-specific government spending questions

Spending preferences	Policy area															
	Food stamps	Welfare programs	AIDS research	Help college students	Assist blacks	Help the homeless	Aid to former Soviet Union	Social security	Science and technology	Child care	Dealing with crime	Protecting the environment	Assist the unemployed	Poor people	Public schools	Aid to big cities
Decrease federal spending	29.6%	42.5%	8.3%	8.0%	24.2%	6.1%	42.6%	4.3%	13.1%	10.0%	3.4%	4.3%	12.8%	6.9%	4.1%	29.9%
Keep spending about the same	52.7	40.4	29.9	31.8	50.5	21.2	40.9	47.1	44.9	39.9	26.4	34.5	47.5	38.1	30.4	49.5
Increase federal spending	17.7	17.1	61.8	60.2	25.3	72.7	16.5	48.6	42.0	50.1	70.2	61.2	39.7	55.0	65.5	20.6

Note. Data are from the 1992 American National Election Study. The number of cases ranges from 2366 to 2441.

compared against the number of programs for which they believed spending should be maintained or increased. Using the 1992 ANES survey, I have divided the government size index described earlier into three categories representing net opposition to large government (scores 0–2 on the original scale), a neutral stance (a score of 3), and net positive feelings about large government (original scores of 4–6). Spending preferences were then sorted in two categories that distinguished spending "opponents" (respondents who said that spending should be maintained/increased in eight or fewer policy areas) and spending "supporters" (who said that spending should be maintained/increased in more than eight areas).[2]

Table 8.2 shows the cross-tabulation between these two categorical variables. The cells in the lower left and upper-right corners of the table contain the respondents with overtly contradictory orientations. They comprise slightly less than one-third of the total observations (30 percent). Of these, the 29 percent in the lower-left cell correspond to Cantril and Cantril's ambivalent critics, that is, people who prefer smaller government combined with some degree of increased spending. The tiny number of ambivalent supporters (1 percent)—people who are comfortable with large government but still believe that spending should be decreased—fall within the upper-right cell of table 8.2. In sum, although the 1992 ANES contains just about the same proportion of seemingly ambivalent respondents as Cantril and Cantril found in their study (32 percent), the ratio of ambivalent critics to supporters is quite a bit larger here.

The results so far show that a basic precondition for citizen ambivalence is met with the ANES data: There is a sizable minority of respondents

Table 8.2   Beliefs about government size/power and attitudes toward policy-specific government spending

Attitude toward policy-specific government spending	Beliefs about a large and powerful federal government		
	Opposed	*Neutral*	*Favorable*
Spending opponents	1.9% (40)	0.0% (1)	1.4% (31)
Spending supporters	28.6% (610)	3.0% (63)	65.1% (1387)

Note: Data are from the 1992 American National Election Study. Table entries are percentages based on the total number of observations in the table ($N = 2132$), with cell frequencies in parentheses. Beliefs about the federal government are measured by collapsing scores on the three-item index described in the text. For the policy-specific variable, opponents are individuals who want to maintain or increase spending in eight or fewer policy areas; supporters are those who want to maintain or increase spending in more than eight areas.

who exhibit inconsistent feelings about governmental size and government spending. But is this a manifestation of *ambivalence?* Recent work, exemplified by Cantril and Cantril, usually assumes that it is. However, such a conclusion is based upon the critical assumption that citizens' spending preferences have more or less the same meaning across all of the policy areas mentioned in the survey questions. Otherwise, the empirical indicator of spending attitudes employed in table 8.2 (and by Cantril and Cantril) makes no sense.

The wide variability in support for government spending in different domains revealed earlier in table 8.1 gives us reason to question this assumption. While the sixteen separate items all refer to "spending," they also mention markedly dissimilar aspects of government policy making. There simply is no *a priori* reason to expect that an individual's reaction toward, say, welfare spending or food stamps will be based on the same underlying attitude as his/her feelings about, say, education or aid to the former USSR. It is therefore necessary to take a closer look at public attitudes toward government spending. As we shall see, citizens appear to make a clear distinction between different categories of expenditures—one that is critical for understanding the meaning of the apparent inconsistent responses observed in the data thus far.

Spending Attitudes: A Closer Look

Instead of simply assuming that all of the spending responses are comparable, it is better to seek an empirical representation that approximates as closely as possible the ways in which people actually think about the issues involved in policy-specific government spending. In order to do this, the analysis that follows will determine how well responses to the policy-specific items conform to a cumulative, or Guttman, structure (see Coombs 1964; Jacoby 1991). If such a model is consistent with the data, it implies that there is an attitudinal dimension or underlying continuum ranging from a preference for reducing spending in all programs to increasing spending in all programs. Other configurations of responses represent intervals along this continuum. The content and relative placement of these intervals reveal information regarding public perceptions of the various policy areas. Basically, popular program areas (i.e., those where large proportions support maintaining or increasing spending) are located closer to the lower, anti-spending pole of the continuum; in other words, it is relatively "easy" to support spending on such programs, even among people with a strong general anti-spending stance. Conversely, it is more "difficult" to support spending in less popular program areas located near the higher end of the continuum; a person would need to maintain a firm pro-spending stance in order to give specific support to spending in such areas. Consequently, scaled locations of the respective programs will show how public support varies across programs.

Individual survey respondents also are arrayed along the continuum, according to their professed preferences. Essentially, each person supports government spending up to a point, but no farther than that. This point varies from one individual to the next, with the point positions themselves being estimated as part of the scaling analysis. The cumulative nature of the scale arises because an individual's responses to *all* of the scaled policies should be predictable from his/her overall point location. The rule is simple: Given a person's position along the continuum, s/he should respond favorably to all spending alternatives that fall at "easier" positions (i.e., to the left of his/her point along the scale) and unfavorably to all spending alternatives that fall at more "difficult" positions (i.e., to the right of his/her point). Hence, the individual responses *cumulate* across the scale.

The cumulative scaling analysis is performed using an approach developed by R. J. Mokken (1971; also Mokken and Lewis 1982). This is a useful strategy for several reasons. First, it is based upon a probabilistic model, unlike the deterministic approach used in traditional Guttman scaling (Jacoby 1991). Second, it is nonparametric in its assumptions about the relationship between empirical responses and the underlying attitudinal dimension, unlike the more stringent assumptions required for parametric item response theory models (Sijstma and Molenaar 2002). Third, it can be used on polychotomous, ordinal, items like the three-category spending questions from the ANES interview schedule (Sijstma *et al.* 1990); there is no need to dichotomize either the individual items or the final scale.

In the Mokken approach, scalability is assessed by comparing the number of observed scaling *errors* (i.e. patterns of responses that are inconsistent with the hypothesized cumulative pattern) to the number of errors that would be expected to occur under a null hypothesis of statistical independence across the items.[3] The ratio of these two numbers is subtracted from one to obtain Loevinger's *H* coefficient. It is a goodness-of-fit statistic in that the larger the value (i.e., the closer to 1.00), the greater the degree to which the data approximate the cumulative structure.

The immediate objective of the Mokken scaling analysis is to find the largest subset of spending items that conform to the hypothesized cumulative structure. The analysis proceeds in a stepwise manner by starting with a pool of items (the 16 policy-specific spending questions) and finding the pair of items that form the two-item scale with the largest possible *H*-value. Then it finds the third item which, added to the first two, produces a three-item scale with the largest possible *H*-value, and so on. The analysis proceeds until the *H* statistic falls below an acceptable level, or the item set is exhausted.[4] This inductive approach to structure in the data produces a variable that is based upon respondents' own patterns of answers to the spending questions, rather than ad hoc decisions or a priori structure imposed by the researcher.

A Mokken Scale of Welfare-Related Spending Attitudes

With the ANES data on spending preferences, a Mokken analysis produces an eight-item scale with an *H*-value of 0.41. Based upon the standards of evaluation that are typical in the scaling literature, this constitutes a very reasonable correspondence between the cumulative scaling model and the empirical data. The eight scalable items are spending preferences toward the following: solving the problem of the homeless, poor people, child care, government assistance to the unemployed, programs that assist blacks, food stamps, aid to big cities, and welfare programs. The substantive nature of the scale is determined by the nature of the scalable items. Here, we see a rather obvious pattern: At least six of the eight items involve policies that are designed explicitly to help disadvantaged groups within the population.[5] There is, then, a coherent structure underlying public thinking about government spending, centering around social welfare policies and programs.

The scaled order of spending alternatives on the eight welfare-related items is shown in table 8.3. Alternatives that lie closest to the "decrease spending on all programs" pole are those deemed acceptable by larger proportions of the general public; as one moves along the scale (that is, a downward direction in the table), the various alternatives are supported by fewer and fewer people until, finally, we reach the "increase spending in all programs" pole, a stance endorsed by very few ANES respondents. Clearly, Americans distinguish systematically between different kinds of public assistance programs. They are relatively likely to believe that spending on programs for the homeless, poor people, child care, and unemployment should be maintained or even increased. In contrast, public support for food stamps, programs to assist blacks, and especially welfare is not nearly as pronounced.

The ordering of the scale alternatives in table 8.3 corresponds to widely held stereotypes about the legitimacy of various beneficiaries of governmental programs. The plight of the homeless, for example, as well as concerns about poor people and children seem to arouse sympathy and compassion, at least as gauged by the willingness to fund programs that

Table 8.3   Scaled order of program-specific federal spending alternatives

Scale position	government spending alternative
0	Decrease spending, all programs
1	Maintain current spending, programs to help the homeless
2	Maintain current spending, programs to help the poor
3	Maintain current spending, child care
4	Maintain current spending, unemployment programs
5	Maintain current spending, programs to help blacks
6	Increase spending, programs to help the homeless
7	Maintain current spending, food stamps
8	Maintain current spending, aid to big cities
9	Maintain current spending, welfare programs
10	Increase spending, programs to help the poor
11	Increase spending, child care
12	Increase spending, unemployment programs
13	Increase spending, programs to help blacks
14	Increase spending, aid to big cities
15	Increase spending, food stamps
16	Increase spending, welfare programs
17	Increase spending, all programs

Note: Based on a Mokken scaling analysis of data from the 1992 American National Election Study.

help these kinds of individuals (Schneider and Ingram 1993). Negative stereotypes about welfare recipients, people who rely on food stamps, big cities, and members of racial minority groups, on the other hand, engender few positive feelings and probably some degree of hostility (Kluegel and Smith 1986; Gilens 1999). Most Americans are willing to support government spending on behalf of disadvantaged segments of American society, but only so long as they are perceived to be deserving and legitimate recipients of public aid (Eismeier 1982; Sanders 1988; Jacoby 1994).

Non-Scalable Spending Preferences

The remaining eight policy-specific spending items (AIDS research, financial aid for college students, aid to countries of the former Soviet Union, social security, science and technology, dealing with crime, improving and protecting the environment, and public schools) are non-scalable according to Mokken criteria. It is important to emphasize that the non-scalable nature of these items does not necessarily imply the existence of "non-attitudes" (Converse 1970) or anything of that sort; it simply means that respondents' spending preferences fail to conform to the cumulative structure exhibited by the survey questions previously discussed. The lack of structure across items could, in fact, mean that people are evaluating policies very carefully on their separate merits. The empirical non-scalability of responses does not, in itself, provide any means of distinguishing between these relatively pessimistic and optimistic interpretations of the data.

It is apparent, of course, that the non-scalable items all pertain to spending in policy areas that are, to varying degrees, substantively different from social welfare concerns. For example, science and technology, AIDS programs, and protecting the environment all focus on research and development issues, whereas assistance to the former Soviet Union obviously deals with foreign policy. As a result, it may not be terribly surprising that citizens respond to spending in these areas differently from the ways in which they think about welfare spending. What is more interesting, though, is that the American public apparently distinguishes between benefits to clearly defined sets of disadvantaged people (e.g., the homeless, the poor, and the unemployed) and programs that are spread out more evenly throughout society, such as education, social security, and crime prevention.

Apart from their failure to form a common scale with the welfare-related items, we should note that attitudes toward spending on non-welfare programs show little internal structure of any kind. For one thing, they do not meet the minimum Mokken scalability criteria for a cumulative pattern of their own. Further, intercorrelations among these items (mean Pearson's $r = 0.130$) are rather small compared to those for questions about welfare spending (mean $r = 0.323$). Thus, the evidence about which items form a coherent cumulative scale and which ones do not suggests that Americans regard government spending on non-welfare policies quite differently from the manner in which they think about welfare spending.

The Subjective Nature of Responses to Government Spending

The observed differences between public attitudes toward government spending on welfare versus non-welfare policies are extremely important. In fact, I argue that citizens base their reactions to the *general* stimulus of "government spending" mainly on their feelings about *welfare* spending, with far less consideration being given to their preferences regarding spending in other, non-welfare areas. The empirical evidence to support this argument is straightforward: As part of the battery of issue questions included in the 1992 ANES, respondents were asked to place themselves on a seven-point scale ranging from "government should provide many fewer services and reduce spending a lot" at one end, to "government should provide many more services and increase spending a lot" at the other end. Notice that the response alternatives only mention governmental actions (spending and services) rather than the specific beneficiaries of those actions. Answers can therefore be interpreted as reflecting individual reactions toward a general frame of the government spending issue.

Consider now the relationships that we find between citizens' policy-specific spending preferences and their general attitudes toward government spending: Bivariate correlations between the eight welfare-related items and the seven-point scale are quite a bit larger (mean $r = 0.323$) than correlations between the eight non-welfare questions and that same scale (mean $r = 0.172$). A difference of such magnitude should not occur if views about spending in general comprise a "mental aggregation" of individuals' attitudes across the full range of policy areas. Instead, people's overall attitudes toward government spending are much more closely aligned with their reactions to welfare spending than with their spending preferences in other policy domains.

The contrasting patterns for citizens' welfare and non-welfare spending preferences imply that it is inappropriate to equate responses across all of the items, as was done earlier. Such a measurement strategy ignores differences in how people think about these two types of government spending. In order to remedy the problem, we can create an additive index for individual responses to the eight welfare-related spending items and another, separate eight-item index for the non-welfare questions. The policy-specific responses are coded zero for "decrease spending," one for "maintain current levels," and two for "increase spending." Acordingly, scores for each of the two additive scales range from zero (for respondents who want to decrease spending in all eight policy areas represented by that scale) to 16 (for people who prefer to increase spending across the board). Reliability coefficients (Cronbach's alpha) are 0.792 for welfare-related spending and 0.545 for non-welfare spending, with the difference between these two values stemming from people's relatively less constrained responses to the latter set of items. The correlation (Pearson's r) between the scales is 0.465, indicating that individuals' beliefs about spending on welfare and non-welfare programs are moderately related even though the underlying structures of public opinion in these two areas are quite different.

We can obtain a more systematic comparison of the ways in which welfare and non-welfare spending preferences impinge on general spending attitudes by regressing the seven-point spending/services item on the new composite measures; results are shown in table 8.4. Because the policy-specific scales have both been created from eight items with identical

Table 8.4   Impact of policy-specific spending preferences
on general attitudes toward government spending

Spending preferences	OLS coefficient estimate	Standard error
Spending preference, welfare-related programs	0.184	0.011
Spending preferences, non-welfare programs	0.090	0.015
Intercept	−0.786	0.268
R^2	0.247	
Number of cases =	1681	

Note: Data are from the 1992 American National Election Study.

response formats, the values of their associated regression coefficients should be comparable to one another. With that in mind, it appears that welfare spending attitudes have about twice the impact of non-welfare attitudes on individuals' overall feelings about government spending. The OLS coefficients are 0.184 and 0.090, respectively, with the difference between them being highly significant ($p \leq 0.001$). Clearly, Americans tend to have welfare programs in mind when they react to the stimulus "government spending."

The distribution of opinion differs markedly across the two categories of policy spending. Figure 8.1 provides histograms for the summary measures (welfare preferences in the top portion of the figure, non-welfare preferences in the bottom portion). As before, the two variables share a common response format so comparisons across them are not problematic. There are two particularly important features of the data to be noted. First, the non-welfare distribution is shifted toward the right, that is, the pro-spending side, relative to the welfare distribution. Second, the non-welfare distribution shows a strong negative skew, while the welfare distribution is much more widely spread out and symmetric about its central region. Taken together, these results indicate that (1) there is a fairly clear consensus that spending on many non-welfare programs should be increased, or at least not cut; however, (2) public opinion toward welfare-related spending is sharply divided, with a plurality of respondents taking a centrist position (i.e., to maintain spending in most programs) but sizable proportions believing that spending should be either increased or decreased.

Even though the separate policy areas captured by these two additive scales both fall under the general umbrella of "government spending," it is critical to distinguish between them. Welfare-related spending remains a

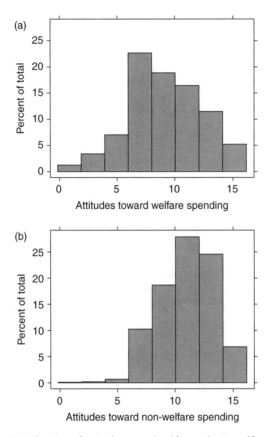

Figure 8.1   Distributions of attitudes toward welfare and non-welfare spending

Note: Each graph shows the histogram of scores on an eight-item summary scale of spending attitudes. In each case, larger scores indicate greater support for policy spending. The data are taken from the 1992 *CPS National Election Study.*

hotly contested and divisive issue in American politics. Non-welfare spending, on the other hand, takes the form of a valence issue where the weight of public sentiment clearly leans in one direction, that is, toward ongoing government expenditures for purposes such as education, scientific research, public health, and social insurance. As we shall see in the next section, the distinction between welfare and non-welfare spending attitudes also helps account for the previously discussed contradictory positions that many people exhibit between their feelings about governmental size and about government spending.

AMBIVALENCE AND INFLUENCES ON SPENDING
ATTITUDES

Having determined that there are two kinds of policy-specific spending orientations held by the American public, we can now return to the more central issue of ambivalence between citizens' attitudes toward spending and their beliefs about the size of government. Specifically, this part of the analysis examines influences on spending attitudes and how they differ across the policy areas identified in the previous section. The logic here is simple enough: Most traditional theories of public opinion hold that specific attitudes are a function of more general orientations (Kinder 1983; Sears 1993; Jacoby 2002). In the present case, this would lead to the hypothesis that preferences concerning the size of government should have a direct impact on attitudes toward government spending: People who oppose government becoming too large and powerful should usually favor reductions in spending, while those who are relatively unconcerned about government size should be more likely to support policy expenditures.

As explained earlier, however, ambivalence might attenuate the preceding relationship with the result that anti-big government sentiments are sometimes accompanied by a preference for maintaining or increasing policy spending, and vice versa. Put another way, ambivalent feelings would be a likely culprit if beliefs about government size were found to exhibit a weak (or even null) impact on policy spending attitudes.[6] One also might anticipate that any such effect would be most pronounced among the determinants of non-welfare spending. Recall the skewed distribution of opinion in favor of spending for non-welfare programs; the consensus evident in figure 8.1b suggests that support for spending may well occur across the entire span of beliefs about governmental size and power. In contrast, welfare preferences are polarized to a noticeably greater degree (figure 8.1a) and therefore seem more likely to coincide with the usual partisan and ideological dimensions of contemporary political conflict.

In order to test these hypotheses, the two policy spending indices are regressed on the three-item scale used earlier to measure individuals' general feelings about the size and power of government. Additional independent variables include three political predispositions known to exert a strong influence upon issue attitudes: party identification, ideology (each of these based on standard ANES seven-point scales[7]), and a four-item index of symbolic racism (see Kinder and Sanders 1996).[8] The direction of coding is such that larger values indicate more Democratic, liberal, and non-racist positions, respectively. Another independent variable gauges self-interest effects by measuring the number of public assistance programs from which a respondent (or someone in his/her immediate family) receives benefits. Finally, family income (in thousands of dollars), race (a dummy variable for African-American respondents),[9] and gender (a dummy variable for females) are included as controls.

The analysis employs *multivariate* (as opposed to *multiple*) regression. It is important to distinguish between these two similar-sounding analytic strategies: Whereas multiple regression implies a single dependent variable, multivariate regression expresses several dependent variables (two in this instance, for attitudes toward welfare and non-welfare spending) as linear combinations of a common set of independent variables (Dunteman 1984). This approach is not seen very frequently in the political science literature, but it is necessary in the present context because the objective is to make comparisons *across* equations. Within each equation, the coefficients and related statistics are identical to those obtained from the usual OLS approach to single-equation estimation, and they are interpreted in exactly the same way. However, because the multivariate approach enables hypothesis tests for linear combinations of coefficients across equations, it is possible to estimate differential influences on citizens' attitudes toward the two categories of government spending.

Results are shown in table 8.5. The two leftmost columns display the coefficients, standard errors, and standardized coefficients for influences on welfare-related spending attitudes, and the next two columns provide the same information for influences on non-welfare spending attitudes. Note that the standardized coefficients are useful for examining the relative effects of different independent variables *within equations*. They cannot, however, be used for comparisons across equations because the distributions of the respective dependent variables are different. Instead, the unstandardized coefficients can be used for this purpose. In addition, to further facilitate comparisons, the rightmost column of the table gives the observed probability values for tests of the null hypothesis, that is, that the corresponding (unstandardized OLS) coefficients are identical across both equations. Smaller values of this probability indicate support for the alternative hypothesis that the effect of a given variable does indeed differ across equations.[10]

Let us begin by considering the results for welfare-related spending attitudes, shown in the left portion of table 8.5. This equation fits the data quite well, with an R^2 of 0.412. The individual regression coefficients have the expected signs, and all but one of them (gender) are statistically different from zero ($p \leq 0.05$, one-sided). Turning to the standardized coefficients, symbolic racism shows the strongest effect (0.278); clearly, feelings about the recipients of public assistance affect individuals' willingness to

Table 8.5   Determinants of attitudes toward government spending

Variable	Attitudes toward welfare policy spending		Attitudes toward non-welfare policy spending		MANOVA probability value for difference between coefficients
	OLS coefficient	Standardized coefficient	OLS coefficient	Standardized coefficient	
Government size/power	0.368* (0.037)	0.239	0.276* (0.031)	0.258	0.019*
Party identification	0.319* (0.044)	0.190	0.061* (0.036)	0.052	0.000*
Ideological self-placement	0.279* (0.063)	0.111	0.161* (0.052)	0.092	0.073
Symbolic racism	0.971* (0.083)	0.278	0.266* (0.070)	0.110	0.000*
Public assistance	0.347* (0.071)	0.113	−0.063 (0.059)	−0.030	0.000*
Family income	−0.009* (0.003)	−0.066	−0.004 (0.003)	−0.038	0.109
African American	0.815* (0.274)	0.070	0.174 (0.229)	0.022	0.026*
Gender (Female)	0.126 (0.154)	0.018	−0.185 (0.129)	−0.038	0.056
Equation intercept	11.141* (0.266)		16.698* (0.266)		0.000*
R^2	0.412		0.148		

Note: Data are from the 1992 American National Election Study. Table entries are regression coefficients, with standard errors in parentheses. Coefficients marked with an asterisk are statistically significant ($p \leq 0.05$, one-sided test). MANOVA probabilities marked with an asterisk indicate that the difference between corresponding coefficients across the two equations is statistically significant.

support spending on programs which provide that assistance. The second-largest standardized coefficient is the one for general feelings about government size and power (0.239), with people who feel that government is too large being quite a bit less supportive of spending than are those who favor a large, powerful national government. Party identification and ideology show the expected effects, although the impact of the former (0.190) is considerably stronger than the latter (0.111). The variable measuring individual reliance on public assistance has a coefficient of 0.113, indicating that there is a large self-interest effect on attitudes toward government spending: People who receive direct benefits from government apparently recognize the source of those benefits, and support spending on the relevant programs that provide them. Finally, higher incomes correspond to less support for government spending on welfare programs while African-Americans are more likely than whites to support spending. These last two effects are fairly weak, however, with standardized coefficients of −0.066 and 0.070, respectively.

Turning to the influences on attitudes toward non-welfare spending, the first feature to point out is the smaller R^2 value (0.148). On the one hand, the attenuated fit for this equation may be due to the lower reliability of the non-welfare spending index compared to that for our measure of welfare-related spending. On the other hand, the size of the difference between these two fit statistics suggests that such a "technical" factor does not tell the entire story. Instead, it seems likely that non-welfare spending attitudes are simply more idiosyncratic and difficult to predict than are welfare spending attitudes.

In the equation for non-welfare spending attitudes, the only independent variables with statistically significant effects are the government size index, party identification, ideology, and symbolic racism. Neither reliance on public assistance, nor any of the demographic control variables show any reliable impact on respondents' non-welfare spending attitudes. The standardized coefficients for this equation reveal that the relative sizes of the effects are quite different than they were with welfare spending attitudes. Here, feelings about governmental size and power have the strongest impact by a wide margin (the standardized coefficient is 0.258); symbolic racism comes in a distant second (0.110), followed by ideological self-placement (0.092) and party identification (a fairly weak 0.052).

Comparing the two sets of estimates, it is immediately obvious that the factors helping to shape welfare and non-welfare spending attitudes are different. First, a multivariate test of the hypothesis that all of the coefficients are identical across equations is easily rejected at any reasonable level of statistical significance. Second, it is clear that virtually all of the independent variables have a stronger impact on welfare spending attitudes than on non-welfare spending attitudes—and in some cases, the difference is pronounced (and statistically significant). For example, the unstandardized coefficients for party identification and public assistance in the welfare spending equation are more than five times larger than their counterparts in the equation for non-welfare spending. Similarly, the impact of symbolic racism on welfare spending attitudes is more than three times its effect on non-welfare spending attitudes. For the size of government variable, the difference is marginally significant (i.e., the null hypothesis would be rejected at the 0.05 level, but not the 0.01 level), though the coefficient is actually fairly large for both types of spending. Ideological self-placement and the three demographic variables appear to have little or no impact on attitudes toward spending in either domain.

On balance, the results presented in table 8.5 are *inconsistent* with the ambivalence hypothesis. The central problem stems from the relatively stable and generally strong impact of beliefs about governmental power on attitudes toward both welfare-related and non-welfare government spending: Once other factors are taken into account, individuals who exhibit concerns about the federal government's scope also tend to favor reductions in all types of spending, while those who are untroubled by governmental size and power prefer maintaining or increasing a broad range of federal program expenditures. As explained earlier, this effect should not occur if people are simultaneously being pulled in two directions by a fear of large government combined with support for expenditures on specific programs (or by the opposite combination of feelings). Consequently, the expected manifestation of ambivalence simply does not arise in these data.

CONCLUSION

The preceding analysis has shown that there are many people who express reservations about a large, powerful federal government, but who nonetheless believe that public expenditures should be maintained or increased across a wide variety of policy areas. These orientations do *not*, however, seem to arise from ambivalent feelings about the role of government in modern society. What, then, can account for the seemingly contradictory combinations of opinion (particularly among those whom Cantril and Cantril labeled "ambivalent critics") that provided the initial focus for this chapter? I believe the answer lies in the nature of the spending issue itself. To the mass public, *government spending* typically means *welfare spending*—and opinions about spending on public assistance programs tend to be explicitly *political* attitudes. As such, the factors that influence their development are highly consistent: symbolic predispositions, beliefs about the proper scope of government, self-interest considerations, and certain personal traits all combine in predictable ways to shape citizens' attitudes about expenditure programs designed to help the homeless, the poor, the unemployed, minority groups, and so on.

The situation is very different for attitudes about non-welfare spending. For one thing, there is much stronger support, across the board, for expenditures on these kinds of programs. Even among individuals who should be most *opposed* to spending on the basis of their symbolic orientations (e.g., conservatives, Republicans, symbolic racists), there is fairly wide support for spending on non-welfare programs related to education, science and technology, AIDS research, social security, and so on. At the same time, the impact of personal political factors (partisanship and ideology) are relatively muted, while perceptions of self-interest (receipt of public assistance) and attitudes toward minorities (symbolic racism) have weak effects at best. The only explanatory variable that shows a robust impact on non-welfare spending attitudes is beliefs about the size and power of government.

Based upon these results, as well as the fact that attitudes toward non-welfare spending are not very predictable in any case, I would argue that citizens' reactions toward spending on non-welfare programs do not constitute *political* attitudes at all. Instead, they reflect a largely consensual belief that modern government is responsible for supporting certain kinds of collective goods, including education, scientific achievement, and broad-based social insurance programs. There is, of course, some latitude for variation within this general consensus: People who are comfortable with powerful government are still more supportive of spending than those who are not. Here, though, the connection between beliefs about government size and spending preferences seems to be based more on logic than on political considerations, and the "limits" within which preferred levels of non-welfare spending vary are quite high in any case. Indeed, non-welfare spending attitudes are largely insulated from traditional sources of public opinion such as partisanship and ideology—and that is precisely why a sizable segment of the American public is willing to profess a desire for smaller government, while still tolerating a fairly high level of government spending, that is, as a concession to the reality of modern society. To call such a configuration of beliefs and attitudes ambivalence would, I contend, stretch that concept to a degree that effectively renders it meaningless.

There is, to be sure, some degree of uncertainty associated with this conclusion, especially since the presence or absence of ambivalence has not been observed directly but rather inferred from patterns that appear in the empirical data. But because it is impossible to know for sure what mental processes actually generated the contradictory responses observed in the 1992 ANES, we need to ask whether invoking the concept of ambivalence provides us with theoretical leverage that would be lacking without it. In other words, can ambivalence account for otherwise unexplainable configurations of beliefs and attitudes? Here, I would contend that the answer to that question is "probably not."

From one perspective, these results may be disappointing in that they represent an area where ambivalence does not appear to be part of the explanation for patterns of mass attitudes. From another perspective, though, the analysis can be taken as an optimistic challenge for scholars: The results presented here remind us, if nothing else, of the complexities inherent in understanding the ways that citizens react to the variegated stimuli that confront them in the political world.

NOTES

1. Virtually identical results are obtained when the analysis presented in this chapter is replicated with data from the 1988, 1996, and 2000 ANES surveys. These other years are not used in this chapter because the interview schedules did not elicit information about respondents' personal use of government benefits. As we shall see, reliance on public assistance exerts a significant influence on attitudes toward certain kinds of government spending.

2. Cantril and Cantril (1999) also used support for spending in eight or more policy areas as their cut off for spending supporters and opponents. Their survey only asked respondents about a total of ten policy areas, however, rather than the 16 policies mentioned in the 1992 ANES battery.

3. In the present context, a scaling error would occur when a respondent supports government spending in a relatively unpopular area (e.g., welfare) while opposing spending for a relatively popular policy (e.g., programs to help the homeless). Of course, the term "error" is somewhat misleading since there is absolutely nothing *wrong* with such combinations of responses; they constitute "errors" only in the sense that they are inconsistent with the cumulative pattern being tested against the data.

4. The Mokken scaling literature usually specifies that the minimum acceptable H-value is 0.30 (e.g., Mokken and Lewis 1982; Sijstma and Molenaar 2002).

5. The inclusion of child care and aid to big cities in a scale dominated by welfare items may seem anomalous. Yet child care is a central concern of women, particularly those with low- to middle-level incomes heading single-parent families; similarly, poverty is often regarded as a major problem facing American cities. As a result, the social construction of these policy concerns leads them to be viewed in welfare-related terms by many citizens.

6. Ambivalence can arise in a variety of contexts. The conceptualization of ambivalence developed in this chapter is actually quite different from that which has been the major focus in much recent political science research. Whereas the latter often points to value conflict as the principal source of ambivalence (Alvarez and Brehm 1995), I am emphasizing contradictions and possible ambivalence between beliefs and attitudes. The distinction is an important one, even though the terms "value" and "belief" often are used more or less synonymously by political scientists (Feldman 1988; McCann 1997; Goren 2001). Values, though, are usually defined as broad, abstract conceptions about desirable and undesirable modes of conduct and end states of human life (Rokeach 1973); they are general feelings that occur across a variety of situational contexts (Schwartz 1996). In contrast, beliefs and attitudes involve the perceived attributes of, and affective reactions toward, specific stimulus objects (Fishbein and Ajzen 1975).

    For both values and beliefs/attitudes, ambivalence would be manifested empirically as contradictory responses to survey questions. However, the *source* of the ambivalence is different in each case: With the former, ambivalence arises from the difficulty in applying strongly held, but potentially conflicting, values (such as freedom and equality) to a given policy controversy (such as affirmative action); with the latter, ambivalence results from people simultaneously supporting mutually incompatible policy goals (such as a smaller, less powerful federal government as well as high levels of government spending in order to achieve desirable social and political objectives). Nevertheless, while the psychological processes may differ, both types of ambivalence are similarly problematic for the development of stable, consistent political attitudes at the individual level.

7. Party identification ranges from strong Republican at one end to strong Democrat on the other (Campbell *et al.* 1960). Ideology is measured by respondents' self-placement on a scale that ranges from extremely conservative to extremely liberal.

8. Respondents were asked to agree or disagree with the following statements: (a) Irish, Italian, Jewish and many other minorities overcame prejudice and worked their way up. Blacks should do the same without any special favors. (b) Over the past few years, blacks have gotten less than they deserve. (c) It's really a matter of some people not trying hard enough; if blacks would only try harder they would be just as well off as whites. (d) Generations of slavery and discrimination have created conditions that make it difficult for blacks to work their way out of the lower class. Answers to each of these statements were recorded on a five-point scale ranging from "agree strongly" to "disagree strongly," with the second and fourth items being reversed to correct for direction of wording; scores were then summed to create a single measure of symbolic racism (alpha = 0.75).

9. It may seem strange at first glance to include African Americans in a model that includes symbolic racism as an explanatory variable, with conventional wisdom suggesting an absence of racist feelings among black respondents. Empirically, however, that is not the case. The symbolic racism scale ranges between zero and four, with lower scores indicating more racist attitudes. On the one hand, it is true that African Americans tend to have higher scale scores (mean = 2.53, standard deviation = 0.87) than whites (mean = 1.55, standard deviation = 0.92). On the other hand, the mean for black respondents is well below the scale maximum, that is, the "least racist" position, and there is almost as much variability in scale scores for blacks as for whites; further, the correlation (Pearson's r) between the dummy variable for African-American respondents and symbolic racism is just 0.34. From a methodological perspective, the latter value is low enough to insure that collinearity is not a problem in the regression model. Substantively, this relatively weak relationship demonstrates that blacks, like whites, are divided in their opinions regarding the experiences, accomplishments, and roles of African Americans in modern society. While such results might be surprising to some, they do not cause any problems whatsoever for the present analysis.

10. Each probability value is obtained from a multivariate analysis of variance (MANOVA) F test that the difference between corresponding coefficients across the two equations is equal to zero. A more general version of this test is used to examine whether *all* of the coefficients are equal across equations (or, equivalently, that observed differences between them are due only to sampling error).

References

Abelson, Robert P. 1959. "Modes of Resolution of Belief Dilemmas." *Journal of Conflict Resolution* 3: 343–352.

Abelson, Robert P. 1988. "Conviction." *American Psychologist* 43: 267–275.

Abelson, Robert P. 1995. "Attitude Extremity." Pp. 25–41 in *Attitude Strength: Antecedents and Consequences*, eds. Richard E. Petty and Jon A. Krosnick. Mahwah, NJ: Lawrence Erlbaum.

Abelson, Robert P., Donald R. Kinder, Mark D. Peters, and Susan T. Fiske. 1982. "Affective and Semantic Components in Political Perception." *Journal of Personality and Social Psychology* 42: 619–630.

Abramowitz, Alan I. 1995. "It's Abortion, Stupid: Policy Voting in the 1992 Presidential Election." *Journal of Politics* 57: 176–186.

Abramowitz, Alan I. 1997. "The Cultural Divide in American Politics: Moral Issues and Presidential Voting." Pp. 211–226 in *Understanding Public Opinion*, eds. Barbara Norrander and Clyde Wilcox. Washington, DC: CQ Press.

Achen, Christopher H. 1975. "Mass Political Attitudes and the Survey Response." *American Political Science Review* 69: 1218–1231.

Adams, Greg D. 1997. "Abortion: Evidence of an Issue Evolution." *American Journal of Political Science* 41: 718–737.

Allport, Gordon W. 1935. "Attitudes." Pp. 798–844 in *Handbook of Social Psychology*, ed. Carl A. Murchison. New York: Russell and Russell.

Alvarez, Michael R., and John Brehm. 1995. "American Ambivalence Towards Abortion Policy: Development of a Heteroskedastic Probit Model of Competing Values." *American Journal of Political Science* 39: 1055–1082.

Alvarez, Michael R., and John Brehm. 1997. "Are Americans Ambivalent Towards Racial Policies?" *American Journal of Political Science* 41: 345–374.

Alvarez, Michael R., and John Brehm. 1998. "Speaking in Two Voices: American Equivocation About the Internal Revenue Service." *American Journal of Political Science* 42: 418–452.

Alvarez, Michael R., and John Brehm. 2000. "Binding the Frame: How Important are Frames for Survey Response?" Paper presented at the 2000 Annual Meetings of the American Political Science Association, Washington, DC.

Alvarez, Michael R., and John Brehm. 2002. *Hard Choices, Easy Answers: Values, Information, and American Public Opinion*. Princeton, NJ: Princeton University Press.

Alvarez, Michael R., John Brehm, and Catherine Wilson. 2003. "Uncertainty and American Public Opinion." Pp. 161–185 in *Uncertainty in American Politics*, ed. Barry C. Burden. Cambridge: Cambridge University Press.

Alvarez, Michael R., and Charles Franklin. 1994. "Uncertainty and Political Perceptions." *Journal of Politics* 56: 671–688.

Anand, Sowmya and Jon A. Krosnick. 2003. "The Impact of Attitudes Toward Foreign Policy Goals on Public Preferences Among Presidential Candidates: A Study of Issue Publics and the Attentive Public in the 2000 U.S. Presidential Election." *Presidential Studies Quarterly* 33: 31–71.

Armitage, Christopher J. 2003. "Beyond Attitudinal Ambivalence: Effects of Belief Homogeneity on Attitude-Intention-Behaviour Relations." *European Journal of Social Psychology* 33: 551–563.

Armitage, Christopher J., and Mark Conner. 2000. "Attitudinal Ambivalence: A Test of Three Key Hypotheses." *Personality and Social Psychology Bulletin* 26: 1421–1432.

Aronson, Elliot, and J. Merrill Carlsmith. 1963. "Effect of the Severity of Threat on the Devaluation of Forbidden Behavior." *Journal of Abnormal and Social Psychology* 66: 584–588.

Bargh, John A., Shelley Chaiken, Rajen Govender, and Felicia Pratto. 1992. "The Generality of the Automatic Attitude Activation Effect." *Journal of Personality and Social Psychology* 62: 893–912.

Baron, Reuban M., and David A. Kenny. 1986. "The Moderator-Mediator Variable Distinction in Social Psychological Research: Conceptual, Strategic, and Statistical Considerations." *Journal of Personality and Social Psychology* 51: 1173–1182.

Bartels, Larry M. 1986. "Issue Voting under Uncertainty: An Empirical Test." *American Journal of Political Science* 30: 709–728.

Bassili, John N. 1995. "On the Psychological Reality of Party Identification: Evidence from the Accessibility of Voting Intentions and of Partisan Feelings." *Political Behavior* 17: 339–358.

Bassili, John N. 1996a. "The 'How' and 'Why' of Response Latency Measurement in Telephone Surveys." Pp. 319–346 in *Answering Questions: Methodology for Determining Cognitive and Communicative Processes in Survey Research*, eds. Norbert Schwarz and Seymour Sudman. San Francisco: Jossey-Bass.

Bassili, John N. 1996b. "Meta-Judgmental Versus Operative Indexes of Psychological Attributes: The Case of Measures of Attitude Strength." *Journal of Personality and Social Psychology* 71: 637–653.

Bassili, John N. 1998. "Simultaneous Accessibility: A Prerequisite to Heated Intrapsychic Conflict." *Response Time Measurement in Survey Research*. Symposium conducted at the 1998 Annual Meetings of the International Society of Political Psychology, Montreal, Canada.

Bassili, John N. and Joseph F. Fletcher. 1991. "Response-Time Measurement in Survey Research: A Method for Cati and a New Look at Nonattitudes." *Public Opinion Quarterly* 55: 331–346.

Baumeister, Roy F., Ellen Bratslavsky, Mark Muraven, and Dianne M. Tice. 1998. "Ego Depletion: Is the Active Self a Limited Resource?" *Journal of Personality and Social Psychology* 74: 1252–1265.

Bell, David W., and Victoria M. Esses. 2002. "Ambivalence and Response Amplification: A Motivational Perspective." *Personality and Social Psychology Bulletin* 28: 1143–1152.

Bennett, Linda L. M., and Stephen Earl Bennett. 1990. *Living with Leviathan: Americans Coming to Terms with Big Government*. Lawrence, KS: University of Kansas Press.

Billig, Michael. 1995. *Banal Nationalism*. London: Sage.

Blank, Thomas, and Peter Schmidt. 2003. "National Identity in Europe." *Political Psychology* 24: 233–240.

Bless, Herbert, and Joseph P. Forgas, eds. 2000. *The Message Within: The Role of Subjective Experience in Social Cognition and Behavior*. Philadelphia: Psychology Press.

Boninger, David S., Jon A. Krosnick, and Matthew K. Berent. 1995a. "Origins of Attitude Importance: Self-Interest, Social Identification, and Value Relevance." *Journal of Personality and Social Psychology* 68: 61–80.

Boninger, Jon A. Krosnick, Matthew K. Berent, and Leandre R. Fabrigar. 1995b. "The Causes and Consequences of Attitude Importance." Pp. 159–189 in *Attitude Strength: Antecedents and Consequences*, eds. Richard E. Petty and Jon A. Krosnick. Mahwah, NJ: Lawrence Erlbaum.

Born, Richard. 1990. "The Shared Fortunes of Congress and Congressmen." *Journal of Politics* 52: 1223–1241.

Breckler, Steven J. 1994. "A Comparison of Numerical Indexes for Measuring Attitude Ambivalence." *Educational and Psychological Measurement* 54: 350–365.

Brehm, John. 1993. *The Phantom Respondents: Opinion Surveys and Political Representation*. Ann Arbor: University of Michigan Press.

Brock, Timothy C. 1962. "Cognitive Restructuring and Attitude Change." *Journal of Abnormal and Social Psychology* 64: 264–271.

Brown, Judson S., and I. E. Farber. 1951. "Emotions Conceptualized as Intervening Variables—with Suggestions toward a Theory of Frustration." *Psychological Bulletin* 48: 465–495.

Browne, Michael W. and R. Cudeck. 1992. "Alternative Ways of Assessing Model Fit." *Sociological Methods and Research* 21: 230–258.

Burden, Barry C., and Janet M. Box-Steffensmeier. 1998. "Vote Likelihood and Institutional Trait Questions in the 1997 NES Pilot Study." Report to the National Election Studies Board of Overseers.

Byrne, Barbara M. 1998. *Structural Equation Modeling With LISREL, PRELIS, and SIMPLIS: Basic Concepts, Applications, and Programming*. Mahwah, NJ: Lawrence Erlbaum.

Byrne, Donn. 1961. "Interpersonal Attraction and Attitude Similarity." *Journal of Abnormal Social Psychology* 62: 713–715.

Byrne, Donn. 1971. *The Attraction Paradigm*. New York: Academic Press.

Cacioppo, John T., and Gary G. Berntson. 1994. "Relationship Between Attitudes and Evaluative Space: A Critical Review, with Emphasis on the Separability of Positive and Negative Substrates." *Psychological Bulletin* 115: 401–423.

Cacioppo, John T., Wendi Gardner, and Gary G. Berntson. 1997. "Beyond Bipolar Conceptualizations and Measures: The Case of Attitudes and Evaluative Space." *Personality and Social Psychology Review* 1: 3–25.

Cacioppo, John T. and Richard E. Petty. 1979. "Attitudes and Cognitive Response: An Electrophysiological Approach." *Journal of Personality and Social Psychology* 37: 2181–2199.

Cacioppo, John T., Mary A. Snydersmith, Stephen L. Crites, and Wendi L. Gardner. 1996. *Bivariate Evaluative and Ambivalence Measures (BEAMS)*. Unpublished manuscript, Ohio State University, Columbus, OH.

Campbell, Angus, Philip E. Converse, Warren E. Miller, and Donald E. Stokes. 1960. *The American Voter*. New York: John Wiley and Sons.

Cantril, Albert H., and Susan Davis Cantril. 1999. *Reading Mixed Signals: Ambivalence in American Public Opinion About Government*. Washington, DC: Woodrow Wilson Center Press.

Carmines, Edward G., and James A. Stimson. 1980. "The Two Faces of Issue Voting." *American Political Science Review* 74: 78–91.

Carver, Charles S., Frederick. X. Gibbons, Walter G. Stephan, David C. Glass, and Irwin Katz. 1979. "Ambivalence and Evaluative Response Amplification." *Bulletin of the Psychonomic Society* 13: 50–52.

Carver, Charles S., and Michael Scheier. 1990. "Principles of Self-Regulation: Action and Emotion." Pp. 3–52 in *Handbook of Motivation and Cognition: Foundations of Social Behavior*, vol. 2, eds. E. Tory Higgins and Richard, M. Sorrentino. New York: Guilford.

Chaiken, Shelly, Eva Pomerantz, and Roger Giner-Sorolla. 1995. "Structural Consistency and Attitude Strength." Pp. 387–412 in *Attitude Strength: Antecedents and Consequences*, eds. Richard E. Petty and Jon A. Krosnick. Mahwah, NJ: Lawrence Erlbaum.

Chong, Dennis. 1993. "How People Think, Reason, and Feel about Rights and Liberties." *American Journal of Political Science* 37: 867–899.

Citrin, Jack, Cara Wong, and Brian Duff. 2001. "The Meaning of American National Identity: Patterns of Ethnic Conflict and Consensus." Pp. 71–100 in *Social Identity, Intergroup Conflict, and Conflict Reduction*, eds. Richard D. Ashmore, Lee Jussim, and David Wilder. Oxford: Oxford University Press.

Cohen, Jacob, Patricia Cohen, Stephen G. West, and Leona S. Aken. 2003. *Applied Multiple Regression/Correlation Analysis for the Behavioral Sciences*. Mahwah, NJ: Lawrence Erlbaum.

Conner, Mark, Paul Sparks, Rachel Povey, Rhiannon James, Richard Shepherd, and Christopher J. Armitage. 2002. "Moderator Effects of Attitudinal Ambivalence on Attitude-Behaviour Relationships." *European Journal of Social Psychology* 32: 705–718.

Converse, Philip E. 1964. "The Nature of Belief Systems in Mass Publics." Pp. 206–261 in *Ideology and Discontent*, ed. David E. Apter. New York: The Free Press.

Converse, Philip E. 1970. "Attitudes and Non-Attitudes: Continuation of a Dialogue." Pp. 168–189 in *The Quantitative Analysis of Social Problems*, ed. Edward R. Tufte. Reading, MA: Addison-Wesley.

Cook, Elizabeth Adell, Ted G. Jelen, and Clyde Wilcox. 1992. *Between Two Absolutes: Public Opinion and the Politics of Abortion.* Boulder, CO: Westview.

Cook, Elizabeth Adell, Ted G. Jelen, and Clyde Wilcox. 1994. "Issue Voting in Gubernatorial Elections: Abortion and Post-*Webster* Politics." *Journal of Politics* 56: 187–199.

Coombs, Clyde H. 1964. *A Theory of Data.* New York: Wiley.

Cooper, Joel, and Jeff Stone. 2000. "Cognitive Dissonance and the Social Group." Pp. 227–244 in *Attitudes, Behavior, and Social Context: The Role of Norms and Group Membership*, eds. Deborah J. Terry and Michael A. Hogg. Mahwah, NJ: Lawrence Erlbaum.

Craig, Stephen C., James G. Kane, and Michael D. Martinez. 2002. "Sometimes You Feel Like a Nut, Sometimes You Don't: Citizens' Ambivalence About Abortion." *Political Psychology* 23: 285–301.

Craig, Stephen C., Richard G. Niemi, and Glenn E. Silver. 1990. "Political Efficacy and Trust: A Report on the NES Pilot Study Items." *Political Behavior* 12: 289–314.

Craig, Stephen C., Michael D. Martinez, James G. Kane, and Jason Gainous. 2005. "Core Values, Value Conflict, and Citizens' Ambivalence about Gay Rights." *Political Research Quarterly.* (in press)

Cunningham, William A., Marcia K. Johnson, J. Chris Gatenby, John C. Gore, and Mahzarin R. Banaji. 2003. "Neural Components of Social Evaluation." *Journal of Personality and Social Psychology* 85: 639–649.

Dawson, Richard E., and Kenneth Prewitt. 1969. *Political Socialization.* Boston: Little, Brown.

De Figueiredo, Rui J. P., Jr, and Zachary Elkins. 2003. "Are Patriots Bigots? An Inquiry into the Vices of In-Group Pride." *American Journal of Political Science* 47: 171–188.

Delli Carpini, Michael, and Scott Keeter. 1996. *What Americans Know about Politics and Why It Matters.* New Haven, CT: Yale University Press.

Dennis, Jack. 1966. "Support for the Party System by the Mass Public." *American Political Science Review* 60: 600–615.

Dennis, Jack, Leon Lindberg, and Donald J. McCrone. 1971. "Support for Nation and Government among British Children." *British Journal of Political Science* 1: 25–48.

Dunteman, George H. 1984. *Introduction to Multivariate Analysis.* Beverly Hills, CA: Sage.

Eagly, Alice H., and Shelly Chaiken. 1993. *The Psychology of Attitudes.* Fort Worth: Harcourt Brace.

Easton, David. 1953. *The Political System.* New York: Alfred Knopf.

Eismeier, Theodore J. 1982. "Public Preferences About Government Spending." *Political Behavior* 4: 133–145.

Emerson, Rupert. 1960. *From Empire to Nation: The Rise to Self-Assertion of Asian and African Peoples.* Cambridge, MA: Harvard University Press.

Fabrigar, Leandre R., and Jon A. Krosnick. 1995. "Attitude Importance and the False Consensus Effect." *Personality and Social Psychology Bulletin* 21: 468–479.

178   *References*

Fazio, Russell H. 1995. "Attitudes as Object-Evaluation Associations: Determinants, Consequences, and Correlates of Attitude Accessibility." Pp. 247–282 in *Attitude Strength: Antecedents and Consequences*, eds. Richard E. Petty and Jon A. Krosnick. Mahwah, NJ: Lawrence Erlbaum.

Fazio, Russell H., Joni R. Jackson, Bridget C. Dunton, and Carol J. Williams. 1995. "Variability in Automatic Activation as an Unobtrusive Measure of Racial Attitudes: A Bona Fide Pipeline?" *Journal of Personality and Social Psychology* 69: 1013–1027.

Fazio, Russell H., and Michael A. Olson. 2003. "Implicit Measures in Social Cognition Research: Their Meaning and Use." *Annual Review of Psycholgy* 54: 297–327.

Feldman, Stanley. 1988. "Structure and Consistency in Public Opinion: The Role of Core Beliefs and Values." *American Journal of Political Science* 32: 416–440.

Feldman, Stanley. 1989. "Measuring Issue Preferences: The Problem of Response Instability." Pp. 25–60 in *Political Analysis*, vol. 1, ed. James A. Stimson. Ann Arbor: University of Michigan Press.

Feldman, Stanley, and John Zaller. 1992. "The Political Culture of Ambivalence: Ideological Responses to the Welfare State." *American Journal of Political Science* 36: 268–307.

Feldman, Stanley. 1995. "Answering Survey Questions." Pp. 249–270 in *Political Judgment: Structure and Process*, eds. Milton Lodge and Kathleen M. McGraw. Ann Arbor, MI: University of Michigan Press.

Fenno, Richard F., Jr. 1975. "If, as Ralph Nader says, Congress is 'The Broken Branch,' How Come we Love Our Congressmen so Much?" Pp. 277–287 in *Congress in Change: Evolution and Reform*, ed. Norman J. Ornstein. New York: Praeger.

Festinger, Leon. 1957. *A Theory of Cognitive Dissonance*. Palo Alto, CA: Stanford University Press.

Festinger, Leon, Henry W. Riecken, and Stanley Schacter. 1956. *When Prophecy Fails*. Minneapolis: University of Minnesota Press.

Fishbein, Martin, and Icek Ajzen. 1975. *Belief, Attitude, Intention, and Behavior: An Introduction to Theory and Research*. Reading, MA: Addison-Wesley.

Frankovic, Kathleen A., and Monika L. McDermott. 2001. "Public Opinion in the 2000 Election: The Ambivalent Electorate." Pp. 73–91 in *The Election of 2000: Reports and Interpretations*, by Gerald M. Pomper et al. New York: Chatham House.

Free, Lloyd A., and Hadley Cantril. 1967. *The Political Beliefs of Americans: A Study of Public Opinion*. New Brunswick, NJ: Rutgers University Press.

Gardner, Wendi L. 1996. *Biases in Impression Formation: A Demonstration of a Bivariate Model of Evaluation*. Unpublished doctoral dissertation, Ohio State University, Columbus, OH.

Gefen, David, Detmar W. Straub, and Marie-Claude Boudreau. 2000. "Structural Equation Modeling and Regression: Guidelines for Research Practice." *Communications of the Association for Information Systems* 4: 1–78.

Gellner, Ernest. 1983. *Nations and Nationalism*. London: Basil Blackwell.

Gilens, Martin. 1999. *Why Americans Hate Welfare: Race, Media, and the Politics of Antipoverty Policy.* Chicago: University of Chicago Press.

Goren, Paul. 2001. "Core Principles and Policy Reasoning in Mass Publics: A Test of Two Theories." *British Journal of Political Science* 31: 159–177.

Graber, Doris A. 1980. *Mass Media and American Politics.* Washington, DC: CQ Press.

Green, Donald Philip. 1988. "On the Dimensionality of Public Sentiment toward Partisan and Ideological Groups." *American Journal of Political Science* 32: 758–780.

Green, Donald Philip, and Jack Citrin. 1994. "Measurement Error and the Structure of Attitudes: Are Positive and Negative Judgments Opposites?" *American Journal of Political Science* 38: 256–281.

Green, Donald Philip, and Peter Salovey. 1999. "In What Sense are Positive and Negative Affect Independent?" *Psychological Science* 10: 304–306.

Greenwald, Anthony G., and Mahzarin R. Banaji. 1995. "Implicit Social Cognition: Attitudes, Self-Esteem, and Stereotypes." *Psychological Review* 102: 4–27.

Gronke, Paul, and John Brehm. 2002. "History, Heterogeneity, and Presidential Approval: A Modified ARCH Approach." *Electoral Studies* 21: 425–452.

Gross, Sharon Ruth, Rolf Holtz, and Norman Miller. 1995. "Attitude Certainty." Pp. 215–245 in *Attitude Strength: Antecedents and Consequences*, eds. Richard E. Petty and Jon A. Krosnick. Mahwah, NJ: Lawrence Erlbaum.

Guge, Michael, and Michael F. Meffert. 1998. "The Political Consequences of Attitude Ambivalence." Paper presented at the 1998 Annual Meetings of the Midwest Political Science Association, Chicago, IL.

Haddock, Geoffrey. 2003. "Making a Party Leader Less of a Party Member: The Impact of Ambivalence on Assimilation and Contrast Effects in Political Party Attitudes." *Political Psychology* 24: 769–780.

Hair, Joseph F., Jr., Ronald L. Tatham, Ralph E. Anderson and William C. Black. 1998. *Multivariate Data Analysis*, 5th ed. Upper Saddle River, NJ: Prentice Hall.

Hanze, Martin. 2001. "Ambivalence, Conflict, and Decision Making: Attitudes and Feelings in Germany towards NATO's Military Intervention in the Kosovo War." *European Journal of Social Psychology* 31: 693–706.

Hass, Glen R., Irwin Katz, Nina Rizzo, Joan Bailey, and Donna Eisenstadt. 1991. "Cross-Racial Appraisal as Related to Attitude Ambivalence and Cognitive Complexity." *Personality and Social Psychology Bulletin* 17: 83–92.

Hass, Glen R., Irwin Katz, Nina Rizzo, Joan Bailey, and Lynn Moore. 1992. "When Racial Ambivalence Evokes Negative Affect, Using a Disguised Measure of Mood." *Personality and Social Psychology Bulletin* 18: 786–797.

Heider, Fritz. 1946. "Attitudes and Cognitive Organization." *Journal of Psychology* 21: 107–112.

Heider, Fritz. 1958. *The Psychology of Interpersonal Relations.* New York: Wiley.

Hibbing, John R., and Elizabeth Theiss-Morse. 1995. *Congress as Public Enemy: Public Attitudes toward American Political Institutions.* Cambridge: Cambridge University Press.

Hill, Jennifer L., and Hanspeter Kriesi. 2001. "An Extension and Test of Converse's 'Black-and-White' Model of Response Stability." *American Political Science Review* 95: 397–413.

Hoch, Stephen J. 1984. "Availability and Interference in Predictive Judgment." *Journal of Experimental Psychology: Learning, Memory, and Cognition* 10: 649–662.

Hochschild, Jennifer L. 1981. *What's Fair? American Beliefs about Distributive Justice.* Cambridge, MA: Harvard University Press.

Hodson, Gordon, Gregory R. Maio, and Victoria M. Esses. 2001. "The Role of Attitudinal Ambivalence in Susceptibility to Consensus Information." *Basic and Applied Social Psychology* 23: 197–205.

Holbrook, Allyson, Jon A. Krosnick, Penny S. Visser, Wendi L. Gardner, and John T. Cacioppo. 2001. "Attitudes toward Presidential Candidates and Political Parties: Initial Optimism, Inertial First Impressions, and a Focus on Flaws." *American Journal of Political Science* 45: 930–950.

Huckfeldt, Robert, Jeannette Morehouse Mendez, and Tracy Osborn. 2004. "Disagreement, Ambivalence, and Engagement: The Political Consequences of Heterogeneous Networks." *Political Psychology* 25: 65–95.

Huckfeldt, Robert, and John Sprague. 1998a. "Extremity, Accessibility, and Certainty: The Role of Ambivalence Regarding Abortion Rights." Paper presented at the 1998 Annual Meetings of the Midwest Political Science Association, Chicago, IL.

Huckfeldt, Robert, and John Sprague. 1998b. "Sources of Ambivalence in Public Opinion: The Certainty and Accessibility of Abortion Attitudes." Paper presented at the 1998 Annual Meetings of the International Society of Political Psychology, Montreal, Canada.

Huntington, Samuel P. 1981. *American Politics: The Promise of Disharmony.* Cambridge, MA: Belknap Press of Harvard University Press.

Hurwitz, Jon, and Mark Peffley. 1987. "How Are Foreign Policy Attitudes Structured? A Hierarchical Model." *American Political Science Review* 81: 1099–1120.

Jacoby, William G. 1991. *Data Theory and Dimensional Analysis.* Newbury Park, CA: Sage.

Jacoby, William G. 1994. "Public Attitudes Toward Government Spending." *American Journal of Political Science* 38: 336–361.

Jacoby, William G. 2000. "Issue Framing and Public Opinion on Government Spending." *American Journal of Political Science* 44: 750–767.

Jacoby, William. G. 2002. "Core Values and Political Attitudes." Pp. 177–201 in *Understanding Public Opinion*, 2nd ed., eds. Barbara Norrander and Clyde Wilcox. Washington, DC: CQ Press.

Jahoda, Gustav. 1963. "The Development of Children's Ideas about Country and Nationality." *British Journal of Educational Psychology* 33: 143–153.

Jamieson, David W. 1988. "The Influence of Value Conflicts on Attitudinal Ambivalence." Paper presented at the 1988 Annual Meetings of the Canadian Psychological Association, Montreal, Canada.

Jamieson, David W. 1993. "The Attitude Ambivalence Construct: Validity, Utility, and Measurement." Paper presented at the 1993 Annual Meetings of the American Psychological Association, Toronto, Canada.

Jewell, Robert D. 2003. "The Effects of Deadline Pressure on Attitudinal Ambivalence." *Marketing Letters* 14: 83–95.

Jonas, Klaus, Michael Diehl, and Philip Bromer. 1997. "Effects of Attitudinal Ambivalence on Information Processing and Attitude-Intention Consistency." *Journal of Experimental Social Psychology* 33: 190–210.

Jöreskog, Karl G., Dag Sörbom, Stephen Du Toit, and Mathilda Du Toit. 2001. *LISREL 8: New Statistical Features*. Chicago: Scientific Software International.

Jost, John T., and Diana Burgess. 2000. "Attitudinal Ambivalence and the Conflict Between Group and System Justification Motives in Low Status Groups." *Personality and Social Psychology Bulletin* 26: 293–305.

Jost, John T., Jack Glaser, Arie W. Kruglanski, and Frank J. Sulloway. 2003. "Political Conservatism as Motivated Social Cognition." *Psychological Bulletin* 129: 339–375.

Kaplan, Kalman J. 1972. "On the Ambivalence-Indifference Problem in Attitude Theory and Measurement: A Suggested Modification of the Semantic Differential Technique." *Psychological Bulletin* 77: 361–372.

Kateb, George. 2000. "Is Patriotism a Mistake?" *Social Research* 67: 901–924.

Katz, Irwin. 1981. *Stigma: A Social Psychological Analysis*. Hillsdale, NJ: Lawrence Erlbaum.

Katz, Irwin, Sheldon Cohen, and David Glass. 1975. "Some Determinants of Cross-Racial Helping Behavior." *Journal of Personality and Social Psychology* 32: 964–970.

Katz, Irwin, David Glass, and Sheldon Cohen. 1973. "Ambivalence, Guilt, and the Scapegoating of Minority Group Victims." *Journal of Experimental Social Psychology* 9: 423–436.

Katz, Irwin, David C. Glass, David Lucido, and Joan Farber. 1979. "Harm-Doing and Victims Racial or Orthopedic Stigma as Determinants of Helping Behavior." *Journal of Personality* 47: 340–364.

Katz, Irwin, and R. Glen Hass. 1988. "Racial Ambivalence and American Value Conflict: Correlational and Priming Studies of Dual Cognitive Structures." *Journal of Personality and Social Psychology* 55: 893–905.

Katz, Irwin, J. Wackenhut, and R. Glen Hass. 1986. "Racial Ambivalence, Value Duality, and Behavior." Pp. 35–59 in *Prejudice, Discrimination, and Racism*, eds. John F. Dovidio and Samuel L. Gaertner. New York: Academic Press.

Kenny, David A., and Charles M. Judd. 1984. "Estimating the Nonlinear and Interactive Effects of Latent Variables." *Psychological Bulletin* 96: 201–210.

Kinder, Donald R. 1983. "Diversity and Complexity in American Public Opinion." Pp. 389–428 in *Political Science: The State of the Discipline*, ed. Ada W. Finifter. Washington, DC: American Political Science Association.

Kinder, Donald R., and Lynn M. Sanders. 1996. *Divided by Color: Racial Politics and Democratic Ideals*. Chicago: University of Chicago Press.

King, Gary, James Honaker, Ann Joseph, and Kenneth Scheve. 2001. "Analyzing Incomplete Political Science Data: An Alternative Algorithm for Multiple Imputation." *American Political Science Review* 95: 49–69.

Klayman, Joshua, and Young-Won Ha. 1987. "Confirmation, Disconfirmation, and Information in Hypothesis Testing." *Psychological Review* 94: 211–228.

Klein, Jill G. 1991. "Negativity Effects in Impression Formation: A Test in the Political Arena." *Personality and Social Psychology Bulletin* 17: 412–418.

Klein, Jill G. 1996. "Negativity in Impressions of Presidential Candidates Revisited: The 1992 Election." *Personality and Social Psychology Bulletin* 22: 288–295.

Klopfer, Frederick J., and Thomas J. Madden. 1980. "The Middlemost Choice on Attitude Items: Ambivalence, Neutrality, or Uncertainty?" *Personality and Social Psychology Bulletin* 6: 97–101.

Kluegel, James R. and Eliot R. Smith. 1986. *Beliefs About Inequality: Americans' Views of What Is and What Ought to Be.* New York: Aldine De Gruyter.

Koriat, Asher, Sarah Lichtenstein, and Baruch Fischhoff. 1980. "Reasons for Confidence." *Journal of Experimental Psychology: Human Learning and Memory* 6: 107–118.

Kosterman, Rick, and Seymour Feshbach. 1989. "Toward a Measure of Patriotic and Nationalistic Attitudes." *Political Psychology* 10: 257–274.

Krosnick, Jon A. 1988a. "Attitude Importance and Attitude Change." *Journal of Experimental Social Psychology* 24: 240–255.

Krosnick, Jon A. 1988b. "The Role of Attitude Importance in Social Evaluation: A Study of Policy Preferences, Presidential Candidate Evaluations, and Voting Behavior." *Journal of Personality and Social Psychology* 55: 196–210.

Krosnick, Jon A. 1990. "Government Policy and Citizen Passion: A Study of Issue Publics in Contemporary America." *Political Behavior* 12: 59–92.

Krosnick, Jon A. 2002. "The Challenges of Political Psychology: Lessons to be Learned from Research on the Projection Hypothesis." Pp. 115–152 in *Thinking about Political Psychology*, ed. James H. Kuklinski. New York: Cambridge University Press.

Krosnick, Jon A., and Robert P. Abelson. 1992. "The Case for Measuring Attitude Strength in Surveys." Pp. 177–203 in *Questions About Questions: Inquiries into the Cognitive Bases of Surveys*, ed. Judith M. Tanur. New York: Russell Sage.

Krosnick, Jon A., David S. Boninger, Yao C. Chuang, Mathew K. Berent, and Catherine G. Carnot. 1993. "Attitude Strength: One Construct or Many Related Constructs?" *Journal of Personality and Social Psychology* 65: 1132–1151.

Krosnick, Jon A., and Richard E. Petty. 1995. "Attitude Strength: An Overview." Pp. 1–24 in *Attitude Strength: Antecedents and Consequences*, eds. Richard E. Petty and Jon A. Krosnick. Mahwah, NJ: Lawrence Erlbaum.

Krosnick, Jon A., and Howard Schuman. 1988. "Attitude Intensity, Importance, and Certainty and Susceptibility to Response Effects." *Journal of Personality and Social Psychology* 54: 940–952.

Larsen, Jeff T., A. Peter McGraw, and John T. Cacioppo. 2001. "Can People Feel Happy and Sad at the Same Time?" *Journal of Personality and Social Psychology* 81: 684–696.

Lau, Richard R. 1982. "Negativity in Political Perception." *Political Behavior* 4: 353–377.

Lau, Richard R. 1985. "Two Explanations for Negativity Effects in Political Behavior." *American Journal of Political Science* 29: 119–138.

Lavine, Howard. 2001. "The Electoral Consequences of Ambivalence toward Presidential Candidates." *American Journal of Political Science* 45: 915–929.

Lavine, Howard, Eugene Borgida, and John L. Sullivan. 2000. "On the Relationship Between Attitude Involvement and Attitude Accessibility: Toward a Cognitive-Motivational Model of Political Information Processing." *Political Psychology* 21: 81–106.

Lavine, Howard, Joseph W. Huff, Stephen H. Wagner, and Donna Sweeney. 1998a. "The Moderating Influence of Attitude Strength on the Susceptibility to Context Effects in Attitude Surveys." *Journal of Personality and Social Psychology* 75: 359–373.

Lavine, Howard, Cynthia J. Thomsen, Mark P. Zanna, and Eugene Borgida. 1998b. "On the Primacy of Affect in the Determination of Attitudes and Behavior: The Moderating Influence of Affective-Cognitive Ambivalence." *Journal of Experimental Social Psychology* 34: 398–421.

Lipkus, Isaac M., Jeffrey D. Green, John R. Feaganes, and Constantine Sedikides. 2001. "The Relationship Between Attitudinal Ambivalence and Desire to Quit Smoking among College Smokers." *Journal of Applied Social Psychology* 31: 113–133.

Little, Roderick J. A., and Donald B. Rubin. 2002. *Statistical Analysis with Missing Data*, 2nd ed. New York: Wiley.

MacDonald, Tara K., and Mark P. Zanna. 1998. "Cross-Dimension Ambivalence Toward Social Groups: Can Ambivalence Affect Intentions to Hire Feminists?" *Personality and Social Psychology Bulletin* 24: 427–441.

Maio, Gregory R., and Victoria M. Esses. 1996. "Ambivalence and Persuasion: The Processing of Messages About Immigrant Groups." *Journal of Experimental Social Psychology* 32: 513–536.

Maio, Gregory R., Frank D. Fincham, and Emma J. Lycett. 2000. "Attitudinal Ambivalence Toward Parents and Attachment Style." *Personality and Social Psychology Bulletin* 26: 1451–1464.

Marcus, George E. 2003. "The Psychology of Emotions." Pp. 182–221 in *Oxford Handbook of Political Psychology*, eds. David O. Sears, Leonie Huddy, and Robert Jervis. New York: Oxford University Press.

Marcus, George E., W. Russell Neuman, and Michael MacKuen. 2000. *Affective Intelligence and Political Judgment*. Chicago: University of Chicago Press.

Marks, Gary, and Norman Miller. 1987. "Ten Years of Research on the False-Consensus Effect: An Empirical and Theoretical Review." *Psychological Bulletin* 102: 72–90.

McCann, James A. 1997. "Electoral Choices and Core Value Change: The 1992 Presidential Campaign." *American Journal of Political Science* 41: 564–583.

McCrae, Robert R., and Paul T. Costa. 2003. *Personality in Adulthood: A Five-Factor Theory Perspective*. New York: Guilford Press.

McCullagh, Peter, and John A. Nelder. 1989. *Generalized Linear Models*, 2nd ed. New York: Chapman and Hall.

McGraw, Kathleen M., Edward Hasecke, and Kimberly Conger. 2003. "Ambivalence, Uncertainty, and Processes of Candidate Evaluation." *Political Psychology* 24: 421–448.

McGraw, Kathleen M., Milton Lodge, and Jeffrey M. Jones. 2002. "The Pandering Politicians of Suspicious Minds." *Journal of Politics* 64: 362–383.

McGregor, Ian. 2004 (in press). "Zeal, Identity, and Meaning: Going to Extremes to be One Self." In *Handbook of Experimental Existential Psychology*, eds. Jeff Greenberg, Sander L. Koole, and Tom Pyszczynski. New York: Guilford.

McGregor, Ian, and Denise C. Marigold. 2003. "Defensive Zeal and the Uncertain Self: What Makes You So Sure?" *Journal of Personality and Social Psychology* 85: 838–852.

McGregor, Ian, Ian R. Newby-Clark, and Mark P. Zanna. 1999. " 'Remembering' Dissonance: Simultaneous Accessibility of Inconsistent Cognitive Elements Moderates Epistemic Discomfort." Pp. 325–353 in *Cognitive Dissonance: Progress on a Pivotal Theory in Social Psychology*, eds. Eddie Harmon-Jones and Judson Mills. Washington, DC: American Psychological Association.

McKoon Gail, and Roger Ratcliff. 1992. "Spreading Activation Versus Compound Cue Accounts of Priming: Mediated Priming Revisited." *Journal of Experimental Psychology: Learning, Memory, and Cognition* 18: 1155–1172.

McNamara, Timothy P. 1992. "Theories of Priming: I. Associative Distance and Lag." *Journal of Experimental Psychology: Learning, Memory, and Cognition* 18: 1173–1190.

McNamara, Timothy P. 1994. "Theories of *Priming: II*. Types of Primes." *Journal of Experimental Psychology: Learning, Memory, and Cognition* 20: 507–520.

Meffert, Michael F., Michael Guge, and Milton Lodge. 2000. "Good, Bad, Indifferent and Ambivalent: The Consequences of Multidimensional Political Attitudes." Pp. 60–100 in *The Issue of Belief: Essays in the Intersection of Non-Attitudes and Attitude Change* eds. Willem E. Saris and Paul M. Sniderman. Amsterdam: The Amsterdam School of Communication Research, Universiteit van Amsterdam, The Netherlands.

Meyer, David E., and Roger W. Schvaneveldt. 1971. "Facilitation in Recognizing Pairs of Words: Evidence of a Dependence Between Retrieval Operations." *Journal of Experimental Psychology* 90: 227–234.

Mokken, R. J. 1971. *A Theory and Procedure of Scale Analysis with Applications in Political Research*. The Hague: Mouton.

Mokken, Robert J., and Charles Lewis. 1982. "A Nonparametric Approach to the Analysis of Dichotomous Item Responses." *Applied Psychological Measurement* 7: 45–55.

Moore, Michael. 1973. "Ambivalence in Attitude Measurement." *Educational and Psychological Measurement* 33: 481–483.

Moore, Michael. 1980. "Validation of Attitude toward any Practice Scale Through the Use of Ambivalence as a Moderator Variable." *Educational and Psychological Measurement* 40: 205–208.

Mowrer, Orval Hobart.1960. *Learning Theory and Behavior*. New York: Wiley.

Mulligan, Kenneth, and Kathleen M. McGraw. 2002. "Value Conflict: The Effects of Competing Principles on Political Judgment." Paper presented at the 2002 Annual Meetings of the American Political Science Association, Boston, MA.

Muraven, Marl, and Roy F. Baumeister. 2000. "Self-Regulation and Depletion of Limited Resources: Does Self-Control Resemble a Muscle?" *Psychological Bulletin* 126: 247–259.

Muraven, Mark, Roy F. Baumeister, and Dianne M. Tice. 1999. "Longitudinal Improvement of Self-Regulation through Practice: Building Self-Control Strength through Repeated Exercise." *Journal of Social Psychology* 139: 446–457.

Muraven, Mark, Dianne M. Tice, and Roy F. Baumeister. 1998. "Self-Control as a Limited Resource: Regulatory Depletion Patterns." *Journal of Personality and Social Psychology* 74: 774–789.

Mutz, Diana C., Paul M. Sniderman, and Richard A. Brody, eds. 1996. *Political Persuasion and Attitude Change*. Ann Arbor: University of Michigan Press.

Myrdal, Gunner. 1944. *An American Dilemma: The Negro Problem and Modern Democracy*, reprint (1997). New Brunswick, NJ: Transaction.

Nelson, Thomas. 1999. "Group Affect and Attribution in Social Policy Opinion." *Journal of Politics* 61: 331–362.

Newby-Clark, Ian R., Ian McGregor, and Mark P. Zanna. 2002. "Thinking and Caring about Cognitive Inconsistency: When and for Whom does Attitudinal Ambivalence Feel Uncomfortable?" *Journal of Personality and Social Psychology* 82: 157–166.

Norris, Catherine J., Jeff T. Larsen, and John T. Cacioppo. 2003. "The Affect Matrix: Indexing Positive and Negative Affect Processes." Poster presented at the 2003 Annual Meetings of the Society for Personality and Social Psychology, Los Angeles, CA.

Nye, Joseph S., Jr., Philip D. Zelikow, and David C. King, eds. 1997. *Why People Don't Trust Government*. Cambridge, MA: Harvard University Press.

Osgood, Charles E., George J. Suci, and Percy H. Tannenbaum. 1957. *The Measurement of Meaning*. Urbana: University of Illinois Press.

Page, Benjamin I. 1978. *Choices and Echoes in Presidential Elections*. Chicago: University of Chicago Press.

Page, Benjamin I., and Richard A. Brody. 1972. "Policy Voting and the Electoral Process: The Vietnam War Issue." *American Political Science Review* 66: 389–400.

Page, Benjamin I., and Robert Y. Shapiro. 1992. *The Rational Public: Fifty Years of Trends in Americans' Policy Preferences*. Chicago: University of Chicago Press.

Patterson, Thomas E. 1980. *The Mass Media Election*. New York: Praeger.

Patterson, Thomas E., and Robert D. McClure. 1976. *The Unseeing Eye: The Myth of Television Power in National Elections*. New York: Putnam.

Paulhus, Delroy L. 1984. "Two-Component Models of Socially Desirable Responding." *Journal of Personality and Social Psychology* 46: 598–609.

Pedersen, Daniel. 1998. "Praying for Time." *Newsweek*. February 2: 66–67.

Peffley, Mark A., and Jon Hurwitz. 1993. "Models of Attitude Constraint in Foreign Affairs." *Political Behavior* 15: 61–90.

Peffley, Mark A., Pia Knigge, and Jon Hurwitz. 2001. "A Multiple Values Model of Political Tolerance." *Political Research Quarterly* 54: 379–406.

Pelham, Brett W. 1991. "On Confidence and Consequences: The Certainty and Importance of Self-Knowledge." *Journal of Personality and Social Psychology* 60: 518–530.

Petty, Richard E., and John T. Cacioppo. 1986a. *Communication and Persuasion: Central and Peripheral Routes to Attitude Change.* New York: Springer-Verlag.

Petty, Richard E., and John T. Cacioppo. 1986b. "The Elaboration Likelihood Model of Persuasion." Pp. 123–205 in *Advances In Experimental Social Psychology*, vol. 19, ed. Leonard Berkowitz. New York: Academic Press.

Petty, Richard E., Curtis P. Haugtvedt, and Stephen M. Smith. 1995. "Elaboration as a Determinant of Attitude Strength: Creating Attitudes That are Persistent, Resistant, and Predictive of Behavior." Pp. 93–130 in *Attitude Strength: Antecedents and Consequences*, eds. Richard E. Petty and Jon A. Krosnick. Mahwah, NJ: Lawrence Erlbaum.

Petty, Richard E., and Duane T. Wegener. 1993. "Flexible Correction Processes in Social Judgment: Correcting for Context-Induced Contrast." *Journal of Experimental Social Psychology* 29: 137–165.

Pratto, Felicia, and Oliver P. John. 1991. "Automatic Vigilance: The Attention-Grabbing Power of Negative Social Information." *Journal of Personality and Social Psychology* 61: 380–391.

Priester, Joseph R. 2002. "Sex, Drugs, and Attitudinal Ambivalence: How Feelings of Evaluative Tension Influence Alcohol Use and Safe Sex Behaviors." Pp. 145–162 in *Mass Media and Drug Prevention: Classic and Contemporary Theories and Research*, eds. William D. Crano and Michael Burgoon. Mahwah, NJ: Lawrence Erlbaum.

Priester, Joseph R., and Richard E. Petty. 1996. "The Gradual Threshold Model of Ambivalence: Relating the Positive and Negative Bases of Attitudes to Subjective Ambivalence." *Journal of Personality and Social Psychology* 71: 431–449.

Priester, Joseph R., and Richard E. Petty. 2001. "Extending the Bases of Subjective Attitudinal Ambivalence: Interpersonal and Intrapersonal Antecedents of Evaluative Tension." *Journal of Personality and Social Psychology* 80: 19–34.

Reicher, Stephen, and Nick Hopkins. 2001. *Self and Nation: Categorization, Contestation, and Mobilization.* London: Sage.

Rieder, Jonathan. 1985. *Canarsie: The Jews and Italians of Brooklyn against Liberalism.* Cambridge, MA: Harvard University Press.

Riketta, Michael. 2000. "Discriminative Validation of Numerical Indices of Attitude Ambivalence." *Current Research in Social Psychology* 5: 63–83.

Rokeach, Milton. 1973. *The Nature of Human Values.* New York: Free Press.

Rokeach, Milton. 1979. *Understanding Human Values: Individual and Societal.* New York: Free Press.

Rosenberg, Milton J. 1968. "Hedonism, Inauthenticity, and Other Goads Toward Expansion of a Consistency Theory." Pp. 73–111 in *Theories of Cognitive Consistency: A Sourcebook* eds. Robert P. Abelson, Elliot Aronson, William J.

McGuire, Theodore M. Newcomb, Milton J. Rosenberg, and Percy H. Tannenbaum. Chicago: Rand McNally.

Roskos-Ewoldson, David R., and Russell H. Fazio. 1992. "On the Orienting Value of Attitudes: Attitude Accessibility as a Determinant of an Object's Attraction of Visual Attention." *Journal of Personality and Social Psychology* 63: 198–211.

Ross, Lee, David Greene, and Pamela House. 1977. "The False Consensus Effect: An Egocentric Bias in Social Perception and Attribution Processes." *Journal of Experimental Social Psychology* 13: 279–301.

Sanders, Arthur. 1988. "Rationality, Self-Interest, and Public Attitudes on Public Spending." *Social Science Quarterly* 69: 311–324.

Saroglou, Vassilis. 2002. "Religion and the Five Factors of Personality: A Meta-Analytic Review." *Personality and Individual Differences* 32: 15–25.

Schatz, Robert T., and Ervin Staub. 1997. "Manifestations of Blind and Constructive Patriotism: Personality Correlates and Individual-Group Relations." Pp. 229–245 in *Patriotism in the Lives of Individuals and Nations*, eds. Daniel Bar-Tal and Ervin Staub. Chicago: Nelson-Hall.

Schneider, Anne, and Helen Ingram. 1993. "Social Construction of Target Populations: Implications for Politics and Policy." *American Political Science Review* 87: 334–347.

Schnell, Frauke. 1993. "The Foundations of Abortion Attitudes: The Role of Values and Value Conflict." Pp. 23–43 in *Understanding the New Politics of Abortion*, ed. Malcolm L. Goggin. Newbury Park, CA: Sage.

Schuman, Howard, and Stanley Presser. 1981. *Questions and Answers in Attitude Surveys: Experiments on Question Form, Wording, and Context*. New York: Academic Press.

Schuman, Howard, Stanley Presser, and Jacob Ludwig. 1981. "Context Effects on Survey Responses to Questions About Abortion." *Public Opinion Quarterly* 45: 216–223.

Schuman, Howard, Charlotte Steeh, and Lawrence Bobo. 1985. *Racial Attitudes in America: Trends and Interpretations*. Cambridge, MA: Harvard University Press.

Schwartz, Norbert, and Herbert Bless. 1992. "Constructing Reality and Its Alternatives: An Inclusion/Exclusion Model of Assimilation and Contrast Effects in Social Judgments." Pp. 217–245 in *The Construction of Social Judgments*, eds. Leonard L. Martin and Abraham Tesser. Hillsdale, NJ: Lawrence Erlbaum.

Schwartz, Shalom H. 1996. "Value Priorities and Behavior: Applying a Theory of Integrated Value Systems." Pp. 1–24 in *The Psychology of Values: The Ontario Symposium (Volume 8)*, eds. Clive Seligman, James M. Olson, and Mark P. Zanna. Mahwah, NJ: Lawrence Erlbaum.

Scott, William A. 1966. "Measures of Cognitive Structure." *Multivariate Behavior Research* 1: 391–395.

Scott, William A. 1968. "Attitude Measurement." Pp. 204–273 in *The Handbook of Social Psychology* (eds.) Gardner Lindzey and Elliot Aronson. Reading, MA: Addison-Wesley.

Scott, William A. 1969. "Structure of Natural Cognitions." *Journal of Personality and Social Psychology* 12: 261–278.

Sears, David O. 1993. "Symbolic Politics: A Socio-Psychological Theory." Pp. 113–149 in *Explorations in Political Psychology*, eds. Shanto Iyengar and William J. McGuire. Durham, NC: Duke University Press.

Sears, David O., and Jack Citrin. 1985. *Tax Revolt: Something for Nothing in California*, enlarged ed. Cambridge, MA: Harvard University Press.

Sears, David O., and Sheri Levy. 2003. "Childhood and Adult Political Development." Pp. 60–109 in *Oxford Handbook of Political Psychology*, eds. David O. Sears, Leonie Huddy, and Robert Jervis. New York: Oxford University Press.

Sherif, Muzafer, and Carl I. Hovland. 1961. *Social Judgment: Assimilation and Contrast Effects in Communication and Attitude Change*. New Haven: Yale University Press.

Sigall, Harold, and Richard Page. 1971. "Current Stereotypes: A Little Fading, a Little Faking." *Journal of Personality and Social Psychology* 18: 247–255.

Sijstma, Klaas, and Ivo W. Molenaar. 2002. *Introduction to Nonparametric Item Response Theory*. Thousand Oaks, CA: Sage.

Sijstma, Klass, P. Debets, and Ivo W. Molenaar. 1990. "Mokken Scale Analysis for Polychotomous Items: Theory, A Computer Program, and an Empirical Application." *Quality and Quantity* 21: 393–408.

Simon, Linda, Jeff Greenberg, and Jack Brehm. 1995. "Trivialization: The Forgotten Mode of Dissonance Reduction." *Journal of Personality and Social Psychology* 68: 247–260.

Singer, Jerome L. (ed.) 1990. *Repression and Dissociation: Implications for Personality Theory, Psychopathology, and Health*. Chicago: University of Chicago Press.

Smith, Kevin B. 1994. "Abortion Attitudes and Vote Choice in the 1984 and 1988 Presidential Elections." *American Politics Quarterly* 22: 354–369.

Sniderman, Paul M., Richard A. Brody, and Philip E. Tetlock. 1991. *Reasoning and Choice: Explorations in Political Psychology*. New York: Cambridge University Press.

Sniderman, Paul M., and Thomas Piazza. 1993. *The Scar of Race*. Cambridge, MA: Harvard University Press.

Son Hing, Leanne, Winnie Li, and Mark P. Zanna. 2002. "Inducing Hypocrisy to Reduce Prejudicial Responses among Aversive Racists." *Journal of Experimental Social Psychology* 38: 71–78.

Sparks, Paul, Duncan Hedderley, and Richard Shepherd. 1991. "An Investigation into the Relation Between Perceived Control, Attitude Variability, and the Consumption of Two Common Foods." *European Journal of Social Psychology* 22: 55–71.

Spinner-Halev, Jeff, and Elizabeth Theiss-Morse. 2003. "National Identity and Self-Esteem." *Perspectives on Politics* 1: 515–532.

Steenbergen, Marco R., and Paul R. Brewer. 2000. "The Not-So-Ambivalent Public: Policy Attitudes in the Political Culture of Ambivalence. Pp. 101–142 in *The Issue of Belief: Essays in the Intersection of Non-Attitudes and Attitude Change*, eds. Willem E. Saris and Paul M. Sniderman. Amsterdam: The Amsterdam School of Communication Research, Universiteit van Amsterdam, The Netherlands.

Steenbergen, Marco R., and Christopher R. Ellis. 2003. "Affective Ambivalence in Electoral Behavior." Paper presented at the Shambaugh Conference on Affect and Cognition in Political Action, University of Iowa, Iowa City, IA.

Stone, Jeff, Elliot Aronson, A. Lauren Crain, Matthew P. Winslow, and Carrie B. Fried. 1994. "Inducing Hypocrisy as a Means of Encouraging Young Adults to Use Condoms." *Personality and Social Psychology Bulletin* 20: 116–128.

Sullivan, John L., Amy Fried, and Mary G. Dietz. 1992. "Patriotism, Politics, and the Presidential Election of 1988." *American Journal of Political Science* 36: 200–234.

Tajfel, Henri. 1981. *Human Groups and Social Categories: Studies in Social Psychology*. New York: Cambridge University Press.

Tajfel, Henri, and John C. Turner. 1986. "The Social Identity Theory of Intergroup Behavior." Pp. 7–24 in *Psychology of Intergroup Relations*, 2nd ed., eds. Stephen Worchel and William G. Austin. Chicago: Nelson-Hall.

Taylor, Shelley E. 1991. "Asymmetrical Effects of Positive and Negative Events: The Mobilization-Minimization Hypothesis." *Psychological Bulletin* 110: 67–85.

Tedeschi, James T., Barry R. Schlenker, and Thomas V. Bonoma. 1971. "Cognitive Dissonance: Private Rationalization or Public Spectacle?" *American Psychologist* 26: 685–695.

Tesser, Abraham. 1978. "Self-Generated Attitude Change." Pp. 290–338 in *Advances in Experimental Social Psychology*, ed. Leonard Berkowitz. New York: Academic Press.

Tetlock, Philip E. 1986. "A Value Pluralism Model of Ideological Reasoning." *Journal of Personality and Social Psychology* 50: 819–827.

Tetlock, Philip E., Orie V. Kristel, S. Beth Elson, Melanie C. Green, and Jennifer S. Lerner. 2000. "The Psychology of the Unthinkable. Taboo Trade-Offs, Forbidden Base Rates, and Heretical Counterfactuals." *Journal of Personality and Social Psychology* 78: 853–870.

Tetlock, Phillip. E., Randall S. Peterson, and Jennifer S. Lerner. 1996. "Revising the Value Pluralism Model: Incorporating Social Content and Context Postulates." Pp. 25–51 in *The Psychology of Values: The Ontario Symposium, Vol. 8*, eds. Clive Seligman, James M. Olson, and Mark P. Zanna. Hillsdale, NJ: Lawrence Erlbaum.

Thompson, Megan M., and Mark P. Zanna. 1995. "The Conflicted Individual: Personality-Based and Domain-Specific Antecedents of Ambivalent Social Attitudes." *Journal of Personality* 63: 259–288.

Thompson, Megan, Mark P. Zanna, and Dale W. Griffin. 1995. "Let's Not Be Indifferent About (Attitudinal) Ambivalence." Pp. 361–386 in *Attitude Strength: Antecedents and Consequences*, eds. Richard E. Petty and Jon A. Krosnick. Mahwah, NJ: Lawrence Erlbaum.

Thurstone, Louis L. 1928. "Attitudes Can Be Measured." *American Journal of Sociology* 33: 529–554.

Thurstone, Louis L., and Edward J. Chave. 1929. *The Measurement of Attitude*. Chicago: University of Chicago Press.

Tourangeau, Roger, and Kenneth A. Rasinski. 1988. "Cognitive Processes Underlying Contest Effects in Attitude Measurement." *Psychological Bulletin* 103: 299–314.

Tourangeau, Roger, Kenneth A. Rasinski, Norman Bradburn, and Roy D'Andrade. 1989a. "Belief Accessibility and Context Effects in Attitude Measurement." *Journal of Experimental Social Psychology* 25: 401–421.

Tourangeau, Roger, Kenneth A. Rasinski, Norman Bradburn, and Roy D'Andrade. 1989b. "Carryover Effects in Attitude Surveys." *Public Opinion Quarterly* 53: 495–524.

Tschirgi, Judith E. 1980. "Sensible Reasoning: A Hypothesis About Children." *Child Development* 51: 1–10.

Vallone, Robert P., Lee Ross, and Mark R. Lepper. 1985. "The Hostile Media Phenomenon: Biased Perception and Perceptions of Media Bias in Coverage of the Beirut Massacre." *Journal of Personality and Social Psychology* 49: 577–585.

Verplanken, Bas, and Rob W. Holland. 2002. "Motivated Decision Making: Effects of Activation and Self-Centrality of Values on Choices and Behavior." *Journal of Personality and Social Psychology* 82: 434–447.

Wald, Kenneth D. 1992. *Religion and Politics in the United States*, 2nd ed. Washington, DC: CQ Press.

Walt, Kathy. 1998. "Death Penalty's Support Plunges to 30-Year Low." *Houston Chronicle*. March 5. Retrieved July 14, 2003 from http:www.chron.com/cgi-bin/auth/story.mpl/content/ chronicle/page1/98/03/15.death.html.

Warner, Stanley L. 1965. "Randomized Response: A Survey Technique for Eliminating Evasive Answer Bias." *Journal of the American Statistical Association* 60: 63–69.

Wason, Peter C., and Philip N. Johnson-Laird. 1972. *Psychology of Reasoning: Structure and Content*. Cambridge, MA: Harvard University Press.

Wegener, Duane T., Norbert L. Kerr, Monique A. Fleming, and Richard E. Petty. 2000. "Flexible Corrections of Juror Judgments: Implications for Jury Instructions." *Psychology, Public Policy, and Law* 6: 629–654.

Wegener, Duane T., and Richard E. Petty. 1995. "Flexible Correction Processes in Social Judgment: The Role of Naive Theories in Corrections of Perceived Bias." *Journal of Personality and Social Psychology* 68: 36–51.

Wegner, Daniel M. 1994. "Ironic Processes of Mental Control." *Psychological Review* 101: 34–52.

Wilcox, Clyde, Lee Sigelman, and Elizabeth Cook. 1989. "Some Like it Hot: Individual Differences in Responses to Group Feeling Thermometers." *Public Opinion Quarterly* 53: 246–257.

Wilson, Timothy D., and Sara D. Hodges. 1992. "Attitudes as Temporary Constructions." Pp. 37–65 in *The Construction of Social Judgments*, eds. Leonard L. Martin and Abraham Tesser. Hillsdale, NJ: Lawrence Erlbaum.

Yzerbyt, Vincent Y., and Jacques-Phillipe Leyens. 1991. "Requesting Information to Form an Impression: The Influence of Valence and Confirmatory Status." *Journal of Experimental Social Psychology* 27: 337–356.

Zajonc, Robert B. 1968. "Cognitive Theories in Social Psychology." Pp. 320–411 in *The Handbook of Social Psychology*, vol. 1, eds. Gardner Lindzey and Elliot Aronson, Reading, MA: Addison-Wesley.

Zaller, John R. 1992. *The Nature and Origins of Mass Opinion*. Cambridge: Cambridge University Press.

Zaller, John, and Stanley Feldman. 1992. "A Simple Theory of the Survey Response: Answering Questions Versus Revealing Preferences." *American Journal of Political Science* 36: 579–616.

Zanna, Mark P., and Colette Aziza. 1976. "On the Interaction of Repression-Sensitization and Attention in Resolving Cognitive Dissonance." *Journal of Personality* 44: 577–593.

Zanna, Mark P., and Joel Cooper. 1974. "Dissonance and the Pill: An Attribution Approach to Studying the Arousal Properties of Dissonance." *Journal of Personality and Social Psychology* 29: 703–709.

Zanna, Mark P., Mark R. Lepper, and Robert P. Abelson. 1973. "Attentional Mechanisms in Children's Devaluation of a Forbidden Activity in a Forced Compliance Situation." *Journal of Personality and Social Psychology* 28: 355–359.

Index